The Present Revelation
In Quest of Religious Foundations

Gabriel Moran

A Crossroad Book
THE SEABURY PRESS · NEW YORK

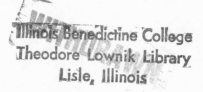

Copyright © 1972 by
Herder and Herder, Inc.

All rights reserved. Printed in the United States
of America. No part of this publication may be
reproduced, stored in a retrieval system, or
transmitted, in any form or by any means,
electronic, mechanical, photocopying, recording,
or otherwise, without the prior written permis-
sion of the publisher.

Library of Congress Cataloging in
Publication Data

Moran, Gabriel. The present revelation.

1. Revelation. 2. Experience (Religion)
I. Title. BT127.2.M597 231'.74 72-2307
ISBN 0-8164-1105-0

CONTENTS

Chapter One : The Question of Revelation

1. A Starting Point

THERE is a middle generation of American Roman Catholics who no longer believe anything. This statement requires some explanation lest it be dismissed as a piece of exaggeration and sensationalism. My interest is not sensational rhetoric but a starting point for inquiry into religious foundations. I wish to start with the stark fact of experience reported in the first sentence. Only by confronting a fact like this will one be impelled to dig deeper into foundational questions. It is so easy to appear to be shaking the foundations when in fact one is merely engaged in a methodological pose. In all likelihood the inquirer is not dishonest; it is just that some of his basic categories have not been shaken up.

Church people often say that we are all "believers" and that we only differ in our object of belief. I have some sympathy with this statement of principle (as well as some reservation about stating the principle too casually). It may seem to be a contradiction to say that a group of people "no longer believe anything." However, the word *anything* is crucial here. I shall presently be dealing with other possible meanings of the verb believe. My reference here is to things like statements of truth.

There is a fairly clear understanding in our language of what it means to believe something. A person believes something when he holds as true some statement of fact that he cannot directly verify for himself. Men and women have always needed this kind of believing to survive at all. There is today a much

1

discussed "credibility problem" which is not cured bv things like the switch of American presidents. The credibility problem in religion is only part of a much larger social, political and cultural question. It has become exceedingly difficult to hold anything as true except in the most tentative way or with the suspicious air that one is liable to get duped at any moment. In either case it is a doubtful use of language to say that a person believes something. If believing anything connotes conviction and certainty concerning specific and identifiable beliefs, then to say that there are people who no longer believe anything is no exaggeration.

If the problem of credibility is a widespread, or even a universal, phenomenon, why concentrate attention on a middle generation of American Roman Catholics? The answer to this question is threefold. First, this book is concerned with the religious question. Although I do not think that religious matters can be adequately examined apart from a full human context, it is only the religious element and not other cultural components of that context with which I can directly deal. Thus, there is the choice of a particular religious group.

Second, I write about a particular generation of that religious body because that is a group I know. A writer, particularly in the field of religion, must write in a vein that is partly autobiographical. A self-conscious narcissism is not desirable but an experiential feeling for the question is. Thus, there is a choice of a particular age group.

Third, the direction of the two previous points is toward the concrete specification of a group. It may help, therefore, to refer to an American experience. The experience which is taken as starting point for reflection is one shared at least in part by other religions, countries and ages. We shall move quickly enough to that fact. It may be worthwhile, however, to pause for a few moments of reflection on this group in whom I am trying to see mirrored a universal truth.

2

There is an identifiable group of American Catholics, I am positing, who constitute an unusual phenomenon for religious study. Like Margaret Mead's generation in the South Seas, who went from Stone Age to Atomic Age in one lifetime, they are an unrepeatable lot whose experience might have an unusual significance because of the convergence of unusual circumstances. The full study of this group must be carried out by sociologists or anthropologists at a later date. I am concerned here with launching a religious or theological essay that springs from those circumstances.

When I refer to a middle generation I do not exactly mean middle-aged but I do intend to designate some grouping by age. There is an older generation who were well set in their ways before Vatican II. For them church changes can never be more than reinterpretations of the historically given church. Most Roman Catholics above the age of forty-five would fall into this category. At the other end, there is a younger generation of Roman Catholics who never experienced the total pattern of church life. For them at the moment the church can hardly be taken seriously. They never experienced induction into the system of Roman Catholicism because that system no longer operated during their maturing years. Most Catholics below the age of twenty-five fall into this category. Finally, there is a group, between the ages of twenty-five and forty-five, who thoroughly accepted Roman Catholicism even into the early part of their adult lives. Today they find all the church paraphernalia not only incredible but a bit preposterous.

It could be objected that any typology like I have just elaborated is arbitrary and inadequate. I would grant that the age lines are only a rough approximation and that each age category has exceptions. However, there is a reason for the existence of the three distinct types. The breakup of Roman Catholicism has been more rapid than anyone could have expected. Effects of historical movements arrive in different places

3

at different times but this historic change has moved with such speed that it has caused almost a clean break between age groups.

I make no claim that all of the people between twenty-five and forty-five have the mentality I am about to describe. The experience remains significant even should it pertain only to a minority. It should be noted that I am not positing a gap be tween the young and the old. This common division of the generations is more difficult to prove and less helpful to use. The young and the old may resemble each other more than either of them resembles the middle.

I began with the assertion that there is a group who no longer believe anything. It is not one religious doctrine or another which gives them trouble. The entire question of doctrine has drifted away from their attention or else religious doctrine has been placed into the hopper of things not to be trusted. Such people have little inclination to join another religion. They suspect, not without reason, that every church is as bad as their own. At the same time, the non-religious options do not carry any glittering promise of stronger freedom and greater wholeness. It is not religious doctrine that is incredible but any elaboration of evidence that goes beyond primitive experience. Even to be an atheist seems to require too much conviction.

Teilhard de Chardin in his time spoke of the dramatic growth of a whole race of spiritual expatriates whom he described as "human beings torn between a Marxism whose depersonalizing effect revolts them and a Christianity so lukewarm in human terms that it sickens them."[1] This race of expatriates certainly exists today but they would in all likelihood see Marxism and Christianity as two variations of the collapsed world rather than the two choices open to them. Marxist-Christian conversations which made a splash in European circles for a time attracted

1. Pierre Teilhard de Chardin, *The Future of Man* (New York, 1964), p. 268.

no more than minimal interest in this country.[2] While many Catholics in this country would have nothing against working with Communists, they would have little interest in Marxist theories. They recognize Karl Marx as a great historical figure but they are not sanguine about Christian theology receiving new life from dialogue with Marxist philosophers. This attitude is not the result of the old time narrow-mindedness which excluded all ideologies but one's own; rather, the attitude springs from an instinctive distrust of all firm ideologies.

The present culture tends to create this distrust. Every objectified expression of truth is also laden with an element of doubt. On the one hand, there is an overwhelming amount of information instantaneously available from all over the world. On the other hand, every last bit of information is subject to manipulation and every formulation can be used for exploitation. Both of these facts have been known for many years but the full impact of their convergence emerged rather rapidly. Thus, the church may have become a non-credible institution at the Renaissance, and knowledge may have become relativized in the nineteenth century. Nonetheless, it was apparently only with the worldwide communication, most dramatically with international television, that the *experience* of these truths became widely available. The experience has not yet been universally accepted but this experience impinges more and more upon the consciousness of everyone, viz., that there is no one set of beliefs for mankind that is normal and true. If a person rides a New York subway train long enough, he must eventually conclude that human patterns are indescribably diverse. If one watches the nightly network news, it becomes impossible to think that there is one set of beliefs which constitutes the normal and obvious way of understanding human life.

2. See: Roger Garaudy, *From Anathema to Dialogue* (New York, 1966); Thomas Ogletree, *Openings for Marxist-Christian Dialogue* (New York, 1969); Herbert Aptheker, *The Urgency of Marxist-Christian Dialogue* (New York, 1970).

5

ın the past ıt was possible to hold some statements as true simply because everyone else ın one's immediate circle believed tne same thing. There are still places in the world untouched by the undermining influence of modern communications. The places in America where this is true have been rapidly shrinking since World War II. A dozen years ago it was possible for Roman Catholics to believe in a doctrine of the Eucharist elaborated in the physical categories of Aristotle. For the Catholics of whom I speak here, it is difficult even to remember or to imagine how such belief was possible.

What has occurred during these recent years is a relativization of all knowledge. Nothing that can be put into human language can be accepted as exhaustively and ultimately true. Every human statement is subject to challenge, correction and contrary points of view. All judgments of truth are human productions and the human is immeasurably diverse and never final.

The nineteenth century had already brought to prominence the *historical* character of knowledge. Human understanding was seen as developmental but the assumption seemed to operate that some positions had finally been gained. A more subtle premise also seems to have functioned, namely, that there is a fixed point which provides the interpretive key fo. understanding historical change. Anyone who grew up in Amerıca previous co current educational reforms learned his history from the viewpoint of American history and that history was very clearcut. Only now can the full force of a world history with no fixed point begin to be felt. Such history does not widen one's views; rather, it is disorienting and it casts in doubt every cherished belief. The effect is highlighted in this passage from Mircea Eliade:

It must be admitted that from a certain point of view the understanding of man as first and foremost a historical being implies a profound humiliation for the Western consciousness. Western man considered himself successively God's creature and the possessor of a unique

6

Revelation, the master of the world, the author of the only universally valid culture, the creator of the only real and useful science, and so on. Now he discovered himself on the same level with every other man, that is to say, conditioned by the unconscious as well as by history—no longer the unique creator of a high culture, no longer the master of the world, and culturally menaced by extinction.[3]

The influx of new scientific and historical knowledge has been the most dramatic factor in the relativizing of all belief systems. Science has repeatedly advanced upon retreating religious beliefs. However, in the area of religion there was a more subtle but in the long run more corrosive factor at work. This factor was the differentiation and specialization of religious institutions. The peculiar character of the religious organization is that it has to maintain a relation to all human concerns. When the religious institutions were willing to accept the position assigned to them by society, *ipso facto* they ceased to be what religious institutions supposedly are.

Science and technology did not have to fight the religious institutions or disprove their claims. The institutions simply became less and less worthy of attention.[4] Once the churches had agreed to become specialists in the religion area they could for the most part be politely disregarded. If one accepts the premises of the churches, their belief systems can still be consistently maintained. Increasingly, however, the premises of such institutions seem insignificant. John Dewey called this specialization of the religious institution "the greatest change that has occurred in religion in all history."[5] He went on to explain the difficulty that anyone now has of giving a serious place to churches:

3. Mircea Eliade, *The Quest: History and Meaning in Religion* (Chicago, 1969), p. 51.
4. See: Peter Berger, *The Sacred Canopy* (Garden City, 1967), pp. 127–153; Jeffrey Hadden, *Religion in Transition* (New York, 1971), pp. 1–14.
5. John Dewey, *A Common Faith* (New Haven, 1960), p. 61.

There are even now persons who are born into a particular church, that of their parents, and who take membership in it almost as a matter of course; indeed, the fact of such membership may be an important, even a determining factor in an individual's whole career. But the thing new in history, the thing once unheard of, is that the organization in question is a *special* institution within a secular community. Even where there are established churches, they are constituted by the state and may be unmade by the state.[6]

The individual in all his judgments, but most acutely in judgments pertaining to religion, is exposed to a bewildering mass of data which cannot be formulated into a set of firm beliefs. When the individual turns to institutions larger than himself he is likely to receive no relief. None of these institutions can prove itself more trustworthy than the others. Each of them has trouble just maintaining itself. Least of all does a religious institution seem capable of dealing with, let alone answering, the serious religious questions.

A long series of upheavals seems finally to have eliminated the hope for an archimedian point of certainty outside the relativities of the human situation. However, most religious groups, particularly the official churches, have resisted this conclusion. As Herbert Muller notes: "Most churchmen failed to meet the challenge of relativity. They simply reaffirmed the absolute truths of Christianity, invoking the authority of the Bible: a sacred knowledge that has been revealed to a minority of mankind, and on the proper interpretation of which Christians themselves have never been able to agree."[7] This tactic h˜ ˙ repeatedly failed and failed badly but that is not the worst of it. The attempt to shore up the untenable position precludes a new starting point being found in the relative itself.

The attempt to make the relative a starting point will never

6. *Ibid.*, p. 61.
7. Herbert Muller, *Religion and Freedom in the Modern World* (Chicago, 1963), p. 38; for further reflection of the same author, see: *The Children of Frankenstein* (Bloomington, 1970), pp. 317–329.

be attempted so long as something still functions as an absolute. Christian writing still seems to presume that there are some divinely bestowed truths, however few or obscure they may be. These truths are thought to provide both a starting point and a touchstone of truth for all consequent inquiry. It is assumed, and sometimes explicitly stated, that to eliminate these revealed truths would cast us into a terrible relativism in which no statement could have more than relative truth value.

What the person who thinks in terms of absolutes cannot seem to grasp is that there might be some positive value in the relative. If there were an absolute truth or absolute perspective, then anything less than that would be "merely relative." But in a world without absolute truths, the more relative a truth is the better. Being relative or related to others becomes the stabilizing and guiding factor for each statement of truth. The whole matrix of interrelationships becomes the starting point for understanding.

When absolute truths begin to go, the world begins to fall apart. The question becomes whether to shore up the remaining system of absolutes by fighting a rear-guard action against de absolutization or to push the process of relativization to its conclusion. Carried to its conclusion, the process bends back upon itself. It will eventually produce not so much a new starting point as a new *kind* of starting point. The doctrines, ideas and institutions that had supplied the normative control are replaced by a level of living which is practical and relational. "The relativizers are relativized, the debunkers are debunked—indeed relativization itself is somehow liquidated. What follows is *not* as some of the early sociologists of knowledge feared, a total paralysis of thought. Rather, it is a new freedom and flexibility in asking questions of truth."[8]

8. See: Peter Berger, *Rumor of Angels* (Garden City, 1969), pp. 52ff.; Michael Novak, *The Experience of Nothingness* (New York, 1970), p. 53.

The untrustworthiness of all *things* (including ideas and institutions) has helped to generate a hope that some meaning, substance and credibility can be found in other *people.* The distinction between "believing things" and "believing in people" is one that is quite ancient in Western tradition. However, "believing in" was never given the predominant and determining position. One always had to get to the point of bridging a gap and accepting the "articles of faith." It is precisely this bridging operation which is rejected today. "Believing in" is thought to be a life's work and consequently all the sustenance of human life is sought for in intense, personal relationships. Such a demand is almost certainly unrealistic but for many people whose belief structure has been obliterated the contact with another human is their only guarantee that they are in contact with reality. Even hatred is a testimony that one's life is substantial and perhaps worth struggling about.

This kind of experience does not provide a great deal of insight into life but it does make complete despair an impossibility. Albert Camus once wrote that the only serious philosophical question is suicide.[9] The fact that people generally do not commit suicide but instead cling tenaciously to their world is a startling phenomenon. Even when every bit of meaning to life is left in tatters and one is unable "to make sense out of anything," the least movement of love for another person will not allow resignation or despair. It is impossible to believe anything but it is just as impossible not to believe that there is some point to the joy and suffering of human exchange.

For the most part this rootedness in the real is confined to exchanges between two people. Pairs of people can be found hovering in the corners of collapsed structures. Sometimes they live in hope of a new building; often they live only in the hope of outlasting the demolition squad. If one person is found want-

9. Albert Camus, *The Myth of Sisyphus* (New York, 1955), p. 3.

ing, it is thought that perhaps the right one or at least another one is somewhere nearby. Even though they may ultimately fail, human beings can be believed in as *there,* that is, as immeasurably more significant than anything institutional.

The strain of anti-institutionalism runs exceedingly deep in the contemporary world. Few individuals deny validity to all institutions but a great many people will not expend any energy to change structures that govern the human. The policy seems to be to avoid institutions as far as possible and to concentrate on what can be experienced as real, namely, interpersonal exchanges. Occasionally, however, the interpersonal is transcended in experiences which are undeniably real. One's unbelief in all things large-scale is tested by certain dramatic occurrences. For some people space exploration may lift them up to a larger perspective of the possible grandeur of man, machines and the universe. In the other direction, some people have been forced to confront larger institutions that produce wars abroad and violence at home; here one is awakened to the possible horror of man, his products and his world. In these and similar cases the reality of the large-scale cannot be dismissed as meaningless. What the meaning is, is not clear, but a search for meaning becomes difficult to avoid.

A particular example of this kind of experience was the extermination of the Jews in Nazi Germany. Anyone who grapples with the fact cannot simply say: "People die every day and human life doesn't mean that much anyway." There is a sense of some unimaginable force for good or ill, some mysterious power that demands a response. In this case the religious issue is unavoidable. Some stance is demanded toward past Jewish history and the ultimate ground of past and present Judaism. The agony of the contemporary Jew is expressed in these words: "Any effort to explain the Holocaust would by that very fact betray the event and our reactions to it. So nothing could be said. Yet unbelief was equally impossible because of

11

the moral affirmation inherent in the very protest. We could not speak but we could not not believe."[10]

The moral affirmation of protest which is referred to here is the counterpart to the individual's refusal to commit suicide. A compassion for suffering mankind is the correlative to passion for irrepressible selfhood. Where passion and compassion still live it is difficult to settle into the conclusion that there is no point at all to life. In this regard, flamboyant announcements of the "death of god" seemed not only premature but too much at the level of another doctrinal formulation. Does one have the energy and the conviction to believe that God is dead? William James once wrote that there are unfathomed realms which "forbid a premature closing of our accounts with reality."[11] This inscrutable mysteriousness of existence survives nihilistic movements even from within Christian theology. In an article on the possibility of faith today, Karl Rahner wrote that one thing sustained him in all "temptations" against faith: "The conviction that we must not allow what has been inherited and transmitted to be consumed by the emptiness of the ordinary, of a spiritual indifference or apathetic and sombre scepticism, but at the most only by something stronger, something which calls us to greater freedom and into a more inexorable light."[12]

These last remarks indicate why a middle generation of Catholics who no longer believe anything still remain Catholic. They would be able to leave only to go to something stronger and more inexorable but these qualities are not easy to come by; nor can this group easily rid themselves of the light and strength

10. Eugene Borowitz, "Hope Jewish and Hope Secular," in *The Future as the Presence of Shared Hope*, ed., Maryellen Muckenhirn (New York, 1968), p. 106; For reflection on the continuing meaning of Auschwitz, see: Emil Fackenheim, "The People Israel Lives," in *Theological Crossings*, eds., Alan Geyer and Dean Peerman (Grand Rapids, 1971), pp. 51–64.

11. Quoted in William Braden, *The Private Sea: LSD and the Search for God* (New York, 1967), p. 31.

12. Karl Rahner, "Thoughts on the Possibility of Belief Today," in *Theological Investigations*, vol. 5 (Baltimore, 1966), pp. 4–5.

that has been transmitted to them. Like Hazel Motes in the novel by Flannery O'Connor, they would like to drop the concern but there is something in the blood and the bones that will not allow it.[13]

There is an older generation of Catholics, I have said, who cannot really suspend belief. Even when the attempt is made it happens as a kind of pose. They have loved their tradition in a way that sets upper limits on the criticism of it. The analyzing of it is necessarily from the inside out. In contrast, the younger generation has never really been inside the tradition and as a result can be quite disdainful of it. Where there is real interest on the part of the young it may get expressed in the form of impatient calls for a new institution.

The middle generation of Catholics I am trying to describe combines in illogical ways a variety of feelings and attitudes. They are affected with a sad nostalgia for a past they have known but is now gone. In the press they may be known as "liberals" but in relation to church reform they have lost heart for what liberals supposedly do in opposition to conservatives. They have no inclination to follow the path of James Kavanaugh tirades. Such action strikes them as kicking the old lady while she is down. Neither does the Charles Davis route make any sense to them since it seems to suppose a purer world that one can go to. The pope tells lies and the Roman church makes untenable historical claims but what should one make of that when one does not believe anything to begin with. What honesty requires in such a situation is not at all clear. "Leaving the church" seems to suppose that the church has clear boundaries (which someone else has defined). It also seems to imply that one has honestly concluded that the church is wrong compared to some other position which is right. One might perhaps sadly drift away but dramatic gestures of exit seem highly inappropriate.

13. See: Flannery O'Connor, *Wise Blood* (New York, 1949).

This description is provided not for psychoanalytic purposes and even less so for the purpose of condemning individuals. My interest is a methodological one, namely, the way of coming to grips with the contemporary religious problem. The people I am describing are the first generation of Catholics who have been able to suspend belief and yet remain Catholics. By suspension I do not mean the didactic maneuver of supposing that Christianity might not be the answer in order to show more dramatically that it is. I mean, rather, the actual experience of considering suicide as a personal alternative because there really might be no point at all. People who have grown up in a world where everything made sense feel strongly the sudden collapse of that world and all worlds. They are not likely to be contented with the business gains or leisure enjoyments which many other people find sufficiently diversionary.[14]

The possibility of suspending belief and yet caring for the tradition carries the possibility of a new kind of religious writing. Practically all Christian writing assumes that the writer *accepts* Christianity, that he takes it to be *true,* that he believes it is *the answer* to life. In this ecumenical age, of course, the phrasing of this assumption is carefully made. Granted that the change of attitude has been real and significant, the basic claim is never given up. To write Christian theology is to accept as controlling factor "the Christian revelation."[15]

Suppose that one neither accepts nor rejects Christianity? Suppose one has an affinity for a Christian life but finds the

14. See: Kathy Mulherin, "Memories of a (Latter-Day) Catholic Girlhood," in *New Theology,* no. 8, ed., Martin Marty and Dean Peerman (New York, 1971), pp. 58–83.

15. In Alistair Kee, *The Way of Transcendence* (Baltimore, 1971), there is an attempt to save Christianity by eliminating God from it. Undoubtedly, some people today find it impossible to believe in God but a problem at least as great as God is the kind of claim made in this book "that Jesus Christ is the very embodiment and final revelation of the way of transcendence" (p. 228). Never once does the author raise the question of whether a "final and definitive revelation" is intelligible not to say acceptable.

14

concept of a "Christian revelation" to be unintelligible? Suppose that one finds Christianity to be an inescapable element of one's life and that one approaches it with care and intelligence but that one cannot possibly believe that it (or anything else) is the norm of one's life. By the standards of ecclesiastical definition one is not a Christian and according to Christian theology one is not a theologian. However, these very definitions could use challenging from some other set of premises.

A typical summary of the attitude of updated, progressive Christian theology would read: "At a point not later than the 1799 publication of Schleiermacher's *On Religion: Addresses in Response to Its Cultured Critics,* systematic theology entered a basically new phase, the consequences of which are not entirely surveyable. From then on in theology it was no longer the many-sided display of Christian truth and the polemics against heresy which was central, but the interpretation of the gospel to a secularized culture.... On the one hand we know ourselves bound to the authority of the books of the Bible in which the truth of God is revealed to us in a unique way; on the other hand we are in spite of ourselves bound up with the way of life of our era."[16]

There is the obvious concern in this passage "to relate to the modern era." However, it is astounding that in the midst of supposed revolution and relativization the key premises are not only unchanged but unchallenged. A Christian theologian apparently has to believe in the "authority of the Bible in which the truth of God is revealed to us in a unique way." Those who do not accept this statement can presumably write about religion as a general phenomenon or in bizarre form but one is no longer in the "theological circle."

At the least there should be questioning of the glib use that Christian theologians make not only of the word God but also of authority, truth, unique and reveal. Is not the word "theol-

16. Hendrikus Berkhof, *Well-Founded Hope* (Richmond, 1969), p. 83.

ogy" itself a pompous claim, especially when preempted by one group of Christian men? Christian writers tend to use theology and Christian theology interchangeably. There may be realism to this usage since Christians have been the group most interested in speaking of God systematically. Many religious groups would have no desire to get a share of the word theology. In any case, if the word theology is to be retained at all, it surely needs broadening at its base to bring in more people doing more kinds of things than the current rules allow.

There has been great progress since the nineteenth century in the investigation of religious issues. At that time one was inevitably forced to be for or against religion. An uncritical spirit of believers was met by a hypercritical attitude of nonbelievers. A conformity that did not allow any objective distance was countered by an apotheosis of objectivity that could not appreciate the reality of a subject's experienced involvement. The rise of phenomenology as a method was particularly helpful to religion since it provided a fresh new alternative to the narrowness of the other two approaches. A phenomenologist of religion, Gerard Van der Leeuw, has described the method in the following way:

Phenomenology, therefore, is not a method that has been reflectively elaborated, but is man's true, vital activity, consisting in neither losing himself in things, nor in the ego, neither in hovering above objects like a god, nor in dealing with them like an animal, but in doing what is given to neither god nor animal, standing aside and understanding what appears into view.[17]

What I am suggesting as a challenge to theological method may be only an extension or qualification of what Van der Leeuw describes as phenomenology. If phenomenology is really as extensive as he makes it, that is, what belongs between animal

17. Gerard Van der Leeuw, *Religion in Essence and Manifestation* (New York, 1963), II, 676; for a more extended definition, see: Maurice Merleau-Ponty, "What is Phenomenology," *Cross Currents,* VI (Winter, 1956), pp. 59–70; Pierre Thevanez, *What Is Phenomenology?* (Chicago, 1962).

and god, then my concern is certainly there. Nonetheless, there may be several ways of standing aside and understanding what appears. More precisely, there is a continuum of involvement of the person understanding with what is understood. Phenomenology has usually connoted a neutrality or impartiality that may need complementing from a position which is still non-judgmental but more personally involving. Suppose one does not believe any of the doctrines of a religious tradition but one is still sustained by some of its beauty, some of its concerns and some of its meaning?

The present essay might be described as an attempt to reconnoiter a position somewhere between phenomenology and theology. Philosophers of religion or free-wheeling devotees of the current scene will probably find the work too restricted and too Christian. Christian theologians will probably see it as too frivolous and not really part of the tradition with which they are concerned. To the former group I am trying to show that one can really care for a concrete religious community without ending up as a propagandizer. To the latter group I am trying to show that the supposed revolution in method of Christian theology has hardly begun.

This work cannot claim to be more than pre-theological by present standards. However, I am suggesting that perhaps one should not be anxious to get to theology. Although there may be a real need for theology, all theologians could profitably spend much of their time in areas that precede theology. "The primary issue of theology is *pretheological*," writes Abraham Heschel, "it is the total situation of man and his attitudes toward life and the world."[18] Those people who pretend to speak theologically must somehow make contact and spend some time with a more primitive experiencing of life.

18. Abraham Heschel, *The Insecurity of Freedom* (New York, 1966), p. 116.

17

Much of twentieth-century theology had its origins in World War I. The shocking collapse of the European world exercised a powerful influence upon Karl Barth and all his heirs. The experience of Nazism reinforced these lessons for a Bonhoeffer breed of theologians a quarter century later. But there are many other sources, both personal and social, that theology should be drawing upon. Despite the way Christian theology looks, European-American civilization is only a small part of the world. The breakdown of Europe was not the collapse of humanity or the end of the world. The kind of sources which should be giving inspiration and content to theology I will presently advert to. Here I wish to stress that there simply may be no way to reform theology from within theology. Many disciplines are undergoing a similar crisis but theology has the severest problem because in striving to go so high it must root itself all the more deeply in strong human soil.

At the end of his book on method in theology, Walter Kasper writes: "The most serious criticism of all may well be that theology has become so faint-hearted and distrustful, so morose and humorless."[19] The humor which Kasper is looking for is not light-hearted frivolity but a zestful engagement of a person's self and the feeling that something surprising or wonderful might happen. The current popular image of theology as a circle (or spiral) is a peculiarly depressing one. If theologians must talk about circular movement, they ought to get outside theology on occasion and meet up with the passionate struggles of a less programmed world.

2. REVELATION AND THEOLOGY

The present work is an experiment in the use of the word "revelation." By choosing to examine this word I am supposing

19. Walter Kasper, *The Methods of Dogmatic Theology* (Glen Rock, 1969), p. 65.

18

that it is possible to establish a viable meaning for the word without directly adverting to the use of the word in Christian theology.[20] I am attempting to offer a meaning of the word which would include Christianity within it. In doing so, I am necessarily breaking the rules of Christian theology or, more precisely, I am challenging their validity.

In 1966 I wrote a book entitled *Theology of Revelation*.[21] In that work I tried to establish the meaning of revelation by working through the established theological channels. Beginning from texts of Vatican I and a traditional Christology, I tried to show that biblical and church sources would themselves lead to a much broader meaning for the word revelation. The conclusion of that work was that revelation is a universal phenomenon, present in the life of every individual and all religions. The validity and worth of such an endeavor seem to me to be still defensible.

With the sequence I have just described there is a nagging problem of methodology. It can be put in the form of the question: If theology *presupposes* revelation, then how can

20. I am thus agreeing with Kai Nielsen, "The Primacy of Philosophical Theology," in *Theology Today* XXVII (July, 1970), p. 165: "We should ask whether the concept of revelation is a coherent concept. The viability of theology (and indeed the viability of the Christian faith, and other faiths as well) hangs on its being a coherent concept. If it is not the whole edifice comes down." It seems to me that Christian theologians do not grasp the extent of this challenge. For example, David Griffin, "Is Revelation Coherent?" *Theology Today*, XXVII (Oct., 1971), pp. 278–294 tries to answer Nielsen by immediately introducing all the Christian claims without apparently grasping the problem of any viable meaning to "a revelation." My own attempt to establish a meaning for the word will probably not satisfy Nielsen but it is an attempt to approach the issue differently. Instead of choosing between philosophy and revelation I am using revelation in a much wider sense that would connect philosophy and religion. I am also asserting that the notion of a "Christian revelation" is incoherent.

21. *Theology of Revelation* (New York, 1966); see also: F. Gerald Downing, *Has Christianity a Revelation?* (Philadelphia, 1966). I agree with Downing on the negative reply to the question of his title, but my conclusion is by a different route. I reject a "Christian revelation" (i.e., a revelation which Christianity *has*) in order to establish a universal revelation in which all participate.

theology *establish* the meaning of revelation? This dilemma has, of course, been recognized in the past but it is amazing how little attention has been paid to the question. The problem has usually been resolved very quickly by the adoption of some philosophical position. Because such adoption has usually been rapid and very often surreptitious, the position adopted has frequently been a limited one. In addition, when theologians look to "human science" for the meaning of revelation, they will turn immediately to some abstruse philosopher. One need not deny a role to the philosopher but artistic experience, psychology, social movements, family life and dozens of other phenomena should perhaps be looked at first.

Since 1966 I have written a dozen pieces on the topic of revelation but each of them has been rather brief.[22] I have found that people either do not understand at all the points I am trying to make or else they believe that my statements are exaggerated or carelessly expressed. What I am trying to do here, with the leisure of space, is to construct a total pattern. This total pattern may be rejected as false or inadequate but at least the individual statements should no longer be misunderstood. Essentially, I am traveling a route which is the reverse of my former book, that is, I am beginning with a universal meaning of revelation and moving toward the Christian community as a possible expression of revelation. I shall not hesitate to use material from Christian tradition but at the same time I presume no special authority for that material.

I am engaged, therefore, in trying to establish a new *paradigm* rather than to add a few more thoughts on the subject. In my former book I called the study of revelation a paradigm for theological study. By that I meant that a correct theological analysis of revelation would be helpful to carrying out the study

22. See my *Experiences in Community* (New York, 1968), pp. 72–76; *The New Community* (New York, 1970), pp. 16–34; *Design for Religion* (New York, 1970), pp. 29–48.

of other theological concepts. Paradigm simply meant a model to be imitated. In this book my meaning of paradigm has shifted in the direction of Thomas Kuhn's usage in his minor classic on the subject.[23] Revelation is a paradigm for theology in the sense that the choice of a patterned use for the word will determine the fruitfulness of theological inquiry to follow. Revelation is not a theological concept similar to others but instead a premise for theological construction as a whole.

The *real* meaning of revelation cannot be found in the bible or other theological sources. Only some wider human experience (which, of course, can include theology) can establish the meaning of revelation. A traditional Christian theology which would charge that this procedure subsumes the "word of God" to human judgment is simply making a gratuitous objection. The objection cannot be taken seriously until some other paradigm is presented. The test of the worth or truth of what I say about revelation is not agreement with any set of statements. The test is the comprehensiveness and consistency with which the word functions in my use. If my usage makes sense out of a great amount of data, does not lead to inner contradictions and opens the way to further inquiry, then this use of the word is justified.

In contemporary theology the word revelation is used with at least a dozen different meanings. Although the word would appear to be rich and flexible, the various meanings do not go together consistently. It could be suspected that any meaning to the word has drifted beyond the clouds of vague metaphors. More likely, however, the various metaphors are allowed to run rampant because the traditional set meaning of the word has not been shaken at all.

The word revelation continues to be used by Christian theo-

23. Thomas Kuhn, *The Structure of Scientific Revolutions* (Chicago, 1962), p. 23; see also: Ray Hart, *Unfinished Man and the Imagination* (New York, 1968), p. 192.

logians as one of their bric-a-brac in the same way as eschaton, sin or sacrament. I would agree with Wolfhart Pannenberg's contention that "the problem of revelation has become the fundamental question in modern theology."[24] But theologians have taken such statements to refer to one of their many concepts and thus to be soluble in purely intramural terms. In many discussions, if one refers to revelation as the central issue, it will be assumed that one is talking about Barth, Bultmann or one of their offspring.[25] However, it may be that all of these supposedly different meanings of the word are all slight variations of the same model. To the extent that the word is not rooted in and filled out from some wider experience than Christian theology, this limitation is inevitable.

The observation has been made that Barth's theology is written from the viewpoint of the preacher while Bultmann's theology is developed from the situation of the listener to the preaching.[26] In one sense they have opposite points of view but their difference is within the same basic model, namely, preaching. Barth or Bultmann cannot be dismissed by such a remark. They are giants whose works cannot be bypassed. But reference

24. Wolfhart Pannenberg, *Jesus God and Man* (Philadelphia, 1968), p. 131; and his essay "The Revelation of God in Jesus of Nazareth" in *Theology as History,* eds. John Cobb and James Robinson (New York, 1967), pp. 101–133; 221–276.

25. In Gerald O'Collins, *Foundations of Theology* (Chicago, 1971), p. 53, the author writes: "Moran's persistent recourse to the category of revelation and relentless application of it as a principle of explanation bears comparison with the thoroughgoing revelation theology practised by Barth, Brunner and Gogarten in the heyday of dialectic theology." I can hardly imagine a more inaccurate summary of my concern with revelation. My interest is in establishing the meaning of revelation on non-Christian premises. O'Collins's description of my work as "pan-revelationism" (p. 53) would be accurate except that he illogically limits the world to the realm of Christian theology.

26. N. A. Dahl as quoted in René Marlé, *Introduction to Hermeneutics* (New York, 1967), p. 37: "The difference in attitude which is apparent since the debate between Barth and Bultmann is due, at least in part, to the theological point of departure, which for Barth is the situation of the preacher and for Bultmann the situation of a hearer of the word."

is made to them here because although they rise above other figures they still retain and solidify the inadequate model which has functioned in theology for centuries. Most of Christian theology seems to come either from the library or the chapel.

My remarks are not meant as an attack upon the men who have written Christian theology. I am merely trying to get behind the statements of theology to the context which produces them. Nearly all theology, up to and including the present, is written by clergymen. Probably only a clergyman could believe that preaching is a good model, let alone the best model, for understanding the religious life of mankind. It would be a near impossibility to find any non-clergymen who think of preaching and sermonizing as significant at all. Most people who give a thought to it conclude that preaching is an anachronism which is allowed existence because it bothers no one. However, if one's professional life is centered on any activity, it is possible to view the whole world in light of that endeavor.[27]

Whether or not the profession of clergyman is an anachronism is not of interest to me here. What is of central concern to this book is that practically all the theology is modeled on the clergyman's work. Theology would not necessarily be better if it were written by teachers, housewives, longshoremen, airline stewardesses or sanitation workers, but it would certainly be different. Any single group's experience and profession are inadequate. Each person works from a perspective determined by his own experience but this limitation can be corrected in part by his awareness of other ways than his own to approach life. What is needed are diversity and cooperation.

Despite some changes that have been made, the model that

27. It could be argued that the work of the clergyman is the result of the accepted meaning of revelation rather than vice versa. Thus, preaching became the Christian thing to do once there was a message to be preached. I think there is a reciprocal relation here so that the role of preacher and the meaning of revelation reinforce each other. In the last chapter I will comment on the different institutional form needed for a different understanding of revelation.

23

operates in most theologians' minds does not really differ from the one traceable at least as far back as Augustine. Gerhard Ebeling may be correct in saying that Catholics and Protestants are distinguishable by their position on revelation,[28] but to out-siders the variation is slight within the same theme. The unstint-ing Christian claim to possess the final revelation of God has inevitably led, when taken at face value, to intolerance and to condemnation of others.[29] The reply that the claim has not been pushed to the limit very often is hardly a sufficient guarantee to those who distrust Christians. It is also no basis for people who would like to find some support for their lives in the Christian religion. The gradual whittling away of pretentious claims to "revealed truth" will never produce a tolerant religious group, especially when the heart of the claim is never touched at all.

The Catholic church's Vatican II document on revelation dif-fered considerably in tone from the pronouncements of Vatican I. Its language reflected the fact that it was worked over by biblical exegetes who were called in to rectify the first disastrous pro-duction of Roman theologians.[30] The final document was hailed as one of the great achievements of Vatican II. Despite some compromises that confuse the second chapter, it managed to be positive sounding and progressive looking. Nonetheless, the key claim goes unchallenged. One severe critic of the church charged that the document still makes "the fantastic assumption that the

28. Quoted in Marlé, *op. cit.,* pp. 82–83.
29. See: Gordon Allport, *The Person in Psychology* (Boston, 1968), pp. 271–272, "The doctrine of *revelation* has led, and can still lead, a re-ligion to claim exclusive possession of final truth concerning the destiny and end of man, as well as sole authority and means for interpreting that end. Held rigidly, this position regards the teaching of other religious and philosophical formulations as a threat to human salvation." John Randall, *The Meaning of Religion for Man* (New York, 1968), p. 119 adds: "Through bitter experience, men have slowly and painfully come to realize that this claim to possess an exclusive and final revelation of the Divine is the most dangerous pretension any group can make."
30. See: Roger Schutz and Max Thurian, *Revelation* (Westminster, 1968); Avery Dulles, *Revelation and the Quest for Unity* (Washington, 1968), pp. 82–99; Henri Holstein, "Les 'Deux Sources' de la Revelation," in *Recherches des Sciences Religieuse,* LVII (1969), pp. 375–434.

Ruler of the Universe had chosen one group of narrowly educated prelates in one Church to be the prime ducts for the transmission of all divine truth to an unenlightened humanity."[31]

The problem pinpointed here is not what was written at Vatican II but the assumption on which Vatican II met. To accuse the writer of the document on revelation with error would be to misunderstand the nature of the problem. Any document that directly deals with "divine revelation" is bound to be inadequate. To the extent that the church cannot yet admit its inadequacy here, any document on revelation is bound to turn out rather badly. Where Vatican II spoke of ecumenism, the Jews or contemporary social problems, it often spoke more genuinely of revelation than did the document which tried to deal explicitly with the subject.

Since the main difficulty with the Christian position is not what is said but what is assumed, the casual way in which the word revelation is used tells more than do definitions. It is fascinating, for example, to see the words "revealed religion" as if the object of the verb reveal is the noun religion. This combination of words is not an unusual one; in fact, it has been customary since Bishop Butler in the eighteenth century to formulate the problem of natural and revealed religion.[32] In tracing the change of meaning in the word religion throughout the centuries, Wilfred Cantwell Smith notes: "We must give very special weight to the concept of 'revealed religion.' This was quite novel, and in fact is revolutionary. The concept of revelation had been standard in Christian thinking from New Testament times. Yet no one before the eighteenth century had ever supposed that what was revealed was a religion."[33]

The claim that there is a revealed religion is an extraordinary

31. Paul Blanshard, *Paul Blanshard and Vatican II* (Boston, 1966), pp. 337–338.
32. See: David Jenkins, *Guide to the Debate about God* (Philadelphia, 1966), pp. 21–30; Wilfred Cantwell Smith, *The Meaning and End of Religion* (New York, 1964), pp. 40–49.
33. Smith, *ibid.*, p. 41.

one, to say the least. But it does simplify things to slide the two words together so often that people forget the nature of the claim being made. Eventually, one can sound the challenge to accept the "revealed religion" of God as if it were merely our stubborn wills that were the problem. A prominent Christian writer can define his "Christian radicalism" by saying: "Here I mean by it that Christianity must be accepted in its revealed totality—accepted absolutely, intransigently, without cultural or philosophical or any other kind of accommodation or adaptation."[34] There is some marvelous assumption here about Christianity in its revealed totality but it is not at all clear to most of the human race what we are challenged to accept.

Even more astounding than connecting revealed and religion is the use of revealed with theology. Presumably if challenged, the user of the phrase "revealed theology" would say: "Of course no one thinks that theology is revealed; that is just a traditional way of speaking which everyone understands." Unfortunately, however, traditional but inaccurate ways of speaking often reflect the fact that some underlying problem is being obscured or avoided. In Ronald Gregor Smith's last book, he wrote: "In the history of man's self-understanding the relationships between the two activities—that is, natural and revealed theology—are so close that the modern assumption of a complete diremption between the two parts can only be described as a historical fallacy."[35] I cite Smith here not to attack him in

34. Jacques Ellul, *Violence* (New York, 1969), p. 145 (footnote).
35. Ronald Gregor Smith, *The Doctrine of God* (Philadelphia, 1970), p. 69. In Randall, *op. cit.,* p. 108: "St. Thomas was expressing this distinction when he held that, while rational theology can demonstrate the existence of God, certain of God's attributes, like goodness, and certain of God's relations to the world, the essential Christian beliefs about the nature of God come from 'Faith,' not from 'Reason.' They were revealed in Christ. Without the aid of this revelation given through the teachings of the Church, Reason cannot alone reach these insights into the character of God, though it can understand their meaning once they have been given. This is the difference traditionally made between the beliefs of 'revealed' theology and those of 'rational' or 'natural' theology." Up to the last sen-

particular; his book is an attempt to overcome this problem. All the more significant, therefore, is the fact that he uses the terms natural and revealed theology without a demur on their legitimacy. Perhaps the "diremption" occurred necessarily because of the choice of categories and the way out of the difficulty is to challenge natural and revealed as words applicable to theology at all.

The word revelation is used in Christian writing with a variety of images. If the word is to be used at all, some metaphor or combination of metaphors is probably unavoidable. The most common phrase associated with revelation is "break in."[36] The dominance of this image may be largely traceable to Karl Barth but the roots of the image go back deep into Christianity.[37] These days what "breaks in" is not usually an angry God but a story or God's word. A religious psychologist writes: "The Judaeo-Christian tradition believes in the irreplaceable part played by the word of God. Revelation has burst in upon history and set up a dialogue of questioning and acceptance which alone is able to show the divine paternity for what it really is."[38] With a revelation that bursts in upon history, the split remains as bad as ever. In addition, there remains the threat of

---

tence Randall is describing St. Thomas's framework but the distinction between revealed theology and rational or natural theology would have been unintelligible to Aquinas. This "traditional" distinction came several centuries later.

36. Sebastian Moore, *God Is a New Language* (Westminster, 1967), p. 131, challenges the metaphor of "break in" by asking: "Does God break in? No, he breaks out, not in the spacial sense that the above question bears, but rather in the sense of an epidemic."

37. See: Rosemary Ruether, *The Radical Kingdom* (New York, 1970), p. 115: "Barth and others that belonged to his circle set themselves to separate what cultural Christianity had joined together, to distinguish the spirit of man from the Spirit of God, to distinguish religious consciousness from revelation, to distinguish religion from the gospel, and to distinguish man's word from God's word.... Revelation is God's Word that breaks in from the other side of this unbridgeable chasm after all of man's ladders to Heaven have fallen short and given way. Revelation is the story of God's ways with man, not man's way with God."

38. Antoine Vergote, *The Religious Man* (Dayton, 1969), p. 168.

intolerance as long as Christians make the assumption that the word revelation is their possession to be defined by them.

The image of a light is frequently made use of, particularly to emphasize the positive and interpretive role of revelation. Lest the word lose all substantiality, however, the light is usually connected with some definite knowledge.[39] A contemporary Catholic theologian writes: "Revelation is a light that aids the light of reason. It is a higher form of knowledge, a foreknowledge that tells man the unerring direction to the Land of Truth and Freedom. As the Scriptures say, the Truth (Revelation) shall make us free. Faith is also seen as a higher light than reason; it is the acceptance of Revelation."[40] The first two sentences of this quotation do not appear to be compatible; in the first, revelation is light, in the second, it is knowledge. Apparently, it is the second which is to be taken literally because in the last sentence faith is a light and what the light accepts is presumably not another light.[41] Shining through the strange combination of metaphors is the clear claim that revelation is a knowledge granted to some people and not to others, granted according to a procedure that prevents its accessibility in the ordinary, regular world of the human being.

Conservative Christian theologians say what they mean in

39. See: Robert Young, *Encounter with World Religions* (Philadelphia, 1970), p. 58: "The meaning of revelation appears in its true significance only when revelation is used to interpret and cast light on other truths. To rely on revelation apart from other truth is as bad as to rely upon prayer without action"; see also: Henri Marrou, *Time and Timeliness* (New York, 1969), p. 25.

40. Eulalio Baltazar, *God within Process* (Paramus, 1970), p. 171.

41. See: Avery Dulles, *The Survival of Dogma* (Garden City, 1971), p. 75: "In the last analysis the question whether revelation is 'light' or 'content' is otiose. It introduces a false dichotomy. Because we ourselves are always involved in the mysteries of which faith speaks, the light of faith is constitutive of the objects on which faith bears." I agree that the argument is badly stated and cannot go anywhere but that does not mean that the question is "otiose." The existence of the question and the impossibility of answering it with "light" or "content" indicate the need for establishing the meaning of revelation on some other basis.

more direct terms: "The peculiar faith of Christianity is that there are two points of view from which every truth must be approached—a human point of view and a divine. There is truth as man sees it from his predicament as man, and there is also truth as God reveals it to man in terms of God's own purpose for man and for the world."[42] Not many people may accept this staggering claim but at least it is fairly clear what is being claimed, namely, that there are a determinable number of truths which did not come from human processes but were directly bestowed by God to Christians.

Progressive Christian theology tends to blur one image on top of the other with little attempt to sort out their relationship. This tendency seems to spring from the belief that if one uses enough images some of them will hit the mark. It also helps one to avoid the charge of naively asserting that somewhere in some place there is an identifiable something called revelation. Thus, revelation is light, encounter, event, word, word-event, story, history, presence, wisdom, Christ, Spirit, scripture, tradition, scripture-tradition, etc. After the profusion of images, however, the main claim still operates throughout Christian theology, namely, revelation is a special source of truth for Christians.

The most concerted attempt to develop a new way to deal with revelation has been to refer to it primarily as *event*. Beginning in the nineteenth century there was a better understanding of the bible achieved by tracing the development of the litera-

42. Daniel Niles, *Buddhism and the Claims of Christ* (Richmond, 1967), p. 23; on the Roman Catholic side, compare the following statement in Jean Danielou, *The Faith Eternal and the Man of Today* (Chicago, 1970), p. 58: "Through religions man tries in an obscure and grasping way to discern beyond visible things the invisible and mysterious realities whose existence he has some vague idea of. Revelation is the opposite movement: it does not go from man to God; it goes from God to man. The essence of revelation is that God came to man; it is a gesture of God. Between man and God there is an abyss that man cannot cross. That is why all pagan religions eventually end in a sort of abyss, where they sense their limitations."

ture in relation to the history of the people who produced it. Great stress was laid upon the fact that God revealed himself not only through statements but through actions. At least for biblical exegetes it was highly significant that the Jewish scriptures emerged not from a school of philosophy but from a nation struggling for its life.

The problem implicit in this concept of revelation surfaced in the later writing of Rudolf Bultmann. Well schooled in New Testament study, Bultmann tried to be fully consistent.[43] He took what biblical scholarship was saying about revelation and attempted to apply it to the present. If revelation is an event in biblical times, then it should also exist today as event. The demand is obvious enough; in fact, it had been made by non-Christian critics for centuries. They have wanted to know why God only spoke in the past and why he retired to heaven leaving his words behind him.

Bultmann's project, however, was at cross purpose with his method—not the Bultmann method but the method of Christian theology. Like any good Protestant theologian, Bultmann went to the New Testament for his controlling definition of revelation.[44] To Christian theologians this was the good part of his project; to most other people this move was illogical. If one is looking for a revelation not frozen in the things of the past, why turn immediately to the pages of a book from the past? This book and many other books may be helpful along the way but it is not clear at all that any writing from the past should be the first or the determining source one should go to.

Bultmann was faced with the dilemma of trusting only the New Testament to supply the content of his belief and yet mov-

43. Rudolf Bultmann, "New Testament and Mythology," in *Kerygma and Myth*, ed., Hans-Werner Bartsch (New York, 1961), pp. 1–44.
44. See: Rudolf Bultmann, "Revelation in the New Testament," in *Existence and Faith*, ed., Schubert Ogden (New York, 1960), pp. 58–91; Joseph Cahill, "Rudolf Bultmann's Concept of Revelation," *Catholic Biblical Quarterly*, XXIV (July, 1962), pp. 297–306.

ing to eliminate any fixed content to belief so that revelation could truly be a present event. The New Testament taught that revelation was an event but it also said that Jesus was Lord and Savior, redeeming mankind by his life, death and resurrection. Since all that the New Testament says about Jesus is difficult to believe today and impossible to prove, this content gets reduced until there is only a single thread above the cross. Like the animal in the fairy tale devouring itself, the New Testament eliminates the New Testament, although the process stops just short of extinction lest there be no basis for asserting revelation to be an event. The only message left from God is that he does not send messages.

My image here is not intended to be deprecatory toward Bultmann. On the contrary, Bultmann, better than most of his contemporaries, was close to the heart of the problem. The inadequacy of his theology is symptomatic of the underlying problem in Christian theology. If revelation is what it is presumed to be in Christian theology then one's ground can only keep getting narrower to the point of disappearance. Much of the theology of recent years has been a pulling back from the abyss that Bultmann faced.[45] Recovering more of the historical Jesus or adding emphasis to words as well as events serve only to patch up the framework that Bultmann shook. The one thing that Christian theology has not been able to contemplate is that there may be no way to deal with revelation from within Christian theology. Or, to put it differently, Christian theology has to face the possibility that there is no Christian revelation.

Rudolph Bultmann is criticized on all sides today but much of the criticism is misleading if not inaccurate.[46] The most com-

45. See: James Robinson, *A New Quest for the Historical Jesus* (Naperville, 1959). Raymond Brown, "After Bultmann What? An introduction to the Post-Bultmannians," *Catholic Biblical Quarterly,* XXVI (Jan., 1964), pp. 1–30.
46. See: Louis Malevez, *The Christian Message and Myth* (Westminster, 1957); René Marlé *Bultmann and the Christian Faith* (Westminster, 1968).

31

mon charge is that he sold out Christian revelation to Heideg-gerian philosophy. This formulation obscures the problem. Bult-mann apparently got much of his inspiration from Heidegger and used some of Heidegger's conceptual apparatus to set up the problematic. But when it came to delivering an answer, Bult-mann went straight to the pages of the New Testament. The result might have been better if he had reversed the process. Certainly, it would have been better if Heidegger and the ex-perience of people today had played some role in developing the notion of revelation. What he took from Heidegger is the im-age of the individual subject in a "fallen world." What is not from Heidegger is the proclamation of the crucified Jesus as savior and that is where the weakness and narrowness of his approach resides. He brought to a conclusion the theologians' rear-guard action of pruning revealed truths. Bultmann is left with one sentence that either inspires faith in the individual or does not. Far from submitting "Christian revelation" to philoso-phy, he leaves the "word of God" perched high above and un-alloyed by human experience, thought or activity.

The other common objection to Bultmann is that he is too concerned with the present to the neglect of past and future. What I have already said suggests that this criticism, too, is dangerously misleading. Bultmann's notion of revelation is par-ticularly deficient in being non-present. I will postpone a full consideration of this point until the next chapter where I can deal with it in greater detail. My interest here has been in pointing to the development of revelation in modern theology as events rather than truths. Catholicism somewhat belatedly fol-lowed Protestantism down this path and spoke of revelation at Vatican II as event and interpretive words.[47] To biblical exe-getes the progress which this marks is significant but it is ques-tionable what significance this has to anyone else. To the extent

47. See: Edward Schillebeeckx, "Revelation in Word and Deed," in *Revelation and Theology*, vol. I (New York, 1967), pp. 33–56.

that the churches talk about a past event they use words to refer back to what is now not available as event. It is not obvious why people should be interested in the events which produced the documents—if the documents are God's word. Roman Catholicism and most of Protestantism, despite the talk about events, rely on the stable given which exists in the form of words. Were anyone to start looking for a revelation in the events available as events, that is, in the day-to-day experiences of his life, he would have to reject any document from the past pretending to define revelation.

Despite the shifting of images, the notion of revelation has changed little in Christian writing. Theologians have done their best to make it appealing ("relevant to modern man"), tolerant and dynamic. However, they are hampered by their starting point and their tools. If the word is defined by ancient documents, the definition can only pertain to that *kind* of thing definable by ancient documents. If something is projected from the pages of a book, it cannot help but be a bookish projection. Books may lead beyond themselves and indeed all good books do. But when that happens, one has a starting point for grappling with human life in which there are no *a priori* truths that take precedence. Every document must be tested against experience. The great documents, of course, should be measured with respect and caution, but experience is the ultimate guide and not the document.[48]

48. Hans Küng, "Hans Küng Replies to Gregory Baum," in *Commonweal*, June 25, 1971, p. 329: "The Gospel, the Christian message, must take on a new form in every age. It must be translated from the language of yesterday into the idiom of today. For this reason one may say, even if it might be misunderstood, that revelation continues to take place in every new proclamation. The mere repetition of biblical verses serves very little use; the contemporary experience of man, the church and society must be included. Together with the Scriptures that experience constitutes the second pole around which Christian theology and proclamation must revolve. ... Although Christian theology and proclamation revolve around two poles, as we have described them, yet the original Christian message must be the decisive pole." Küng's identification of scripture and revelation here makes

33

Christian theology has not believed that it is possible to accept this principle. The proof that it does not is the fact that its concept of revelation is not developed from human experience but is dictated by Christian sources. I do not see how Christian people can be "relevant" to modern problems unless they join in the quest for meaning with everyone else. Christians are still at the game of delivering their revelation instead of cooperating with all men and women to develop a meaning of revelation. For the first time Christians are being challenged with the prospect of developing a theology that must take its place and prove itself on the stage of world history.

The above criticisms of Christian theology are enough to indicate in an anticipatory way how I intend to use the word revelation. Here I am choosing a starting point; the remainder of the book is an attempt to fill in the meaning of the word. In trying to elaborate on the word I will have to use words and images that are not fully adequate. As I have tried to show, the great problem is not the use of metaphors and analogies but the inadequate context in which each of these functions. Unless the word can be established on its own as a non-Christian and even non-religious word it is always going to pose an insoluble problem in Christian theology. It will always be that inexplicable little blip that one has to accept to get the whole thing moving.

Some people would object that "revelation" is a word with such religious and Christian connotations that it is unrealistic to establish a viable meaning outside of that realm. This point is a serious and debatable one but my answer consists in the entire project that follows. I am aware that there could be a subtle imperialism in trying to use the word revelation to cut across

---

it impossible for him to understand what is demanded for contemporary experience. Obviously in translating texts, the original text is determinative. But revelation has very little to do with translating texts. Revelation does not "continue" so much as it is totally the present; it is not mainly in the "proclamation" of Christian scriptures but the experience of the human race.

religious traditions. For example, Confucianists may say they have no revelation because their *Way of Ritual* is a book of human insight. They reject what they understand to be the Western meaning of revelation. What I have to offer is a meaning of revelation that would enable this particular word to be a link between East and West. Perhaps there are other links and better links still to emerge but I think there is some reason to believe that the notion of revelation might be particularly appropriate in relating East and West.

Revelation in the English language is a noun and would seem to refer to some object or thing. Embodied in the word, however, is a verbal quality which enables the word to carry some flavor of doing or making. Revelation is what one engages in and the word immediately conveys that there is at least one person engaged in it. For the revelation to be completed there must be at least one other person.

The words reveal and revealing are more commonly used than the word revelation. Nonetheless, the word revelation can regularly be found in the book reviews, theatre gossip, political intrigues or sports pages of the daily newspaper. When the noun revelation is used in ordinary discourse it usually is in reference to some guarded secret that has suddenly been exposed. In that sense, the revelation is the secret revealed by the revealer; but even ordinary usage grasps that the revelation is not only of the secret but of the one who is revealing secrets. Christian writing likes to make this point but then it immediately proceeds to dismiss this fact and to attach the word revelation to the things supposedly revealed. In non-religious discourse one does not get into trouble by deciding to use the word revelation of the things revealed. I will, nevertheless, maintain that human life is better understood by placing the word back at the level of the persons exchanging. In the religious area the identification of the word with things said to be revealed is disastrous beyond repair. It forces one into maintaining that there are some things

35

that come from God as opposed to other things which do not.

I wish to fix the primary meaning of the word at the most comprehensive level where it will not lead down a blind alley. I am stretching the common usage but not doing violence to it. In using revelation as I do, I claim to relate aspects of life that can be called religious and non-religious and to clarify poles of experience that can be called human and divine.

Revelation is relation qualified by the fact that the poles of the relation initiate activity toward the other. Thus, revelation in its primary sense is capable of being as extensive as all reality. The only words more fundamental would be words like being, relation or activity. All of these words are at the same level of ultimacy. To be and to act are inseparable and being or to be is necessarily relational. Revelation refers to the relational character of being. The word specifies, however, that at least one of the poles in the relation is what humans experience as a knowing, awareness or conscious pole. In human experience revelation is most obvious as a relation between two persons; it is less obvious but still possible between a person and a tree; it is not apparent but should not immediately be ruled out between two trees. What man calls knowing may be only one form of communing, that is, the mutual giving and receiving in which each grows more itself by unity with the whole.

It would be inadequate simply to identify revelation as relationship because this latter word might be taken in a static sense. Revelation is relationship in which the relata really relate. Furthermore, revelation is not one of the relations but the entire set of relations that constitute the universe. Experientially, humans know many foci in the matrix of relationships. Even though one tendency of religion is to deny the ultimate reality of these foci, experience begins with the poles of the revelatory relationship being many.

What is said above may have some resemblance to one philosopher or another. My intention, however, is not to deduce religion from philosophy nor to use one metaphysical system to line up reality. The sources for my description are less esoteric, as I shall shortly mention. Philosophy obviously plays some role in trying to set out a comprehensible and consistent pattern but the driving force comes from many sources including religious ones. It would be fairly easy to stay on the plane of asserting that revelation is the unveiling of being but such statements approach tautology in their abstraction. To try to imagine, to point to, to express bodily or verbally what revelation means is bound to be a frustrating expedition that is finally doomed to failure. The magnificent thing about religious traditions is that they try and even their defeats have been worth the effort. The disastrous end of religions is for them to think that they possess a revelation given to them by the gods. Such a possession would short-circuit their need to cooperate with all men in understanding the whole revelational structure of the universe.

With the meaning I am proposing for revelation, it is almost impossible to put any adjectives before the word. Of course, one can use an adjective and claim that it is a shorthand way of saying something else. To make my point clear I am going to be especially insistent about challenging the adjectives because they constantly mislead. One could perhaps put the word personal before revelation but that would seem to be redundant. A revealing pole would seem to be personal although one could debate the meaning of the word person. I will return to this point in the subsequent chapters. Since all the revelation that man can experience by definition includes the human, then human revelation would also seem to be redundant unless by contrast to the divine. Whether and how the word divine comes in here will also be examined in more detail later. Suffice it to say here that any divine revelation is by definition also a human revelation. If there is a divine pole to the revelational structure it is within relation, i.e., one focus of giving and receiving.

The adjectives "natural" and "supernatural" are not helpful

as descriptions of revelation. Although the terms are not cited often the remnants of the distinction still operate in theology. I would agree on this point with Eugene Fontinell's statement: "The category of the supernatural was developed over against a specific view of nature—nature which was fundamentaly closed and finished. Given such a view of nature, I think that the construction of the category of the supernatural was a necessary and liberating moment in the development of human consciousness. If, however, one views nature as open, as alive with unrealized but realizable possibilities and as radically developmental, then the category of the supernatural would appear less useful and indeed quite misleading."[49] I suspect that the reason the term supernatural has survived is because it was necessary for justifying the existence of a church. The church reluctantly put aside the claim that "outside the church there is no salvation" but it held on to the premise of that belief, namely, a supernatural revelation available only through the church. If revelation, that is, the only revelation there is, is everywhere, then those who are in charge of the church will see themselves in trouble.

There are other distinctions which I suspect are traceable to the instinct of church leaders to prop up the church's need to exist. The term "Christian revelation" epitomizes the need and the claim. Logically, one would speak of a "Christian revelation" only if there were other kinds of revelation, e.g., Buddhist revelation. That is indeed what is said today but through Buddhist revelation may be given courteous respect by Christians, the Christians know that their revelation is best. The category of "Christian revelation" is a cul-de-sac and the only way to avoid the dead end is by giving up the term. If Christians were to talk about the universal revelation of which Christianity is a limited expression, they could stop being condescending and/or intol-

49. Eugene Fontinell, "Transcendent Divinity and Process Philosophy," in *New Theology, no.* 7, eds., Martin Marty and Dean Peerman (New York, 1970), p. 183.

erant. They could make any claim they wished to (and then try to sustain it in the arena of human experience) as long as they stopped talking about the divine revelation which they possess.

For similar reasons I would object to the phrase "biblical revelation." There is no specific revelation that can be called biblical even if one believes that the Christian bible is a most helpful piece of writing in trying to make sense out of life. The phrase "biblical revelation" is consistent with a fundamentalism which holds that each statement of the bible is a truth revealed by God. Very few people believe that today but most of theology still lives off the pale shadow of that belief. In Christian theology today revelation is not the statements of the bible but it does come to us in the bible, giving us the (true) biblical revelation as opposed to those other (not so true) non-biblical revelations.

More subtly misleading is the term "historical revelation."[50] Sometimes the term is used as synonymous with biblical revelation and is objectionable for the same reasons. When the word means more than this, it tends to become equivalent to personal and human. Historical revelation then approaches redundancy because in the most comprehensive sense of history all revelation is historical. More often, however, historical revelation is used in clear contrast to non-historical revelation, corresponding to the difference between Jewish-Christian tradition and all other religions. An important thing is at issue here concerning Jewish and Christian contributions to world history. The point is inevitably clouded by the contrast drawn between historical and nature religions.

There is finally the common distinction between a general and special revelation.[51] This distinction could be closer to the mark

50. See: Louis Monden, *Faith: Can Man Still Believe?* (New York, 1970), p. 87.
51. The inadequacy of the distinction between general and special revelation is pointed out by Joachim Wach, *Comparative Study of Revelation* (New York, 1958), p. 49; also in Van der Leeuw, *op. cit.*, p. 566: "The

but of itself it is inadequate. General and special was a way of possibly breaking down or sliding around the Christian claim to have the truth. In practice the distinction became equivalent to natural and supernatural. There is a general body of truths available naturally but the important truths can only be got via the special source, the church.

The helpful distinction which sounds close to general/special is that between universal and particular. A universal revelation would require concrete and particular realization. In contrast, a general revelation would be a matter of generalities which are not very enlightening until one gets the special data available only in the church. Since revelation is a relational structure with a unity including diversity, some distinction is probably necessary to speak at all. Thus, I will speak of the one, universal revelation and the particular, concrete expressions of it. A particular expression of revelation is not identical or equivalent to revelation nor is it a part of revelation (in the sense of a divisible segment).[52] Christian may be a particular way of expressing revelation but it is misleading to refer to Christian revelation.

3. BELIEF AND UNBELIEF

Further light can be thrown on the use of the word revelation by bringing into the discussion the word faith. Obviously, faith is a category that is very closely related to revelation. However, they are by no means synonymous words. There is an unfortunate tendency in theological writing to refer to the question of "faith and revelation" or "faith or revelation." The latter refer-

distinction between a 'general' revelation to everyone, and a 'special' revelation bestowed upon the faithful alone and in some particular way, is very mischievous. For in so far as it is always originally given to myself, revelation is never 'general' but always 'special.' "

52. See: Nels Ferré, *The Universal Word* (Philadelphia, 1969), p. 17: "If the ultimate is universally related, any revelation concerning the ultimate at its center must constitute a universal word. Consequently revelation at its full heart cannot be limited to or by any historical faith."

ence is the more misleading since it presumes that the words are interchangeable and that to describe faith is to deal with revelation. For many writers on faith, revelation is a skeleton in the closet which they never face.

The word faith is used more frequently in ordinary language and in literature than is the word revelation. Partly for that fact, faith is a more ambiguous term, or, perhaps better, it is a word more diverse in meaning. Whereas it is feasible with the word revelation to choose one meaning as primary and to relegate all the others to a pattern of secondary meanings, it is much more difficult to do the same thing with faith. However, the meanings of faith do break down rather evenly into two sets: one relating to the objective world, the other pertaining to subjective attitudes. It is this split, which is impossible to overcome with the word faith itself, that makes faith a category of limited value for beginning theology.

Until recently Roman Catholics usually used the word faith in a highly objectified sense. Thus, a person "had the faith" or "belonged to the faith" and he might "lose the faith." The person with all of his attitudes was involved but the key question was whether the person would accept or reject the faith. He could have difficulties but not doubts since doubt did not belong within faith. Temptations against faith were to be resolved by being avoided.

Less common among "the faithful" but present in Catholic theology was the use of the word faith as a subjective light. Here the word was used in the distinction between "faith and reason." This distinction could have been a helpful one if faith and reason had been placed as functions or attitudes in reference to a larger human context. Unfortunately, faith and reason came to be thought of as two independent sources of information about the world. There were natural truths known by reason and in addition there were (supernatural) truths known only by faith.

41

Catholic theology was confident that it had covered the whole problem since it had included in discussion of faith, the inner and the outer, the subjective and the objective. The presumed solution was more like a restatement of the question and to the extent the statement acquiesced in the split between subjective and objective, it was a poor restatement of the question. Lip service was paid to both objective and subjective but when it came to a test of which was the important meaning no one had any doubt. In any conflict between the subjective and objective, the faith demanded that one submit. The ultimate proof that one had the faith was the willingness to abide by the faith of holy mother church. For purposes of achieving conformity the church's faith was available in the clearest, unmistakable terms.

In the 1950's and 1960's a rash of books by Catholic authors raised a challenge to the operative meaning of faith in Catholicism.[53] Prodded by biblical exegesis, these authors had begun to rediscover the riches of the notion of faith in the New Testament, in patristic literature and in contemporary writing. They joined with the Protestant tradition which from the day Luther had read the Epistle to the Romans had placed faith at the center of personal reflection. In sharp contrast to Catholicism, Protestantism had generally nourished the subjective side of faith. To be a Protestant believer was to have received the gift of faith which enabled one to respond to God's word. To be in possession of such faith was more important than anything one might do. The proof that one had the faith resided not in conformity to an external rule but in an inner confidence or testimony of the Spirit.

Catholic writers have continued to mine this rich vein of biblical and Protestant tradition of faith. When Catholic philosophers get mixed up in the theological fray they nearly always

53. For example: Romano Guardini, *The Life of Faith* (Westminster, 1960); Jean Mouroux, *I Believe* (New York, 1959); Eugene Joly, *What Is Faith?* (New York, 1958); Carlos Cirne-Lima, *Personal Faith* (New York, 1965).

use faith as their central category.[54] In fact, it is amazing that there are numerous recent books on faith and extremely few on revelation.[55] Some of the books on faith are valuable works which can enrich the lives of Catholics. These books also have a built-in limitation which prevents them from coping with the underlying problem of a Christian religious group in the contemporary setting.

The advantage of the word faith and the reason that philosophers can feel comfortable with it is that the word has currency outside of the Christian and religious area. As a word descriptive of a basic human attitude, faith can easily bear a secular interpretation. Philosophers, anthropologists, psychologists or sociologists can discuss faith as a searching, open trust that is necessary for all human beings. However, any attaching of the word faith to external data can only be looked upon as a corruption of faith. For example, John Gardner writes of some people in society: "When such individuals talk of their search for meaning or faith or something to believe in one gets the impression that they conceive the object of their search as a kind of wonderful secret room they will someday stumble into. Once they find it the struggle will be over. No more effort. No more doubt."[56] Gardner is contrasting here faith as a genuine human attitude to what most people would still call a religious faith. The wonderful secret room of revealed truths is what a religious faith is supposed to have found.

Much can be done and has been done to overcome the opposi-

54. For example: Michael Novak, *Belief and Unbelief* (New York, 1965); Josef Pieper, *Belief and Faith* (New York, 1963); Leslie Dewart, *Foundations of Belief* (New York, 1969); Eugene Fontinell, *Toward a Reconstruction of Religion* (Garden City, 1970); Baltazar, *op. cit.*

55. Nearly all books on revelation are expositions of scripture or of a theology only slightly removed from scripture; for example, Heinrich Fries, *Revelation* (New York, 1969); Claude Tresmontant, *La problème de la Révélation* (Paris, 1969).

56. John Gardner, *The Recovery of Confidence* (New York, 1970), p. 135.

tion between a religious faith and a human attitude of faith. However, there is ultimately no way out of an opposition if at some point faith has to accept a revelation. And that is exactly what does happen and must happen with books on faith which leave the category of revelation untouched. Revelation, insofar as it is qualified by words like biblical, historical or Christian, implies a set of data external to faith. At some point one must jump the gap from inner to outer. People who are writing on faith today are very reticent on this point (in contrast to someone like Kierkegaard who had to face the problem and faced it head on).

Philosophers perhaps have an excuse in leaving the investigation of revelation to theologians. Nonetheless, I think that this division of work is an unfortunate one. Furthermore, there is danger in philosophers seeming to suggest that the question of revelation is a relatively minor one, which is either implicitly solved by their treatment of faith or can be finished off with dispatch by continuing in the same direction. The category of revelation will not reconceptualize itself; it is at least as difficult to reconstruct as faith. For the viability of Christianity and other religions it is more in need of examination. So long as revelation stands as a "something" to be accepted by humans, Christian theologians and their religion are running down a dead-end corridor.

The net result in Catholic writing so far has been that faith and revelation are now correlates. Great emphasis is placed upon faith as a subjective act involving the whole person. The faith response is said to be to God's call or word. God reveals and man believes.[57] There is very little talk about *articula fidei* but these have been replaced by a biblical and historical revela-

57. See: Oliver Rabut, *Faith and Doubt* (New York, 1967), pp. 104–110; Alfonso Nebreda, "Role of Witness in Transmitting the Message," in *Pastoral Catechetics*, eds., Johannes Hofinger and Theodore Stone (New York, 1964), pp. 67–86.

44

tion. The new phrases are certainly more attractive than the old ones. If faith is in a word of promise for the future, then there is a sense of dynamism and progress. Nevertheless, it is amazing that so little has changed. One either accepts the revelation or not; one is still asked to believe that at some point God has bestowed some words of promise available through transmission by official channels. As I shall try to show presently, this scheme of faith and revelation still shows little awareness of the chief complaint about Christianity by sincere and intelligent men of today.

Revelation, I am claiming throughout this work, is either the central notion in the reconstruction of the Christian and religious or else it cannot find a place at all. It is not one of the categories of theology nor can it be set up as the correlative of faith. One must choose a meaning for revelation which implies a meaning for faith or else reverse the process. Nearly all the writing in this area begins with faith and projects a meaning for revelation. The result is an attractive-looking path but one that ends in disaster. Because faith is examined as a personal attitude (and rightly so because this is where the wider use of the language places the word) the only thing left to do with revelation is to correlate it to faith as an external call, word, event, etc.

Revelation is a less propitious-looking word to start with but that is part of its strength. What is needed at the base of religion is a category that is relational, social and practical (that is, including action). Revelation can be developed this way but faith cannot. If revelation is developed in this way then all the recent writing on faith can be retained, appreciated and strengthened by a wider context. In such a context revelation is the structure of all experience and faith is an element or basic component of the revelational process. Faith is directed not toward revelation but toward people and the universe. Revelation is not the answer to faith but the underlying reality which gives sense to faith as an open-ended search.

I am simply affirming completely what is constantly said in Christian writing, namely, that "believing in" is the primary meaning of faith. At no point does one have to jump from "believe in" to "believe that."[58] If revelation is not "something" there is no need to "believe that" something is true. This move does not eliminate doctrinal expressions by a religious group. It might even make the verbal expressions more important for holding the group together. Protestantism could push aside the need for verbal, material, social expressions but only because it could always go back to its doctrinal bedrock, the Christian scriptures. Catholicism has been more concerned with the verbal exposition but usually as a shibboleth of orthodoxy. The path I am advocating undercuts both Catholic and Protestant positions with the hope of re-establishing them on a firmer, experiential base. Verbal formulations have to arise from the continuing interaction of people; doctrine then becomes the constantly changing expression of the group's commitments to one another. None of the statements, including those of the bible or church councils, is God's revelation. Of nothing formulable into human words can it be said: You must "believe that" that is true because God has revealed it.

In summary, I have warned that it is dangerous to slide back and forth between faith and revelation as if they were synonymous, or else to treat the two as correlatives equally basic to understanding. All attempts to project a meaning for revelation from a document of faith or an attitude of faith are bound to failure because the starting point is too restrictive. The meanings of both faith and revelation must be derived from the widest possible experience. Whereas this approach has been adopted for faith, this approach has not been used for revelation. The reconstruction of revelation is the more necessary since it subsumes and determines faith whereas the reverse cannot be true.

58. On the irreducibility of "believe in" to "believe that," see H. H. Price, "Belief 'in' and Belief 'that'" in *The Philosophy of Religion*, ed., Basil Mitchell (New York, 1971), pp. 143–167.

46

Eventually one might return to speaking of "a Christian faith" or "the Christian faith" although I would not particularly recommend this way of speaking. At no point can one come to speak of "a Christian revelation" or "the Christian revelation." In contrast to faith which is a determinate attitude that might be specified and specify a particular group (e.g., Christian as distinct from Hindu), revelation is the encompassing reality that is expressed everywhere but is nowhere portioned out into sections called Christian or Hindu.

The relation I have drawn between faith and revelation can be supported by considering the rise of atheism in the modern West. Unless there is a redoing of the notion of revelation, the writing on faith will not come to grips with the issue raised by the "non-believer." Much of Christianity seems to believe that in the Christian conflict with the modern world one simply has evidence of the sinfulness of men and that it is the modern world which has to change rather than Christianity. Karl Barth was probably the most eloquent spokesman of this position. "Barth suggests that our problem is not with a world come of age but with 'a world which *regards* itself as of age (and proves daily that it is precisely not that).' In such a situation, Barth says that it is dangerous to approach modern man 'with some sort of gibberish, which, for the moment, is modern' because what we have to say both to other men and ourselves 'is a strange piece of news.' "[59] His reaction to a "world come of age" is understandable and has some validity to it. However, Dietrich Bonhoeffer, who was most responsible for the phrase "world come of age," also understood the point which Barth is making here. It would be silly to think that Bonhoeffer did not grasp the ambiguity of a "world come of age" as he waited for execution in a prison camp.[60] What Bonhoeffer also grasped was that the

59. William Hordern, *Introduction to Theology* (Philadelphia, 1966), p. 152.
60. Regin Prenter, "Bonhoeffer and Barth's Positivism of Revelation," in *World Come of Age*, ed., Ronald Smith (London, 1967), p. 93.

Christian church itself was part of the condition, if not the cause, of the virulent atheism which the churches loudly condemn. In the same way that authoritarian police regimes are part of the reason for law breakers, so modern atheism is the counterpart of religious development in the West.[61] One of the best ways to penetrate the Christian position on revelation is to understand modern objections to it. Perhaps at the end of this study the churches can still dismiss the objectors as sinners, but Christian theologians must examine the objections of atheism and consider if there is not some validity to them.[62]

After the founding age of the Christian church there slowly developed a doctrine about God, that is, an omnipotent, omniscient, immutable ruler of the world. The concept of such a God, wrote A. N. Whitehead, was "clear, terrifying and unprovable," but "to dissent was death."[63] There were never lost in medieval Catholicism other elements that helped to soften the picture: the loving Jesus, the tender virgin, the interceding saints. But "having a Christian revelation" at all led inevitably to a God who was outside the human struggle. For those who have grown up in the West, even those who reject the whole doctrine, it is almost impossible to imagine that there may be a different way of approaching the matter. The operative model for God's relation to the world could be entirely different. "The form of Christianity differs from the form of nature because in the Church and in its spiritual atmosphere we are in a universe that has been *made*. Outside the Church we are in a universe that has

61. See: Fyoder Dostoevsky, *The Idiot* (New York, 1958), pp. 527–529; Carl Jung, *Psychology and Religion* (New Haven, 1938), p. 23: "The Catholic who has turned his back on the church usually develops a secret or manifest inclination toward atheism.... The absolution of the Catholic church seems to demand an equally absolute negation."
62. Johannes Hoekendijk, *The Church Inside Out* (Philadelphia, 1966), p. 19, points out that the skeptic and the drunkard are the two classical types that Christian evangelism seeks out. The modern rejection of the Christian church does not fit into this framework.
63. Alfred North Whitehead, *Religion in the Making* (New York, 1960), p. 72.

grown. Thus the God who made the world stands outside it as the carpenter stands outside his artifacts but the Tao which grows the world is within it. Christian doctrine admits, in theory, that God is immanent, but in practice it is his transcendence his otherness, which is always stressed."[64]

I am particularly interested here in the reverberations of Christian doctrine in the modern, scientific era. The reasons for the rise of critical, scientific method in the West are complicated ones, but it seems to have been both a result of and a reaction to Christianity.[65] In any case, a new era arose and a new world came to be. The fact that this world was incompatible with the world of "Christian revelation" was at first hidden. The founders of this new world, like Galileo and Newton, were conservative Christian believers.[66] Nonetheless, despite their personal beliefs, they had initiated a process that shifted power from God to man. It became only a matter of time until the earth took back the power bequeathed to heaven. "Man becomes an atheist," wrote Proudhon, "when he feels himself to be better than his God." The thought of man which can create the concept of *ens realissimum* someday becomes strong enough to slay its own creation.[67]

As happens in the struggle of an oppressed people, there is a first stage of claiming equal rights. If this first stage succeeds, the result is not contentment and truce but a more dramatic and often violent opposition to all remnants of oppression. At this stage the cry is not for equality but for a different world. In the early stages of modernity the slogan was "dare to be wise" but

64. Alan Watts, *Nature, Man and Woman* (New York, 1970), p. 40.
65. See: Alfred North Whitehead, *Science and the Modern World* (New York, 1967); Herbert Butterfield, *Christianity and History* (New York, 1950).
66. See: Lewis Mumford, *The Pentagon of Power* (New York, 1970), pp. 39–76; Allen Whelis, *The End of the Modern Age* (New York, 1971), pp. 10–24.
67. See: Bernhard Welte, "The Philosophical Knowledge of God and the Possibility of Atheism," in *Is God Dead?* (Glen Rock, 1966), p. 125.

this path eventually led to Nietzsche's scream: "He crawled into my dirtiest corners; this God had to die; man cannot bear that such a witness live." The turning point at which the desire to "think from below" became thinking without limits is often attributed to Immanuel Kant. Once again this fact is obscured by Kant's orthodox and conservative Christian position which conflicted with the proclaimed direction of enlightenment in Kant's philosophy: "Enlightenment is man's exodus from his self-incurred tutelage. Tutelage is the inability to use one's understanding without the guidance of another person."[68]

Below the surface of the nineteenth century, and occasionally emerging in figures like Marx and Nietzsche, there were the tortured cries of men making an all-out stand against the tyrant God of Christianity. These were the men who with Rilke declared: "It is high time that the impoverished earth took back that which was borrowed from it to fit out the beyond." The struggle was an unreasonable one, contorted back upon itself because it was forced to use the products of Christian tradition against that tradition. The method and imagery, however, were unavoidable because as Nietzsche knew better than anyone: "I was born in a parsonage. . . . Philosophy has been corrupted by theologians' blood."[69]

Astounding as it may seem, Nietzsche's passionate, half-crazed screams were turned into clichés a century later. *Time* essays could solemnly comment on various interpretations of the death of God. The mediating force was a small group of theologians who coined the strange phrase "death of God theology." The phrase sounded suspiciously like many other theological slogans that had preceded it. Whether it was the fault of theologians or of news media to which they were unaccustomed, the sensationalism of theological movements seemed outdone only by their

68. See: Schubert Ogden, *The Reality of God* (New York, 1966), p. 10.

69. See: Eric Przywara, "St. Augustine and the Modern World," in *A Monument to St. Augustine* (New York, 1945), pp. 249–286.

brevity. Thus, whatever movement there was within Christian theology in the 1960's to deal with the religious problem of today was obscured by what seemed to be another intramural squabble.

The wider response of the Christian churches has been to insist that God is not the wicked tyrant attacked by atheism but is instead a loving and beneficent father. At first sight, this emphasis seems to be an adequate rejoinder to complaints about the divine. On closer examination this Christian picture turns out to be a dangerous misreading of the situation. There is a moment in rebellion when paternalism is found preferable to authoritarianism; the acceptance of paternalism, however, is only the prelude to worse revolt. "A God who is simply a benefactor will always be paternalistic. It is better than being a tyrant, but it is still a subtle form of alienation. Only a God capable of sharing his spontaneity can guarantee the salvation and dignity of the spirit."[70] Few Christian theologians seem capable of grasping this objection to a kind and loving God. They are like concerned parents saying to an eighteen-year-old child: "We only want to help you," and being dumbfounded by the reply: "The only way you can help is by leaving me alone."

The heart of the problem with "Christian revelation" is not *what* is there but *that* it is there. Changing what is there or eliminating part of it is not even going in the right direction. Adjusting "Christian revelation" to fit "modern man" can convey the impression that some soft-sell persuasion is afoot. Even if one goes the whole route, which I described with reference to Bultmann, the remaining thread of "Christian revelation" is not likely to impress people today. So long as there is one truth, one speck of "Christian revelation," it will appear not only as thread but also as apron string or umbilical cord. People who do not comprehend this seeming irrationalism do not grasp what human autonomy means. George B. Shaw put the matter in brief-

70. Henri Dumery, *Faith and Reflection* (New York, 1969), p. 177.

est terms: "I'm not a Christian, I'm a man." The unchallenged concept of "Christian revelation" shows that this main point of modern atheism has not been grasped. Theology which presupposes a "Christian revelation" can never, no matter how hard it works, eliminate the concept of a "Christian revelation." Only by stepping outside of the theological circle can one begin to reconstruct some understanding of a religious and revelational way of living.

The Christian criticism of modern notions of freedom is often irrelevant. That is, it is often asserted that autonomy is never complete because man is dependent on reality that goes beyond him. Therefore, Christians assume, there should be no objection to the Christian God. This line of argument fails to understand the modern desire for autonomy. No one but the most deluded man has ever supposed that an individual is self-sufficient. Relationship to others is inherent to the human individual's experience of autonomy. The building of a human world can only be undertaken through sharing and cooperation. It is not relationship but one particular kind of relation that is incompatible with freedom, namely, that arrangement whereby someone else is in control and has the answers before the questions are asked. "What would be left to create, if there were gods?" asked Nietzsche; "if god exists, then man is superfluous."

The freedom that constitutes man as man is not won an inch at a time. It is given with humanness and must be experienced and asserted as the primary category of life.[71] If such freedom does not find room for expression it can become isolated megalomania. If, on the other hand, the modern premise that experience must be trusted all the way were encouraged and criticized by religious traditions, a richer, creative and cooperative freedom might emerge. Yet, in churches across the land every Sunday morning preachers sprinkle references to "almighty God." It is highly doubtful that the phrase is intelligible, let alone true.

71. Nicolas Berdyaev, *Truth and Revelation* (New York, 1963), p. 71.

"If, as Hartshorne holds, power is a meaningful concept only if it entails the notion of opposing power—if, that is, power is in *in principle* shared—the doctrine that God has limitless power simply does not make sense."[72] In any case, those people who begin to experience creativity and to explore the universe are ro. likely to find that an almighty father is an intelligible image.

For many people atheism is at its peak and attacks upon God are at their demonic height. Undoubtedly, one can cite evidence for this claim but one could also suggest that the peak of atheism passed some decades ago. People today who are not church members are not likely to designate themselves as a-theist. They are no longer caught in Nietzsche's contortion of having to define one's life by what one denies exists. Before the believers prematurely celebrate the passing of atheism, they should note that the alternative to atheism is not necessarily theism, certainly not the particular form of Christian theism which is traceable to the ancient and medieval worlds. From a Christian point of view the passing of atheism should probably be viewed as an ambiguous phenomenon. The protests of atheism were indicative of a strong Christian theism against which it protested. It may be that Christianity has become so weak that protest against it is no longer necessary and that the churches in the modern world are free because they are innocuous.

On the other hand, one cannot overlook the possibility that the twentieth century may be at that time when, in Jaspers' words "the world has lost its naïveté." The so-called believers and so called non-believers may finally be ready to cooperate. Their motives may differ but both groups may find that they have common desires and the need to work together. Desperation and hope intermingle in the awareness of people who have faced the abyss of non-being and are now searching for a new

72. Eugene Peters, *The Creative Advance* (St. Louis, 1966), p. 95. For his reference to Charles Hartshorne, see: *The Divine Relativity* (New Haven, 1948), pp. 134–142.

way. "Modern man, when he lost the certainty of a world to come, was thrown back upon himself and not upon the world; far from believing that the world might be potentially immortal, he was not even sure that it was real."[73] Those people who thought that the main enemy was God have not found satisfaction in their victory. They are not in a mood to turn the clock back (as the Christian church seems to demand) but neither are they about to settle down into a comfortable atheism. Getting rid of God does not of itself settle the problem of human meaning, as Nietzsche found toward the end of his life. "Where is my home? For it do I ask and seek, and have sought but not found it. O eternal everywhere, o eternal nowhere, o eternal useless."[74]

In the nineteenth century Marx had felt compelled to see atheism as "humanism mediated by the suppression of religion." To restore man to himself and his earth it seemed essential to destroy religion. Today there is less certainty among Marxists that the connection between humanism and the suppression of religion is a necessary one. A modern interpreter of Marx can see a good side to religion even within the definitions that make it the moan of an oppressed creature and the sentiment of a heartless world. "In the very text in which we find the famous formula, 'Religion is the opium of the people,' Marx emphasizes several lines further that '*religious* suffering is at the same time an *expression* of real suffering and a *protest* against real suffering.' We have here an initial dialectical approach to the religious fact."[75]

In a similar vein, the philosopher Maurice Merleau-Ponty sees Christian saints as engaged in the same struggle as humanists today. He sees only this difference: "They merely tried to believe that their fight was already won in heaven or in history. Men today no longer have this resource. Contemporary man's hero is

73. Hannah Arendt, *The Human Condition* (Chicago, 1958), p. 320.
74. Quoted in William Luijpen, *Phenomenology and Atheism* (Pittsburgh, 1964), p. 259.
75. Garaudy, *op. cit.*, p. 100.

not Lucifer, nor even Prometheus, but simply man."[76] If there were agreement on this last point it would serve not as conclusion but as premise to investigating issues under the categories of faith, religion and revelation. The exploration of dimensions of human experience that would fill out religion will be dealt with in the following chapters. What should be clear from this description of modern rejections of religion is that the concept of a "Christian revelation" is an insurmountable obstacle to progress in this direction.

4. SOME SOURCES TO BEGIN

As a concluding section to this first chapter I would like to advert to several cultural influences which are of significance to my theme. These developments are at the very least inspirations for elaborating a new meaning for the word revelation. To some extent they may also provide some of the content of the discussion. It is difficult to cite these factors without seeming to introduce frivolous material, that is, fads which might be interesting but are not part of serious theologizing. I have already admitted that this book is not one on Christian theology and therefore the following factors are not necessarily part of a Christian theological method. I would claim, however, that these movements should influence the questions that are asked in theology and might provide the context for making sense of what theology says. The three influences I would like to cite are: (a) Human Science (b) The Struggle for Human Rights (c) Ecology.

a). *Human Science.* During the past century the study of the human person has become more and more central to the sciences. Of course, the human had never been excluded from scientific study but because man was subsumed within the study of other phenomena, there was no distinctive study of the nature of human being. In the early period of modern science the model

76. From *Le héros, l'homme,* as quoted in Vergote, *op. cit.,* p. 257.

for understanding the universe was the machine. The constant comparison of the universe to a clock may seem to us a little silly but to an era fascinated by the making of mechanical timepieces it was a great key to learning.[77] Unfortunately, the unabated growth of technology has perpetuated remnants of the mechanical model of man. Even though it is clearly inadequate, the data-processing machine is widely presumed to be a model for human knowledge. Sigmund Freud, whose contribution to the understanding of human nature was immense, still presumed a mechanical model of parts and pressures. People who were sick seemed to need tinkering with so that their systems would be readjusted to conform to the blueprints. The fact that B. F. Skinner's work was given serious and sympathetic consideration indicates that the old mechanical model is not dead yet.[78]

During the last century all of science has been undergoing changes of model. The physical sciences have struggled since the early nineteenth century to incorporate new finds from the micro-physical world and the macro-physical universe. The biological and then evolutionary sciences began to challenge the mechanical scheme as the model for all understanding. The psychological and social sciences both began to emerge in the late nineteenth century but it took a while for them to find common ground. At first, psychology tried to imitate the physical sciences which were more mature and better accepted. The alternative to Freud seemed to be behaviorism. What I have said of the presumption of a mechanical model in Freud would be even more true of behavioristic psychology.

The last few decades have seen the growth of a "third way" in psychology.[79] This development is somewhat inadequately described by the adjectives existential, personalistic or human-

77. See: Mumford, *op. cit.,* pp. 75–84.
78. B. F. Skinner, *Beyond Freedom and Dignity* (New York, 1971).
79. See: Abraham Maslow, *Motivation and Personality,* 2nd ed. (New York, 1970); Orlo Strunk, "Humanistic Religious Psychology," in *The Psychology of Religion,* ed., Orlo Strunk (New York, 1971), pp. 116–123.

istic. There are strong differences among the men involved in this movement but some common points of interest join them. Two of these themes are that a search for meaning is central to understanding the human and that human life can be studied only in a relational way. I shall comment briefly here on these two points and continue discussion of them in the next chapter.

Interest in the relational character of human existence received a great stimulus by Martin Buber's little classic, *I and Thou*.[80] In a kind of delayed action, psychologists several decades later began to realize how important this idea is in understanding man. The "interpersonal" took on a special character of its own. Instead of being one phenomenon among many, the interpersonal relation has come to be the prime analogue for understanding everything else. The "I–thou encounter" has become a term of everyday language with the consequent danger that the profound meaning of the phrase may be lost. Nonetheless, the recognition that all that is human can only be understood relationally is an insight whose limits we have yet to discover. Psychologists themselves may be only at an early stage of developing their categories in a properly relational way. The concepts of "insanity" and "mental sickness" may be misleading and may stem in large part from the "sane" world's inability to relate.[81]

The other theme mentioned above is the search for meaning.[82] The human person cannot be reduced to a machine or one variety of the animal world. He is the animal that laughs and weeps because he can see the difference between what is and what could be. The concept of meaning is certainly in Freud but its relationship to human behavior was left somewhat con-

80. Martin Buber, *I and Thou* (New York, 1937).

81. See: R. D. Laing, *The Divided Self* (Baltimore, 1965); Thomas Szasz, *The Manufacture of Madness* (New York, 1970).

82. See: Aaron Ungersma, *The Search for Meaning* (Philadelphia, 1967); for a summary of the "meaning of meaning," see: Robert Holmes, *The Academic Mysteryhouse* (New York, 1970), pp. 33–63.

fused.[83] Just as the interpersonal has emerged as a primary notion, so the peculiarly human interest in meaning has also become of crucial concern. "The concept of meaning, in all its varieties, is the dominant concept of our time."[84] Victor Frankl, whose approach to psychology is called logotherapy, postulates that the primary need of human beings is meaning. Frankl often quotes the words of Nietzsche: He who has a why to life can bear almost any how.[85]

The most dramatic expression of the quest for meaning is what Abraham Maslow described under the term "peak experience." I will examine this concept as a link between the second and third chapters of this book. With the study of phenomena called peak experience or transcendence, psychologists have moved into an area formerly thought to be a strictly religious area.[86] In addition to high points of meaning there may be special significance in low points of life. Both ends of the meaning spectrum may dramatize the relational, revelational and religious dimensions of life. Frankl has written of low level meaning: "Ever more patients complain of what they call an 'inner void,' and that is the reason why I have termed the condition the 'existential vacuum.' In contradistinction to the peak-experience so aptly described by Maslow, one could conceive of the existential vacuum in terms of an 'abyss experience.' "[87]

Although the significance of these movements for religion should not be exaggerated or prematurely praised, the importance of them is nonetheless great. At the least, religious questions are being recognized as legitimate issues in the human sciences. In fact, "contemporary existential and humanistic

83. See: Herbert Fingarette, *The Self in Transformation* (New York, 1965), pp. 15–73.
84. Susanne Langer, *Philosophical Sketches* (Baltimore, 1962), p. 55.
85. Victor Frankl, *Man's Search for Meaning* (New York, 1963).
86. See: Abraham Maslow, *Religions, Values and Peak-Experiences*, 2nd ed. (New York, 1970), p. 20.
87. Victor Frankl, *The Will to Meaning* (New York, 1969), p. 83.

psychologists would probably consider a person sick or abnormal in an existential way if he were not concerned with these 'religious' questions."[88]

Freud had placed religion into the category of *illusion*, a term which for him is different from the usual connotations of the word.[89] Illusion for Freud has the negative sense of a crutch that people need in order to live; however, illusion has meaning and may even have truth. "According to the whole doctrine of repression, 'substitute gratifications'—a term which applies not only to poetry and religion but also to dreams and neurotic symptoms—contain truth: they are expressions, distorted by repression, of the immortal desires of the human heart."[90] A generation of post-Freudians is interested in following the implications of this issue beyond the point where Freud left it.

I am not looking to prove the existence of God by psychology nor am I suggesting that psychology is a substitute for religion. I am merely describing a meaning for the word revelation in immediate, human, experiential terms. Unless arbitrary limits are set upon the human experience of revelation, the religious question will inevitably arise. The religious question should not put one into some other realm called faith where one accepts or rejects a "Christian revelation."

One of the roles of human science today is to pursue the religious aspects of revelation instead of either implicitly condemning religion or else prematurely giving it over to believers and theologians. Behavioristic and mechanistic psychologies have no way of understanding revelation as a peculiarly human phenomenon; the deficiency here is not first religious but psychological.[91] A more humanistic psychology, in exploring the

88. Maslow, *Religions, Values and Peak-Experiences*, p. 18.
89. Sigmund Freud, *Future of an Illusion* (New York, 1964), p. 72.
90. See: Norman O. Brown, *Life against Death* (New York, 1959), p. 13; Leslie Dewart, *The Future of Belief* (New York, 1966), pp. 20–37.
91. Erwin Goodenough, *The Psychology of Religious Experiences* (New York, 1965), p. 62: "We, too, crave to come into the peace and dignity

realms of the interpersonal relationship and the search for meaning, discovers some exciting, new dimensions of the human. When no *a priori* limits are placed upon human experience, some surprising outlooks return even within psychology. J. F. Bugental puts it in the strongest terms: "Perhaps I can best summarize what existential psychology means to me by using this phrase: 'It restores our divinity.' I am not content to see man as mechanism or robot or even as organism. Man must partake in whatever he means by the concept of God."[92] Religions will each have their own way of distinguishing man and God but probably all of them do agree in trying to express how man partakes in the concept of God.

b) *Struggle for Rights.* The second source or inspiration for a new meaning or revelation is the struggle of oppressed peoples. A vast literature on revolution, oppression and civil rights already exists. I wish only to single out a theological or pre-theological implication. Each struggle has its own particular character which makes any sweeping generalizations hazardous. Blacks and Puerto Ricans in New York City, although grouped together by whites, have neither the same historical problem nor the same current discrimination. In turn, neither of them faces the same kind of oppression as Mexican-Americans in Texas.

Despite all the differences in the various struggles of the oppressed, there is a commonly recurring theme. Whether pro

---

that justice meant to Plato and Paul, and we similarly know that in igno rance we blunder and that in knowledge of reality alone can we hope. Modern psychology, psychiatry, and sociology no longer assume that we have that knowledge through biblical and ecclesiastical revelation." It is beyond doubt that human sciences cannot derive knowledge from "biblical and ecclesiastical revelation." However, it is possible that psychology and religion might be mutually enriched if they met within the category of revelation. Goodenough's pale concept of "religious experiences" could use some enrichment.

92. J. F. T. Bugental, *The Search for Authenticity* (New York, 1965), p. 20.

test comes from youth or the aged, women or homosexuals, Asians or Africans, the plea carries a similar message: Each human being must be free from self-oppression and group oppression so that the human race can have more unity and more diversity at the same time. It is not so much *equality* that is needed (although a guarantee of equality before law is a necessity) but a changed society with different relationships. For purposes of illustration I will comment on these representative movements: Black, Indian, youth, feminine.

1. Ancient prophets saw in vision a world that could be one and they embodied in themselves the terrible struggle of mankind to find itself. In our own day this struggle has taken concrete embodiment in figures like Malcolm X and Martin Luther King. At the time of King's death, Herbert Richardson wrote a short but penetrating essay on the theological significance of King's work.[93] Richardson sees in King the answer to the supposed problem of the relativism of truth. King understood that relativism is not a theoretical problem to be resolved by compromise but is instead the motive for action in the public sphere. A sense of the unity of all people to be realized by a reconciling kind of action is the beginning point of theology. Given this start, theology would proceed by reflecting upon what religious people are doing to achieve a world of brother–sisterhood. This context would provide an operational meaning of faith: "Faith is the commitment of man to oppose the separation of man from man. It is a commitment to struggle against attacks on the common good, against racism and segregation, and against the fragmentation of man's intellectual and spiritual life. ... The one who responds to evil asymmetrically, returning good for evil, is the man who lives by faith."[94] I would add to this that revelation is situated in the struggle itself and faith

93. Herbert Richardson, "Martin Luther King—Unsung Theologian," in *New Theology, no. 6,* eds., Martin Marty and Dean Peerman (New York, 1969), pp. 178–184.
94. *Ibid.,* p. 180, p. 182.

is the personal attitude within this process of revelational expression.

In recent years there has developed a category of writing called "black theology."[95] This development seems to be an offshoot of the black power–black pride movements. Despite the significance of current books on "black theology," I suspect that they are transitional works. Black people have a more profound contribution to make to theology than can yet be tapped by a few black men working in the white man's world.[96]

Much of the "black theology" today has a Barthian tone in which the word of God preached from the bible is a judgment upon sinful society. There will remain the need for this element in a Christian theology but to be effective it must be set in a far larger framework. In the future "Christian revelation" will not be the thing brought out of the past to judge the current scene. Rather, the language, history and culture of the black man will change the meaning of the word revelation. How the divine and the human are related will be reconceived on the basis of an acceptance of blackness. Seen at the deepest level, the conflict of black and white has real religious overtones. The black man frightens the white because there is intimated in the relation a whole other world that the white man does not grasp. It is frightening when one begins to suspect that one's rational schemes do not control all reality. "We do not expel this black family from our neighborhood in order to make the neighborhood a nicer place, although that is what we tell ourselves. In the end the blacks could be blue or brown or green, what we are afraid of is that something 'other' will come to matter to us, and then we might be hurt by our own exploration of 'otherness' "[97]

2. The struggle of the American Indians for their freedom

95. See: James Cone, *Black Theology and Black Power* (New York, 1969); Albert Cleage, *The Black Messiah* (New York, 1969).

96. For a sympathetic but strong criticism, see: Rosemary Ruether, "The Black Theology of James Cone," in *Catholic World*, Oct., 1971, pp. 18–20.

97. Richard Sennet, *The Uses of Disorder* (New York, 1970), p. 43.

had received scant attention until the end of the 1960's.[98] The extermination of the Indians by the "Christian" settlers did not seem to bother the consciences of many white people. The chief source of information for most people seemed to be the cowboy movies. In the white-settler mythology, the cowboy was the man and the Indian was the savage; the triumph of humanity over savagery could only be applauded. During recent years some whites have begun to recognize the terrible injustice done to the red man. What is more difficult to recognize is the staggering idea that culturally and religiously the white man has much still to learn from the red man.

A few years ago whites, practically unaware of what they were doing, began adopting Indian clothing and ritual. Many American youths began to find more affinity with Indian religion than with the Christianity they were brought up on.[99] Some of the externals in the Indianization of America can be dismissed as passing fads. But there is something in the yearning for new tribes and a new earth which is not going to go away. In particular, as ecology becomes central, a new appreciation of Indian attitudes is certain to accompany this awareness. How far the movement will go cannot be predicted. Few people would agree with the conclusion of Vine Deloria, but his is a thesis which bears consideration: "The ultimate conclusion of American society will be that even with respect to personal safety it was much safer and more humane when Indians controlled the whole continent. The only answer will be to adopt Indian ways to survive. For the white man even to exist, he must adopt a total Indian way of life. That is really what he had to do when he came to this land. It is what he will have to do before he leaves it once again."[100]

98. See: Dee Brown, *Bury My Heart at Wounded Knee* (New York, 1971); T. C. McLuhan, *Touch the Earth: A Self-Portrait of Indian Existence* (New York, 1971).
99. See: Theodore Roszak, *The Making of a Counter Culture* (New York, 1969), pp. 245–268.
100. Vine Deloria, *We Talk, You Listen* (New York, 1970), p. 197.

63

3. The so-called youth movement was the one which attracted the most attention on an international level in the 1960's. The possibility here of establishing a new meaning for both revelation and religiousness is great. Unfortunately, so is the possibility for misunderstanding an enormous cultural change as simply a rebellion of young against old. Every single person is young at one time and old at another (whereas everyone is not sometimes black and sometimes white) which distinguishes this movement. It should be clearer here than anywhere else that what is at stake is a new society for everyone. There is a cataclysmic change which is generally more apparent among youth than elsewhere. But the young people who may be leading the protest should not be trying to create a youth society but should be striving for a human society. The latter phrase is not a redundancy since what people face in varying degrees is an inhuman or dehumanizing world.

To write on the "youth scene" and have neither a condemnatory nor a pandering attitude has been a near impossibility for American adults.[101] Dismissing the protests of young people because of the inadequacies of their proposed alternatives has been all too easy. On the other hand, adults who adulate over youth are often playing out their own problems or joining forces with the most corruptive aspects of American advertising. The equation of youth with goodness is an old American myth which needs dismantling not reinforcing. The hope that youth will save us places an impossible burden upon people who already have enough troubles.

The movement to release certain "youthful qualities" (e.g., vitality, zest, enthusiasm, courage, dignity, openness) may in fact be led by young people but it is a process which involves everyone. The society that is needed is one where everyone would be respected whatever his age, race or profession. Young

101. For example, Charles Reich, *The Greening of America* (New York, 1970).

people who do not understand this point ought to be criticized as severely as their parents. When the so-called youth movement is understood this way then chronological age is not the decisive factor in the conflict. For example, the young and the old should be natural allies in the struggle because both groups want a world where people are respected not first for what they can produce but for who they are. Retired people have as much stake in that world as adolescents do. Thus, the old people with "youthful" qualities can join hands with the young. If one draws any generational lines, therefore, it makes far more sense to see not a struggle of young against old but of young and old against the middle.[102]

A new meaning for love and a new meaning for work are desperately being sought for by millions of people. The demand is often made by people who do not look like loving and working people because they cannot fit themselves into the accepted meanings of love and work. The current administrators of society can be very harsh in their judgments upon these people. Probably society's guardians should be highly critical but they had better try to find out the meaning of what is happening. For example, things begin to make sense when one starts with Mumford's premise that the young are living as if the catastrophe had already occurred, still using (and abusing) the technological apparatus of today but acting in ritual as if it had all been destroyed. In this situation they "recover an elemental animal faith, perform acts of mutual aid, hospitality, and love, share freely whatever food or drink they can get hold of, and get pleasure simply out of each other's presence."[103] The possibility of new meaning and new relationships surfaces within this description.

4. The most universal case of oppression and subjugation

102. See: Philip Slater, *The Pursuit of Loneliness* (Boston, 1970), pp. 142–143.
103. Mumford, *Pentagon of Power*, p. 373.

would seem to be found in the relation of women to men. What other conflict can match the struggle of one-half the human race against the other? The words oppression, subjugation and conflict seem to many people to constitute exaggerated and inflammatory rhetoric. Many women profess to be quite content with their lot and not at all in agreement with their reputed leaders. Nonetheless, there is some powerful change afoot in this area and my interest is in locating the significance of the change.

Similar to the "youth movement" a women's movement is a movement toward a more human society. As there is a need for everyone to develop his or her youthful qualities so everyone ought to be able to express both the masculine and feminine aspects of person. Women can be liberated only as men are liberated and both can be liberated only as they can develop the sexual mix within themselves. One of the most universal of all stories is the androgynous myth which supposes that each person was orignally bi-sexual. In much of Asian mythology the interplay of *yin* and *yang* dominates the cosmic as well as the personal realm.[104]

The current struggle for the liberation of the sexes does not have an adequate name; sexual, woman and feminist all have limitations. In any case, the struggle which must focus on the freeing of women from past stereotyped conditions is also a movement to free men. I use the words masculine and feminine to refer to the polarity within each person. Not everyone accepts this usage of masculine and feminine. They need not but unless some kind of distinction is introduced to designate the interplay of complementaries in each person, the movement will always be contorted against itself. Caught in the limitations of its own

104. Mircea Eliade, *The Quest*, p. 172; also Brown, *Life against Death*, p. 132; "At the deepest level the androgynous or hermaphroditic ideal of the unconscious reflects the aspiration of the human body to overcome the dualisms which are its neurosis, ultimately to reunify Eros and the death instinct. The dualism of masculine-feminine is merely the transposition into genital terms of the dualism of activity and passivity."

terminology, it will strike out bitterly at "man" while grasping for equality with what is being attacked. If each person is a relationship of masculine and feminine then inequality need not mean subservience and the enemy is not man but a domination of masculinity. It is not by accident that it is nearly impossible to use the English language without equating man and human. What is needed is not the replacing of man by woman but the subsuming of man by the human.

An acquaintance with religion and mythology would help those people leading this movement. Many writers, like Kate Millett, are keenly and correctly aware of the discrimination against women in organized religion of the West.[105] But this is by no means the most significant issue in the religious area. The organization of western churches simply reflects their inadequate religious attitudes pertaining to a concept of God, personal relation, sexuality and the roles assigned to women. I am claiming that all of these deficiences have their roots in an inadequate notion of revelation, namely, in a father giving commands to his children. If women had had any significant part, surely the result would have been different. The question, therefore, is not what does "Christian revelation" have to say about women but what do women (and the feminine side of men) have to say about revelation. A "theology of women" could simply be another case of "man's world, woman's place,"[106] that is, a special-interest section is tolerated while the mainstream remains untouched. What is needed rather are women theologians in significant number who by their presence will change the meaning of both theology and revelation.

105. Kate Millett, *Sexual Politics* (Garden City, 1970), pp. 46–54; see also Germaine Greer, *The Female Eunuch* (New York, 1971); for applications of this to theology, see Mary Daly, *The Church and the Second Sex* (New York, 1968), pp. 137–149; for some interesting historical reflections, Herbert Richardson, *Nun, Witch, and Playmate* (New York, 1971).

106. The title of an excellent book by Elizabeth Janeway published in New York, 1971.

Nearly all religions have a father god and a mother god.[107] Judaism, as is well known, developed the notion of father to the exclusion of any female consort. One might have expected that the Christian doctrine of the Trinity would have led to God being called either they, she or it, with the main emphasis being put on Spirit. Christianity did not go that route at all. Instead, it went the route of psychological imagery for the Trinity only to desiccate to the point of meaninglessness the doctrine of a relational God. Furthermore, it tried to obliterate the concept of a feminine god. The attempt was bound to fail. The Virgin Mary or some other substitute came to play the role of the feminine god.

Although the divinization of the Virgin has consistently been condemned by the official church, Roman Catholicism has lived in places for centuries by adoration of the virgin-mother. F. S. C. Northrup began his tour de force of scholarship, *The Meeting of East and West,* with a study of Mexican religion. He saw in this presumably primitive religion some common ground for East and West. His central theme was the attitude to the Virgin: "The fact is, this image of the Virgin conveys in some direct and effective way a basic, intuitively felt element in the nature of things and in the heart of human experience which is spontaneously natural and convincing to the native Mexicans. In some way, the Virgin of Guadalupe and the story of her revelation, directed especially to the Indians, call forth from the Mexican spirit a devotion and sweeping response not equalled by any other influence in Mexico even today."[108]

The strength of Roman Catholicism still largely resides in its feminine capacity to survive the most masculinized organization.[109] In Protestantism, and to some degree in Catholicism

107. Van der Leeuw, *op. cit.,* p. 99.
108. F. S. C. Northrop, *The Meeting of East and West* (New York, 1966), p. 26.
109. Vergote, *op. cit.,* p. 186: "It is an everyday occurrence in the life of a practising Catholic to distinguish between the functions attributed to God

today, the figure of Jesus has taken on the feminine as well as masculine role. This development may be a good one but it must be wondered whether the figure of Jesus can carry the entire weight of this religion. It is to be hoped that the movement for the rights of women will both find inspiration and give inspiration to the joining of Eastern and Western religions. It is unlikely that Catholicism or Protestantism will by themselves discover this ancient wisdom of the East:

> He who knows the masculine and
> yet keeps to the feminine
> Will become a channel drawing
> all the world to it
> Being a channel for the world, he
> will not be severed from the
> eternal virtue,
> And then he can return again
> to the state of infancy (i.e.
> to spontaneity) [110]

c. *Ecology.* The final source for a new meaning of revelation is ecology. This movement is related to the protests described above. Possibly one could describe ecology as the supreme protest movement, that is, the cry of the oppressed universe against the dominant species. In any case, the sense of relationship within wholeness is the key notion here just as it was in the previous two sections. As was also true above, I am mainly interested in how ecology throws light on the meaning of revelation. There is religious connotation in what at first sight appears to be a non-religious movement.[111]

---

and those attributed to the Virgin Mary. The image of God is depicted in conformity with a lawmaking Father, a distant Judge, whereas the Virgin fulfils the role of a divinized mother, one who consoles, protects, is near, seeks forgiveness for her children."

110. Ch'u Ta-Kao as quoted in Watts, *op. cit.,* p. 113.

111. Lynn White, *Machina Ex Deo: Essays in the Dynamism of Western Culture* (Cambridge, 1968), p. 84: "What people do about their ecology depends on what they think about themselves in relation to things around them. Human ecology is deeply conditioned by beliefs about our nature and

The empirical facts that ecology deals with are easy enough to state even though most people seem incapable of assimilating the significance of these facts. Everyone knows what foul air or polluted water means; everyone, it may be safely added, is against pollution. However, as René Dubos notes, not everyone is ready to appreciate "the human value symbolized by phrases such as the good earth, a brilliant sky, sparkling waters, a place of one's own."[112] Furthermore, many people seem to have little sense of the origin of attitudes that have brought on the ecological crisis.

In regard to this last point, there is a grave misunderstanding about ecology which can lead to self-defeating practices among conservation groups. The attempt to protect nature by simply opposing human activity is not a workable approach and is wrong in principle to begin with. The ecological movement is threatened with becoming a movement that is anti-urban, anti-technological, anti-modern.[113] Nature cannot be saved from man nor can man flee back to nature. Rather, the relation of man to nature has to be reconceptualized. Man and nature, in fact, are not adequate categories in which to discuss this problem.[114] One ought to talk about sub-personal (including that in man) which must be respected and loved as over against the personal which is everywhere striving for emergence to love, care and direct the whole.

We must beware of freezing reality into concepts that look

---

lestiny—that is, by religion. To Western eyes this is very evident in, say, India or Ceylon. It is equally true of ourselves and of our medieval ancestors."

112. René Dubos, *Reason Awake* (New York, 1970), p. 168.

113. See Barry Commoner, *The Closing Circle* (New York, 1971); Richard Neuhaus, *In Defense of People* (New York, 1971), raises some good questions about the ecology movement but unfortunately in a way that cannot avoid being polemical. Neuhaus is trying to sound a warning against the ecology movement becoming anti-urban and anti-modern.

114. Frederick Elder, *Crisis in Eden* (New York, 1970), tries to deal with this problem but his own typology is inadequate and misleading.

clear enough but are actually misleading. If the words man and nature are used often, one begins to assume that they designate separable things. The closely related pair of words, nature/history has been the source of trouble in Christian theology and the trouble remains to this day. An "historical revelation" has no chance of making sense if history has been set over against nature. One does have to pick pairs of words to describe distinct elements within a larger unity. The word nature might best be reserved to refer to the experienced whole. Then one could proceed to investigate the relation between the human and the non-human, the personal and the non-personal, the living and the non-living insofar as these relations characterize the universe and each thing in it.

Among primitive people the sense of distinctive unity had not fully emerged. The capabilities of the free element which emerges in man had not been recognized or accepted. Particularly within western civilization, the individual person emerged as a distinct element in the universe. A human mind arose that could contemplate the rest of the world but man had to pay the price of being expelled from his former friends. The Christian religion played a major part in severing man from his own natural roots.

Christian man in the West strove to escape this lingering illusion that the primitives had projected upon nature. Intent upon the destiny of his own soul, and increasingly urban, man drew back from too great intimacy with the natural, its fertility and orgiastic attractions. If the new religion was to survive, Pan had to be driven from the hillside or rendered powerless by incorporating him into Christianity—to be baptized, in other words, and allowed to fade slowly from the memory of the folk. As always in such intellectual upheavals, something was gained and something was lost.[115]

What was gained in the West was the great flowering of empirical science and powerful technology. Unfortunately, the

115. Loren Eiseley, *The Invisible Pyramid* (New York, 1970), p. 143.

images that accompanied the growth of technology were "rivalry with nature" and, worse, "conquest of nature." The conquest of space was from the start America's self-appointed mission. In the midst of man's exaltation of himself above nature, a subtle transposition of values took place. "If the goal of technics was to improve the condition of man, the goal of man was to become ever more narrowly confined to the improvement of technology. Mechanical progress and human progress came to be regarded as one; and both were theoretically limitless."[116]

Human progress may be limitless but the role of conqueror and exploiter of nature is definitely limited. It could only be a matter of time before the supplies on "spaceship earth" began to grow scarce.[117] Worst of all man found that the supplies he was using were secreted from his own body. Suddenly and desperately he needed not only anti-pollution laws but a new attitude to trees, animals, water, machines, leisure, love, work, entertainment and much else.

In the third part of this book I will pick up the thread of the religious implications of ecology. Here I am merely saying that a new meaning for the word revelation should have arisen in Christian theology but has not. The bifurcation of man and nature remains as bad as ever when it comes to the idea of revelation.[118] Biblical positivism and existential demythologizing both try to remove man from his natural environment. Revelation is still either something delivered to man's mind from the past or

116. Mumford, *Pentagon of Power,* p. 197.

117. The image of "spaceship earth" was used by Adlai Stevenson in his last speech: "We all travel together, passengers on a little spaceship, dependent on its vulnerable supplies of air and soil; all committed for our safety to its security and peace, preserved from annihilation only by the care, the work, and I will say the love we give our fragile craft." quoted in René Dubos, *So Human an Animal* (New York, 1968), p. 234ff.

118. H. Paul Santmire, *Brother Earth* (New York, 1971), rightly bewails the separations which destroy but his bringing to the problem the "biblical message" only helps to perpetuate the splits. The attempt to solve human problems by the application of texts is part of the problem not the answer.

72

else it is the isolated decision of the moment having no roots in the fanciful, mythical world of nature. Ancient man with Pan in the woods was closer to the truth. Unless a sense of brotherhood can be established with the earth and all the animals man cannot find himself and the word revelation cannot function with a fully human meaning.[119]

In all three of these sources for developing the notion of revelation I have tried to show that what is needed is a relational and practical category. Placed within the context of human experience, revelation will always involve as one pole of relation the bodily–temporal–social being. At the same time experience invites to some greater wholeness which is not evident but which man already has some intimation of. In the next two chapters I will try to exemplify and to elaborate on this description.

119. White, *op. cit.*, p. 93, after suggesting Francis of Assisi as a model for present attitudes, concludes: "Both our present science and our present technology are so tinctured with orthodox christian arrogance toward nature that no solution for our ecologic crisis can be expected from them alone. Since the roots of our trouble are so largely religious, the remedy must also be essentially religious whether we call it that or not."

Chapter Two : Revelation: Human Aspects

1. EXPERIENCE AND RELATION

My preliminary definition of the word revelation in the first chapter has situated the word as a human phenomenon. Revelation in my usage always includes the note of a human subject who is engaged in the revelational process. The phrase "human revelation" would seem, therefore, to be a redundancy because any revelation which man could be aware of would be human. However, "human aspects" of revelation is intended to be in contrast to non-human aspects. I am leaving open at this point the applicability of the word divine here. If the word divine is used to describe revelation, then presumably revelation will be described as a divine-human relationship.

My last sentence is stated in a tentative way so as to anticipate a possible objection to my whole approach. It may seem that my approach has already locked God and the world into a paired relationship whereas the main message of some religions is the non-dual character of reality (*Advaita*). It is true that I have begun by accepting the apparent duality of a relational world. This starting point would still be valid even if, in the course of examining experience, relationship comes to be seen as illusory. We may find that "the unique relation that one can form with Brahman is the rupture and negation of every alleged relation."[1]

1. Raymond Panikkar, "Toward An Ecumenical Theandric Spirituality," in *Journal of Ecumenical Studies V* (1968), pp. 507–534; the elimination of all duality and distinction is not clearcut even in the East: R. Tagore, *The Religion of Man* (Boston, 1961), p. 202: "Such an ideal of the utter extinction of the individual separateness has not a universal sanction in

Before we come to any conclusion about what is ultimately real, the human ought to be looked at in all of its relational complexity. Perhaps it is possible to understand relation in a way that does not issue either in God being outside man or man being swallowed inside God. I think we must look carefully at human models of relationship (as opposed to mechanical and spatial models). At this point I want simply to examine the human while keeping open the question of the divine.

The evidence for the reality of the divine will be examined in the next chapter. My division of material is somewhat arbitrary and the division could lead to the separation I am trying to avoid. This limitation is inherent to speech and writing. One cannot say everything at once; some sequence is unavoidable. I wish to reiterate, however, that in this chapter I am not excluding the divine but neither will I directly advert to it. If the divine is present in human life, it will be implicit in what I am saying. I wish to move slowly in that direction because the premature introduction of religious considerations can obscure the perception of some simple but important realities.

Since I have said that the phrase human revelation is redundant it may seem that a chapter on human aspects of revelation is superfluous. However, there are various ways in which the human being can participate in a process. Abraham Heschel writes: "I was born a man and now my task is to become human." This paradoxical statement contains a profound truth. Each of us is a human being and has at least a *minimum* grasp of what human means. On the other hand, no individual nor all of us together has an *exhaustive* understanding of the human. We can only try to devise ways that will enable us to progress in understanding what the human can mean.

The word revelation is a good, comprehensive category for understanding the human. It is not necessary to presume that it

India. There are many of us whose prayer is for dualism, so that for them the bond of devotion with God may continue for ever."

is the best of all ideas to comprehend the human. However, if the religious element is taken seriously there are very few other categories which can embrace the religious and the non-religious in a comprehensive and consistent pattern. Since I am taking revelation to be my primary category I have to move back and forth with it. That is, I am trying to show that revelation is a notion which helps to make sense out of human data and at the same time I am filling in the meaning of the word revelation with that human data. This procedure is not a vicious circle. There is no way to get started here except by accepting some tentative framework for immediate experience. If the choice of starting point is a good one, then continued study should lead to an ever widening understanding of the phenomena in question. The test of one's starting point is whether it eventually leads into a cul-de-sac or whether it keeps opening out on new worlds that do not obliterate the old.

In starting with the word human I am leaving somewhat vague the place of the sub-human. As I shall try to show, a full examination of the human will include a significance for the sub-human. In this regard, the word human is preferable to a closely related word, person, which for many people has exclusivistic connotations. In twentieth-century philosophy, the words person, personal and personalistic came to have special meanings which I think are too restricted. My previous writing on the topic of revelation has often been described as personalistic. I would not accept the description unless I could also fill out the meaning of personalistic in a way that avoids exclusivism.

The particular problem that developed with the word personal was that it tended to become equivalent to "interpersonal." Thus, when one speaks of a personal relationship it is assumed one is referring to a relation between two people. Logically, one would have thought that all the relations that a person has are personal relations. There is certainly nothing wrong with emphasizing relationships between two people but it is misleading and unhealthy to suggest that this is the only relation in life. Even if we say that the interpersonal is the highest reality we know, we would also have to remember that the highest can be the worst if it is ripped from the context of the whole. My intention here is to situate the personal in a context and to show that the meaning of the personal cannot be assumed without question. For purposes of comprehensiveness, therefore, I begin with the word human rather than person even though I recognize that the word human has its own inherent limitations.

The noun which I join with human is the word "experience." This word, too, has its own difficulties. Nonetheless, I know of no word in the American language which has as good a chance to function in the comprehensive way that is desirable.[2] I begin with the premise that human experience is where one looks to grasp anything that can be grasped about revelation. Correlatively, the category of revelation will be the most helpful in making sense of human experience.

An immediate objection from religious traditions should be dealt with here because it challenges the premise on which I am beginning. Most of orthodox Christian tradition would probably deny that experience is the most ultimate or comprehensive category. The supposition has always been that some document or something or someone from the past is the ultimate "norm" against which today's experience is to be measured. To many Christians, the thesis that experience is final judge would seem to be an adjusting of God to our level, a refusal to allow for the possibility of men being shaken from their apathy and self-centeredness.

It could be true that the emphasis upon experience is a cutting down of reality to our puny size. There is no reason, however, why this must be so. The beginning of clarification can be

2. For the word experience, see: Fontinell, *op. cit.*, pp. 37–72; also see: John Dewey, "The Need for a Recovery of Philosophy," in *On Experience, Nature and Freedom*, ed., Richard Bernstein (Indianapolis, 1960), pp. 19–69.

made by distinguishing my use of experience from a meaning of experience common in the West since the rise of empirical science.[3] During the seventeenth, eighteenth and nineteenth centuries the scientific method was propagated on the basis that science dealt with experience and that science described what appeared before the senses in raw experience. In this conception of the world, an individual *had* experience and the measuring of the data was the attaining of the object of experience.

In the second half of the nineteenth century the confident assurance that experience was under control began to get undermined from within the sciences themselves. This movement issued in the scientific revolutions of the twentieth century. This century has not settled back into a single world view and united methodology. Beginning with Edmund Husserl, philosophy joined in the challenge from outside.[4] What had imperiously come to be known as "science" was not the whole of knowledge. The "atomic facts" of these particular sciences did not constitute the whole of experience. There is a more primitive kind of experience from which the mathematical/empirical sciences abstract. Although these sciences have demonstrated their value by their amazing fruitfulness, their very success may blind men to other aspects of experience.

Many men in the contemporary world still accept experience to be whatever the mathematical/empirical sciences say it to be. However, the great thinkers, artists and doers have for a century past been launching a devastating assault on this assumption. Sometimes, as in Marx, Husserl and Dewey, "the scientific approach" was spoken of as the ideal while at the same time these men were undermining the narrow scientific method which surrounded them.[5] Sigmund Freud is often credited with giving the

3. See: Northrop, *op. cit.*, pp. 165–219.
4. See: Edmund Husserl, *Cartesian Meditations* (The Hague, 1960); *Phenomenology and the Crisis of Philosophy* (New York, 1965).
5. For example, see: Dewey, *A Common Faith*, p. 33.

decisive blow in the battle against a narrow scientific rationalism. After Freud no one could easily explain everything without
his explanations being analyzed for hidden meaning outside his
consciousness. Defense of rationalism became nearly impossible
once defense itself had become suspicious.

At the least there is much more room today to investigate the
meaning of the word experience.[6] If one begins by assuming that
experience is the totality of interaction between organism and
environment, then one will never presume to have control over
it. Experience is not what I have but what we are engaged in or
enveloped by. I can never get a full, clear, "objective" picture of
experience because I am part of the experience. Whatever experience ultimately means, it is not reducible to "sense data" or
"empirical facts."

"The error of empiricism," Gabriel Marcel wrote, "is to take
experience for granted and to ignore the mystery; whereas what
is amazing and miraculous is that there should be experience at
all."[7] Marcel was the chief architect of the notion of "mystery"
in philosophy. He admitted borrowing the notion of mystery
from religion but he showed that it could render valuable service
in philosophy. His contrast between mystery and problem has
become part of the language and may be a help to keeping open
the meaning of experience.

When a man begins to question deeply he finds himself immersed in mystery, that is, the questions he asks envelop the
questioner. There is no clear beginning, no certain resolution and
no obvious method when I begin to ask: Who am I? What is
death? Can I trust this person? and hundreds of other urgent

6. Robert Jay Lifton, *Boundaries* (New York, 1970), p. 111: "Today's
young have available for their formulations of self and world the great
twentieth century insights which liberate men from the senseless exclusions of
the experiential-versus-rational bind. These insights can expand the boundaries of man's thought and his feelings in their varied combinations."

7. Gabriel Marcel, *The Philosophy of Existentialism* (New York, 1962),
p. 128.

79

questions. To suppose that these questions can be adequately answered by measurement, calculation and logic would do violence to the complex structure of experience. This supposition would be what Marcel calls the reduction of mystery to problem. He sees this reductionism as an inevitable tendency in human life. Although it is sometimes helpful to measure the problematical elements in life, the tragedy of life would be to see nothing but the solving of problems.[8]

Gabriel Marcel in his own particular terminology and description is trying to keep people awake to a meaning of experience which could be neglected precisely because it is so all-encompassing. There may be more to experience than *what* is experienced. All kinds of implications may be overlooked by a person who never lets up from the pursuit of the facts of experience. The more intently one tries, the more one might set up an obstacle to getting at the full range of experience. It might be that people are not so desirous as they think they are to experience life. It may be safer to use one's head all the time than to drop one's guard and let experience flow in and out. Sidney Jourard writes of such experience: "This hidden dimension of self, sought for centuries by men who have longed for personal fulfillment beyond rationalism, is usually dreaded by the average person. It could be called 'experiencing possibility.' It sometimes 'peeps out' when one permits himself to be unfocused and aimless, unintegrated, not going anywhere or doing anything; but it is 'tamped back' in anxious haste, for it is experienced like the contents of Pandora's box."[9]

Human experience as the locus of reflection does not specify what data or kinds of data might eventually emerge. In the past there has usually been some group powerful enough to decide what the limits of experience are and what the correct interpre-

8. For a detailed contrast between mystery and problem, see: Abraham Maslow, *The Psychology of Science* (New York, 1966), pp. 104–107.

9. Sidney Jourard, *Disclosing Man to Himself* (New York, 1968), p. 45.

tation of experience is. The images of man current in a society tend to function as the upper limit to what is admissible within experience.

The problem is not that human experience is made the measure of things but that human experience is imagined to be so limited. Christian writers have frequently attacked the saying of Protagoras, usually translated as "man is the measure of all things." The dictum was indeed worthy of attack, as Plato immediately realized, but not for the reason which became customary after Plato. What Protagoras had said was that "man is the measure of all 'use-things' (*chrēmata*)," that is, things are to be judged on the basis of how they can be used. "Plato saw immediately that if one makes man the measure of all things for use, it is man the user and instrumentalizer, and not man the speaker and doer or man the thinker, to whom the world is being related."[10]

Ironically, it was in the "Christian West" of modern times that the very thing Plato warned about has come to pass. While churchmen ridiculed the classic text of Protagoras they were reinforcing a Protagorean world. The Church handed over "natural" man to man the user in return for "supernatural" man. Deference was then paid to a realm of truth outside of the human while human experience underwent a progressive narrowing. The abandonment of the natural religious ground as experience paved the way for the secularism and materialism that the Churches loudly denounce. The result was predictable: "*Homo faber* will eventually help himself to everything and consider everything as a mere means for himself. He will judge everything as though it belonged to the class of *chrēmata*, of use objects, so that, to follow Plato's own example, the wind will no longer be understood in its own right as a natural force but will be considered exclusively in accordance with human needs."[11]

10. Arendt, *The Human Condition*, pp. 157–158.
11. *Ibid.*, p. 158.

In ancient times this possibility was merely material for philosophical discussion. Modern times have made this issue the ordinary stuff of life through the application of technology. Obviously, if the wind or sea or earth can be used to alleviate human needs, this use is all to the good. The key word in the above quotation is "exclusively." The use that technology makes of any part of nature must never be equated with the whole meaning of the thing. As soon as nature is conceived to be exclusively for man's use we are on the way to the "conquest of nature" and the destruction of man.

I doubt whether the above reflection will satisfy some religious people who wish to establish their religion on ground more firm than human experience. But I am asserting that the demand for a divine revelation outside or above human experience is a search for idols. Some theologians perhaps flirted with experience in Schleiermacher and liberalism but then turned back to the "givenness" of revelation.[12] Their attitude is that experience was tried and found wanting. However, the narrow channel that runs through Schleiermacher to contemporary theology may not have exhausted the meaning of experience. My premise, very simply, is that we must look to human experience for whatever is to be found. No limits are to be set either at the beginning or the end for what might somehow be in, with or under experience.

In the following pages there is a single recurrent theme which is used for the examination of human experience. It is not evi-

12. See: Friedrich Schleiermacher, *On Religion: Speeches to Its Cultured Despisers* (New York, 1958), pp. 26–101; Stephen Sykes, *Friedrich Schleiermacher* (Richmond, 1971), pp. 1ɔ–43; my difference from Schleiermacher on experience and revelation is indicated in this passage of *Christian Faith* (Edinburgh, 1928), pp. 49–50; "All will at once agree that the word 'revealed' is never applied either to what is discovered in the realm of experience by one man and handed on to others, or to what is excogitated in thought by one man and so learned by others; and further that the word presupposes a divine communication and declaration." I would not be ready to agree that this is the way the word reveal must be used.

dent beforehand and it cannot be proved before starting that this is the best theme to use. The proof, if there is any, will be the fruitfulness of the following attempt to give a comprehensive, consistent and profound understanding of human experience.

The theme that I refer to is one of distinctions within unity. The number and kinds of distinction seem to be limitless but in each case the distinctive elements function within some more comprehensive unity. This theme can be found in many contemporary phenomena and it is also one which runs back through the earliest philosophy and religion. For example, Carl Jung uses the notion of *enantiodromia,* or the running together of opposites, which he traces back to Heraclitus. Experience seems best understood as the relation of pairs of contrasting qualities.[13]

When relation is taken seriously, that is, when the relata really relate and the relata are real by relating, then one has a set of dynamic movements and sub-movements. The complex of relational processes can be called a *field.*[14] This word field is a helpful complement to the word relation. When the word relation is used alone, there are two limiting tendencies. One tendency is to think of relation as simply external to the isolated th'ngs which are placed into relation. The other tendency is to assume that relations are dyadic, that is, one thing is related to another thing without regard to a larger context. The notion of field conveys a sense that things emerge at the intersection of sets of relationships.

The notion of field should break through the walls between "academic fields" so that psychology, sociology, anthropology, theology, ecology, etc., overlap one another. This fact does not

13. C. G. Jung, "On the Psychology of the Unconscious" in *Two Essays on Analytical Psychology* (New York, 1953), pp. 82–84; on the general theme of man as *homo duplex,* see: Anton Zijderveld, *The Abstract Society* (Garden City, 1970).

14. Fontinell, *loc. cit.,* p. 175.

mean that all lines between things are obliterated. Parts of reality can be understood within the approach of a disciplined framework. However, the understanding of anything requires a progressively wider framework of interrelations. An *exhaustive* understanding of any point in the field would require a grasp of how that point is related to every other point.

There are two opposite errors regarding the field of experience: (1) unity is demanded without accepting the distinct relational elements within unity (2) unity is not accepted and one settles for the separate pieces. Both of these errors mask themselves under terms which hide the problem. Often, one error sounds much more like the other error. For example, people who *talk* about unity are often people who accept a juxtaposition of fragments as their meaning of unity.[15] This confusion is not so surprising when one realizes that both of the errors cited above are manifestations of the one fundamental rejection of distinction-within-unity.

Norman O. Brown quotes several times a line from William Butler Yeats:

> Nothing can be sole or whole
> That has not been rent[16]

Experience is to become whole but first it must be accepted as rent. It is difficult to grasp both of these facts together, namely, that it is to *become* whole (it is not yet entirely whole but it should be whole) and it *is rent* (there is separation but it need not be so). By the time people begin to *think* about unity they are already rent. No one begins with a unified field in which he can make helpful and accurate distinctions. Whether or not it is necessary to project back into the past some original fissure, fall or sin, each individual seems to be born with a split self.

The almost inevitable tendency is to take rentness for unity

15. See my *Design for Religion* pp. 49–71.
16. Norman O. Brown, *Love's Body* (New York, 1966), p. 80.

and in so doing to misunderstand both. Especially in a world that prides itself on analytic thought, each man presumes that he is a unity opposed to other unities. His conceptual thought tells him so. This presumption cannot usually be sustained in the face of other kinds of evidence that he is far from unified. Instead of trying to return to some more primordial unity that preceded thinking, the individual may use his dividing thought to find the parts of himself that are really the units (e.g. mind and body). Not only is the conclusion incorrect but the direction in which the answer is sought is the wrong one. Dismantling what had first seemed united is not the way to unity but it is the only thing analytical thought knows how to do.

The way toward unity is to preserve or to re-establish the primordial experience from which thinking arises. Thinking cannot establish the ground of thinking. If the problem is that thinking divides, then it does no good to think harder about the problem of unity. Whether there is some wider field of activity that subsumes thought is, of course, a major concern of this book. My point for the present is that the act of thinking is limited. The question is not whether to be for or against thinking but how it relates to a larger field. Classical philosophy and medieval philosophy were not unacquainted with this problem. However, as we look back on Aristotle or Aquinas, their trust in reasoning and ideas now seems a little naive. Christian thinkers in the middle ages did place reason at the service of a divine revelation. When the Christian concept of a revelation became discredited, reason tried to take over the top perch. The hegemony of reason and thinking was bound to be short-lived. The reason of a man is not fully in control of even himself, let alone the whole cosmos. Beginning with Kant and more dramatically in Husserl and Heidegger, modern times have been turning the tables on thought and demanding a new starting point for thinking itself. When this principle is translated into politics it is liable to unleash the furies. If revolutionary movements dispense

85

with reason as a criteria of action, then politics, and man with it, is in danger of extinction. Nonetheless, there is no reversing the process which has led to the distrust of reason and thought. Their credibility must be re-established on the basis of their service to a wider ideal of action and experience.

One of the consequences of this admission that thinking is limited, is that there are no *final* answers. Furthermore, just as there is no way to get to the end of the story, there is no way to the beginning. There is no *direct* way to get a picture of the whole thing from its origins. This fact leads to a discussion which can be both perplexing and irritating. The following pages have a single theme interwoven through many examples of distinction within unity. In each case I wish to show that what we take to be opposites are complementary aspects of experience and that these aspects must be held together within a larger context. The unity cannot be *said;* what can be expressed in words is already one level removed from unity. The use of words that comes closest to conveying the whole as whole is poetry. This fact led Heidegger to turn to the poetry of Holderlin as the best approach to the regrounding of metaphysics.[17]

The alternative, if one is not a poet, is to repeat the same theme in a kaleidoscope of imagery. Each choice of words is to some degree arbitrary and the meaning of each of these words is unavoidably ambiguous. The pairs of words I will describe vary in their connotations for different people but the contrast is nonetheless definite and real. The methodology involved can be demonstrated in the following example. I shall take the words active and passive as descriptive of human life. At first sight, these two words appear to be opposites but further consideration leads to the conclusion that these two words have to be interrelated. At that point it becomes debatable how to use the words and which of the following paths to follow: (a) broaden the

17. See: Martin Heidegger, *Poetry, Language, Thought* (New York, 1971).

meaning of active so as to include being passive as an activity (b) broaden the meaning of passive so that activity can be a form of passivity (c) coin a new word which both active and passive relate to. The third way would seem the easiest but it is almost impossible to carry it through in practice. The other two ways have some artificiality and will never be entirely successful. My general tendency will be to develop circumlocutions which are not new words but expressions which are puzzling enough to give the reader pause. Thus, in the present example, I say that human experience is best understood when it is seen as "actively passive and passively active."[18] This kind of expression may look like an obscurantistic playing with words. Actually, it is a serious attempt to describe what cannot be described more simply in any other form.

One of the most common images for understanding the complications of experience is the pendulum. It is a particularly unfortunate choice of imagery. The question of the active and passive in life is not resolved by saying that there should be a balance between the two. If life appears too active, it is presumed that the pendulum ought to swing toward the passive. This solution is dear to people who see no great mystery to life; balance and common sense, they believe, resolve all problems. If there is ever to be progress in understanding experience, the image of clocks and pendulums has to recede to the background to be replaced by imagery more organismic.

Some further preliminary comment can be made here on the general notion of relation. A note of warning has to be attached here before taking up the interpersonal relation as the model relationship. I have already mentioned that there is a danger in looking at the relation of two things in isolation. Two things in exclusive relationship to each other are still in isolation. It is often assumed that an interpersonal approach is equivalent to a

18. See: Teilhard de Chardin, *The Divine Milieu* (New York, 1960), pp. 13–68.

social approach but these two are not necessarily the same. In fact, strong involvement with one other person often sets off an asocial, non-political move on the part of individuals. This danger does not invalidate personal encounter as a model relationship but it should make us wary of using this model as the all-sufficient image for understanding reality.

The difficulty of working in this area is exemplified by Martin Buber's classic, *I and Thou*.[19] Even the title of the book can mislead. The use of the conjunction *and* easily leads to the assumption that relation is a juxtaposition of two realities. In trying to posit that "in the beginning was relation," Buber wished to avoid the *I* facing other persons and things. His primary word, I-Thou, is one word not two; likewise, his other basic word is I-It. In his concern with personal encounter, Buber was led to stress the intention and the attitude of the I component in the I-Thou word. As a result of this emphasis he could never quite reach the point where "meeting" and "the between" would in fact be the primordial reality.[20]

Both the strength and the weakness of Buber's work resides in the use of a language that has particular and concrete experience tied to it. He could have described what he was after in some other terms than I-Thou since it is a more generalized relation than that which includes two persons. His use of the standard terms I and Thou to make up a new term I-Thou roots the new word in concrete experience. The accompanying danger in this choice is that the new word will be trivialized and the new insights will be lost.

With the above reservations in mind we can now look at interpersonal encounter as a source for better understanding of relationship. Several of the themes to be explored here are touched upon in the following statement by Buber: "The primary word *I-Thou* can be spoken only with the whole being.

19. Martin Buber, *I and Thou* (New York, 1937).
20. See: Smith, *The Doctrine of God* pp. 133–134.

Concentration and fusion into the whole being can never take place through my agency, nor can it ever take place without me. I become through my relation to the *Thou,* as I become I, I say Thou."[21]

We should note first the emphasis here on mutuality or reciprocity in relations. The more real or genuine a relation, the more each partner both gives and receives. A unilateral relation is the limit point for what can be called relation at all. Relationship at anything but the minimal level implies an exchange that moves toward the full engagement of both parties. This fact does not mean that the two parties have to be equal, certainly not equal in every respect. It does mean that there is some common ground of experience on which they both stand. At any moment either partner may play the more significant or more dynamic role. Nothing would be more destructive of the relationship of two persons than the assumption that one of them is at a fixed point trying to move the other. In any "helping relationship" each partner is helpmate to the other. A doctor does not heal unless the patient also heals the doctor. A teacher cannot teach unless in some way the student teaches the teacher.[22]

In talking about mutuality I could not avoid introducing another aspect of the matter, namely, the helpful or growth character of relationships. There are many criteria one could set out for what constitutes growth and help. For my present purpose I can define a good, genuine and helping relation as one in which greater unity with the whole is accompanied by a developing sense of personal autonomy. The experience of this dual growth is the closest one can come to proving that all of reality is relationally structured. Two self-identities are needed to constitute a relation and the relationship itself helps to establish two self-identities.

21. Buber, *I and Thou,* p. 11.
22. Carl Rogers, "The Characteristics of a Helping Relationship" in *The Planning of Change,* eds., Warren Bennis, Kenneth Benne and Robert Chin, 2nd ed. (New York, 1969), pp. 153–166.

The relation is helpful as it calls forth what is latent in each partner. By drawing out what was there but not visible, each partner is strengthened because the reality of his own person is now more accessible. The concentration into a whole being, as Buber says in the above quotation, can never take place through my own agency but neither can it take place without me. It takes place as I answer to the invitation from another; and I continue to receive so long as I continue to give. "Disclosure begets disclosure," Sidney Jourard writes, "I believe that trust and hope are not *contributors* to healing. Rather they are the experienced aspect of a *total* organismic healing or reintegration process. Trust and hope are indications that the healing or reintegration or transcendence process *has been set in motion.* Trust and hope don't cause healing. They *are* healing."[23]

The reference to healing has not been introduced artificially. The healing of the rent in the whole is at the heart of reality. What has only begun to be explored is the power of personal attitudes or gestures in the healing process. It is not so much *what* is given from one to the other because no *what* is really given at all. In a therapy situation, the doctor gives to a client his own person as the other pole in a healing relationship. The therapist's person is given through a what, that is, as embodied in words and gestures. But it is the doctor's giving of himself which is the chief healing power.

We may note in passing that the religious traditions usually speak of healing, saving or redeeming as central to the religious process. Often, however, there is little intrinsic connection between the healing element and revelation. In fact, in Christian theology they have usually emerged as quite separate processes. One of the indications that revelation was inadequately understood is shown by the fact that revelation was not of itself a healing process. Between two human beings, to the degree that there is revealing there is healing. If the process does not move

23. Jourard, *op. cit.,* pp. 23, 68.

in the direction of healing, then what is going on is not a revealing of persons. It is more likely a concentration on revealing certain things which are actually a mask to prevent a revealing of the person.

This concealing of the person by hiding behind things is a final aspect of the notion of personal relationship. A person, even with the best will and effort, can only slowly move into the dynamism of an open-ended relationship. The person has to be patient with himself and others in this step-by-step process. At every point he can give himself only to the degree he can direct his whole self and he can give only to the degree that the other is ready to receive. The sense that there should be a greater wholeness or totality to the experience is the motive force for further effort but at the same time it is the source of frustration and anxiety.

Every attempt to "unveil" the truth is at once a veiling and unveiling of the whole truth. Revelation, as human beings experience it, is always in part a process of concealing. One might expect that revelation makes everything clear and eliminates mystery. Religious spokesmen often seem to suppose just that, but if they looked closely at human relationships they would see otherwise. Human beings cannot reveal themselves totally nor can they place themselves into clear words and unambiguous gestures. If people can accept this as a fact of life they can move gradually in the direction of greater wholeness and light. The attempt to strip bare the psyche all at once is tied to a fear of what is left unexposed in oneself and others. "Talking a great deal," said Nietzsche, "is a way of concealing oneself."[24] One who seems desperately intent on revealing all is more likely desperately afraid that his true self might be revealed. People who have little fear of revealing themselves do not usually give the impression of being in a hurry to do so.[25]

24. Friedrich Nietzsche, *Beyond Good and Evil* (Chicago, 1955), p. 88.
25. See: Soren Kierkegaard, *Fear and Trembling, Sickness unto Death* (Garden City, 1954), pp. 182–200.

2. ONE AND ALL

We can turn at this point to various kinds of interrelationship that fill out or complement the interpersonal exchange. The interpersonal, I have warned, would be falsified if ripped from its organic context. There is another way of looking at the relational character of life which may not be as immediately fruitful as interpersonal encounter but which is just as important. What two people experience as love toward each other is at the same time an experience of some greater whole. It is this experience of *all* or *totality* that I wish to consider here. This inquiry can be carried out apart from any religious meanings that may be attributed to such words.

Each individual is confronted with "the other." He can focus attention on one other thing, that is, his attention can be restricted to one thing or another. In addition, a person can experience himself as encompassed by the otherness of world or being. Philosophical reflection leads to a confrontation of man with the question of to be or not to be. "Why should there be something rather than nothing?" or perhaps: "Why should there be something and nothing?" The question of his own personal death concentrates the question but at a metaphysical level the question is what does it mean to be. Whatever answers there are to the question, the question itself is a peculiarly human one. Man in raising the question reveals something of being and the question reveals the being of man. Karl Rahner, who has dealt at length with this issue, writes: "Man is the being in whose being being is at issue. Man is that being which always has a relationship to itself—one of subjectivity, not simply of nature. Man is always a person; he is not simply 'there' but is always aware of being there."[26]

Rahner works here from the same framework which Heideg-

26. Karl Rahner, "On the Theology of Freedom," in *Freedom and Man*, ed., John C. Murray (New York, 1965), p. 208.

ger had developed.[27] Man is the locus of being, the place where being comes to light in questioning. Man in turn becomes "authentic" by becoming part of the process of the truth as emergence into the light. Only by continually raising the question of being or to be (as distinct from questions about beings) can man remain in contact with his true self and what is real. Heidegger sees the history of philosophy in the West after Socrates to be a "forgetting of being" and a contentment with things to be used.[28]

When a person comes to conscious awareness he confronts what appears to be other than himself. He then uses his mind to interpret his relation to the other. As I have previously suggested, mind or rational thought as the primary medium of interpretation is liable to mislead. Conscious, reflective thought starts from the givenness of an ego and opposing things. It does not raise the question of to be or not to be. There is some more primordial kind of unity which man has a sense of belonging to. If he is jolted into awareness of this unity by something other than rational thought, the unity will provide a new context for thinking. Likewise, there is a more primordial relation of man to world which cannot be directly examined by thought.

The organism begins developing attitudes or stances toward its environment long before its first conscious thought. The environment together with the complex of attitudes is the person's "world." Husserl, Heidegger and Merleau-Ponty tried to get at these structural ingredients of human experience that can be brought to light only indirectly. Heidegger's treatment of "care" and his examination of death are two primary illustrations of this special kind of analysis. A person's fundamental dispositions toward the world are refracted through (and thereby indirectly

27. See: Martin Heidegger, *Being and Time* (London, 1962); William Richardson, *Heidegger* (The Hague, 1962); Karl Rahner, *Spirit in the World* (New York, 1968).
28. See: Martin Heidegger, *An Introduction to Metaphysics* (New York, 1961).

available through) what he thinks and says about the world.

The terms "self-conscious" and "self-understanding" have probably been misleading in recent philosophy and theology. The movement of understanding is a bringing to light the presence of being among men. Understanding is always of people together in a world. The focal point at which this happens is an individualized self but the process is always more encompassing than a self. The term "self-understanding" may be legitimate shorthand for this process but it easily leads to the untenable supposition that understanding is an isolated act of self-searching. If one starts with a "self" as the first category there is no way out to a social framework. There is no way to overcome an opposition from within the opposition itself. If, in contrast, one begins with relation or field, then the understanding of self can be expanded without limits but understanding will never be apart from what is recognized as other though also recognized as not entirely other.

It is not easy to put together the personalistic approach described previously and the metaphysical approach described above. Even though one does not seem to flow into the other, it is imperative to keep some hold on both of them. The metaphysical outlook alone always threatens to swallow all sense of personal autonomy in the face of the all-encompassing other. The interpersonal experience taken alone seems to give a premature solution to the great problems of autonomy and wholeness but only to lead to later disillusionment.

Perhaps the best definition of the word love would be an experience which combines the interpersonal and metaphysical outlooks. Lovers might scoff at such a statement since metaphysics is hardly their concern in the first flush of love. It is obvious that in human love there is a moment of apparent exclusivity when the movement toward the other is intensely directed to the other. It is also apparent, however, that love must have a moment of inclusivity when nothing is excluded and the loved one is recognized as the embodiment of some universal good. The fact that this latter aspect of love is often only dimly grasped in an individual's awareness does not negate its necessary place in all human love.[29]

Wherever there is human love, the partners are revealed, and in a true sense created, as embodiments of the universal value of being.[30] The relational character of reality is nowhere better demonstrated than here. The detached observer cannot understand what is going on. He attributes what is happening to a blindness caused by emotion. Undoubtedly, it can happen that a supposed love interferes with a person's perception of reality. It is just as certain that the opposite can be true, namely, that engagement in the relationship of love is the only way to perceive some levels of reality. The full individuality of a human being can only be revealed by love. "It is commonly thought that, of all people, lovers behold one another in the most unrealistic light, and that in their encounter is but the mutual projection of extravagant ideals. But may it not be that nature has allowed them to see for the first time what a human being is, and that the subsequent disillusion is not the fading of dream into reality but the strangling of reality with an all too eager embrace?"[31]

Integration of the person with the whole can only take place as a person becomes integrated within himself. The unification of the world and the unification of the person must go together. In much of history, the individual has been divided into parts; the most common division has probably been into body and

29. See: Erik Erikson, *Insight and Responsibility* (New York, 1964), p. 128; Carl Rogers, *Freedom to Learn* (Columbus, 1969), p. 252.
30. Abraham Maslow, *Toward a Psychology of Being* (New York, 1962), p. 41: "In a profound but testable sense love creates the partner. It gives him a self-image, it gives him self-acceptance, a feeling of love-worthiness and respect-worthiness, all of which permit him to grow. It is a real question whether the full development of the human being is possible without it."
31. Watts, *op. cit.*, p. 183; see also: John McMurray, *Persons in Relation* (London, 1961), p. 33.

95

spirit. This split did not originate solely from religious tradition although it has nearly always carried religious or moral overtones. Man is rent; whatever be the names of the combatants, some kind of conflict is waged in the human self.

The scandal of much of religious tradition has been to choose sides in this conflict. The easiest way out of war seems to be quick and decisive victory by one side. But as nations have discovered in this century, unconditional surrender may not be the most appropriate objective. For a just and lasting peace we need not a definitive conquest by one side but a new awareness of the uselessness of war and the need to work toward cooperative alliances. Conflict may be not only inevitable but creative if it is approached with patience and care, but destruction and annihilation should have no place. If man is to be saved, we need for the first time in the race the clear and full acceptance of the fact that "there is no beast in man. There is only man in man and this we have been able to release."[32]

In modern times the body/spirit split has lost considerable ground among educated people. Insofar as the rejection of this doctrine was a rejection of the identification of man with a supposed part of man, the movement was a healthy one. It is not at all clear, however, that the problem which gave rise to this split has been squarely faced. Denying that there is any conflict at all in the heart of man is not a solution at all. The nineteenth-century doctor, who solemnly announced that he had found no soul, was announcing the unification of the human. Unfortunately, he was either being silly or a bit less than candid. Equally disingenuous, however, was the religious solution that solved the problem of unity by reducing people to their souls.

32. Carl Rogers, *On Becoming a Person* (Boston, 1961), p. 105; see also: Nathaniel Cantor, *Dynamics of Learning,* 2nd ed. (Buffalo, 1961), p. 241: "If the 'bad' self is accepted with the 'good' side, neither aspect of the personality has to be denied, and there is no need for justification or rationalization. To accept oneself means to be responsible for one's decisions without feeling too much guilt."

The fissure in man does not go away despite all the denials. The twentieth century has had to develop new conceptualizations to wrestle with the problem. Perhaps the most dramatic and most helpful of these descriptions is the notion of conscious/ unconscious. One must be careful to understand from the start that this conceptualization is an attempt to describe the relationship that *is* man. The advance which this description represents is that conscious and unconscious are not metaphysical entities, nor does one word represent the good side and the other the bad. We are therefore not reintroducing under slightly altered terms the former division into parts. Rather, we are describing the relational character of human experience and looking for distinguishable poles of activity within a growing unity.

It must be admitted that Freud himself was not entirely clear on this point. Through the development of a set of brilliant techniques, Freud was able to unlock the door to a whole side of humanness that had been neglected or denied. But this discovery was easily misinterpreted to mean that the human being was "nothing but" this underside brought to light. A related but contrasting error was to suppose that the newly discovered "unconscious" was the bad part to be eliminated as far as possible. The objective for an individual would be to transpose material from the unconscious to the conscious. Freud's dictum "All that has been id shall be ego" reflects this turn of mind. Burdened with the mechanical model of man that a rationalistic age had bequeathed to him, Freud could not escape making a value judgment on the unconscious. His choice of the term "reality principle" for describing the objective world to which the individual must conform issues from that bias. It would have been impossible for Freud to suppose that dreams, magic, mystery and madness have as much claim on "reality" as the "objective" world which demands conformity.[33]

Much of post-Freudianism has been in the direction of chal-

33. See: Sigmund Freud, *The Future of an Illusion* (Garden City, 1964).

lenging this bias. Of course, the reductionistic tendency of Freudianism remains a dominant motif of our era; that is, any activities which seem to come from high ideals and intense dedication can be explained away as beastlike compulsions which secretly drive the person. This popularized version of the unconscious is a perpetuation of the age-old refusal to look at man for what he is: neither beast nor angel but man. This view also trivializes the unconscious instead of recognizing the profound implications of the concept.

The unconscious, then, is not a closet full of skeletons in the private house of the individual mind; it is not even, finally, a cave full of dreams and ghosts in which, like Plato's prisoners, most of us spend most of our lives. The unconscious is rather the immortal sea which brought us hither; intimations of which are given in moments of "oceanic feeling"; one sea of energy or instinct; embracing all mankind, without distinction of race, language, or culture; and embracing all the generations of Adam, past, present, and future, in one phylogenetic heritage; in one mystical or symbolic body.[34]

In this passage, Norman O. Brown cannot avoid a language that is metaphorical, lyrical and mystical. This fact is itself significant since one might have presumed that such qualities are inherently inferior to logic and objectivity. Allowing the lyrical, metaphorical and mystical to be valid and even necessary modes of discourse for getting to truth and reality is one of the immediate conclusions that should have been drawn from the discovery of the unconscious.

The failure to draw this conclusion springs from assumptions which place the unconscious within a mechanical model of the individual. What should have been the context of understanding is the conscious/unconscious man in organic relation to the universe. The difference of models is crucial and the practical consequences are enormous. In an organic model, material is not dredged up from the unconscious and transferred to conscious-

34. Brown, *Love's Body*, pp. 88–89.

ness. Instead, consciousness and unconsciousness grow together. "As the islands of consciousness grow broader the surrounding seas of the unconsciousness grow deeper."[35] A grasp of this fact would alter some of the rhythm and pattern in attempts today to "form community" or liberate the individual. Brutal, frontal assaults or intense, focused activity may be inadequate ways to cope with the delicate interplay of the conscious and unconscious.

A further advantage to this new model would be a better understanding of what is wrong, bad or evil about man. The former picture, traceable in part to religion, saw one part of a man or something in man that was evil. The consequent plan of action was clear even if painful, namely, to act against the "natural" tendencies in order to get "self-control." In recent times the metaphysical or religious belief that supported the program was gradually eroded and it was declared that man is good. An era of no control succeeded to a long history of repression. Many people in the twentieth century, however, have begun to suspect that there is still something lacking in what the human race is doing to itself. We do not need less "permissiveness" and more rigid control but we still do need a better understanding of the human.

There is something wrong with men, a fact which can be ascertained and articulated without recourse to any metaphysical position on evil or religious discourses on sin. The attempt to correct what is wrong by providing general education for everyone (combined with therapy for those who still do not act correctly) can obscure the profundity of the problem. Education and therapy may be among the greatest needs of the race but before programs are outlined in both areas the human model

35. Robert Bellah, *Beyond Belief* (New York, 1970), p. 206 referring to the work of Philip Slater; see also William Johnston, *The Still Point* (New York, 1971), pp. 47–63 for the same point in Zen Buddhism and the interpretations of Zen by Carl Jung.

which is presupposed should be examined. Unless the human is understood as the mutual relation of conscious and unconscious in mutual relation to a beyond, education and therapy might only worsen matters. When man is assumed to be a mechanism of two parts, education which is highly rational alternates with education that is irrational. The slow, organic growth of the whole is represented by neither of these educational approaches. Within the same framework, therapy which centers on explaining rational acts by delving back into hidden controls of the unconscious alternates with schools of therapy that stimulate explosive emotions apart from any critical reason.

There are indeed urges and forces in man which are frightening. The eruptions from the dark, unfathomed side are suspected of being the source of trouble. The suspicion is justified. What is less often realized but should be a main concern of education and therapy (not to mention religion) is that these forces are also the source of man's potential greatness. "I tell you," wrote Nietzsche, "one must harbor chaos if one would give birth to a dancing star." The elemental urge is the force of life and death.

Rollo May, in trying to describe this powerful force, reaches back into classical times for the word *daimonic*. As May describes it, the *daimonic* does not have the wholly negative connotations that derivatives of the word (demon, demonic) have in popular speech. It is simply the urge to reach out to others, to exert power and to increase life.[36] One can indeed go a long way toward stamping out the *daimonic* force but the price is very high, namely, the stamping out of life itself. The point was well understood by Rilke: "If my devils are to leave me, I am afraid my angels will take flight as well."

A better policy than trying to get rid of the dark side is the acceptance of it, the willingness to live with it and the gradual integration of it into a mutual relationship with the rational side of life. Integration, it should be noted, does not mean absorption

36. See: Rollo May, *Love and Will* (New York, 1969), p. 146

or elimination.[37] Integration, as the black man has been making clear to the white man, means greater diversity within unity. As the unconscious is integrated with the conscious, the former does not cease to exist but instead becomes more powerful, more imperative and more directed to the universal than is consciousness alone. "The more I come to terms with my daimonic tendencies, the more I will find myself conceiving and living by a universal structure of reality. This movement toward the logos is *transpersonal*. Thus we move from an impersonal through a personal to a *transpersonal* dimension of consciousness."[38] The word transpersonal here means, at the least, going beyond an individual person. There is no solution for the individual in trying to integrate himself. Genuine contact with his own life will push him toward integration with what goes beyond his individual self.

These reflections on the conscious/unconscious would be helpful in understanding both the creative person and the insane individual. Nothing shows more clearly a society's understanding of itself than its attitudes toward the creative and the sick. It is not by accident that I refer to these two categories in the same sentence. The realization that these two are intimately related ought to play a central role in understanding both phenomena. The relation is expressed by Cohen and Murphy in the following way: "When the dissolution of the reasoning self occurs in a chaotic manner, the result is called psychosis. When the state is not accompanied by panic or anxiety, it is perceived as mystical, and creative solutions for (or at least an armistice with) life problems could result."[39]

The preceding statement is clear and forceful but it leaves unresolved the question of who will decide the meaning of chaotic and panic. Who is so sane that he can set up himself to be the

37. For reflections on the "dark side" of life, see: Loren Eiseley, *The Night Country* (New York, 1971).
38. May, *op. cit.,* p. 177.
39. Quoted in Braden, *Private Sea,* p. 26.

decider of sanity and insanity. G. K. Chesterton once said that "rationalism is a peculiar kind of insanity in which one has lost everything but one's mind." His remark is more widely applicable than he could suspect. Sickness and health are misunderstood when it is supposed that some of society's members are sick and some healthy. Yet, this kind of "insanity" applies to much of the human race including the doctors who are trying to restore "the insane" to the "real world." Any society that defines part of itself as "insane" has a problem on its hands but not the problem it has just defined. The bigger problem is its conception of health and consequently the means that are adopted to achieve health. If sanity and insanity are valid terms, they apply along a continuum to each person. There is no guarantee that some of the people who are most certain of being sane are in fact among the least insane.

The person who is defined today as a schizophrenic does have something wrong with him but his sickness is the opposite of what many people suppose it to be. The schizophrenic, far from being cut off from reality, is unable to shut off experience at the point he can bear it. The "normal" person is the one cut off from most of what is happening whereas in schizophrenia false boundaries are disintegrating. "Schizophrenic thought is 'adualistic'; lack of ego-boundaries makes it impossble to set limits to the process of identification with the environment."[40] There is a striking similarity here to some forms of religious experience.

The schizophrenic person may be closer to the truth than the normal person but it is a truth too heavy to bear for that individual. Thus, the person with such an affliction reveals the problem which affects others in less obvious ways. Rollo May refers to the Cassandra figure in Mycenae predicting the doom she sees will occur all about her. "Today, the person with psychological problems bears the burdens of the conflicts of the time in his

40. Brown, *Love's Body*, p. 159.

102

blood, and is fated to predict in his actions and struggles the issues which will later erupt on all sides in the society."[41] The majority who define themselves as sane would prefer to exclude from the human what is frighteningly different. For everyone, that is, for each human being who is sane/insane, we must enlarge the concept of the human so that it will include everything that appears.

A few comments on the creative person are appropriate here. As I have indicated, the creative person is often seen to be at the borderline of sanity and insanity. Often, it is not certain which category the person belongs to, a fact which in itself should collapse most of the naive assumptions about insanity. The creative person's greatest significance is not found in what he creates but in the challenge and inspiration he gives to every person's creativity and unconscious. The result ought to be the recognition that creativity, too, is a continuum. Everyone is creative; some are more creative than others.

The highly creative person is usually assumed to be a "loner," that is, to be cut off from the people around him and working at the edge of solipsism. This conception is completely inaccurate. "The creative man (though often this is not evident) is deeply bound up with his group and its culture, more deeply than the common man who lives in the security of the cultural shell, and even more deeply than the actual representatives of this culture."[42]

In cases of creativity, the possibilities and limitations of a society find a receptive point of expression. At first, the individual seems to be playing out some peculiar problem of his own. It always remains his personal "call" which he alone faces. At the same time this personal calling can become a cosmic

41. May, *op. cit.,* p. 24; see also: Jourard, *op. cit.,* p. 38.
42. See: Erich Neumann, *Art and the Creative Unconscious* (New York, 1959), p. 99; see also: Robert Nisbet, *Community and Power* (New York, 1962), p. 236.

struggle which is embodied in his person. Erik Erikson, in his study of Luther, describes this struggle:

A creative man has no choice. He may come across his supreme task almost accidentally. But once the issue is joined, his task proves to be at the same time intimately related to his most personal conflicts, to his superior selective perception, and to the stubbornness of his one-way will: he must court sickness, failure, or insanity, in order to test the alternative: whether the established world will crush him, or whether he will disestablish a sector of this world's outworn fundaments and make a place for a new one.[43]

Creativity is a topic closely related to the discussion of conscious/unconscious. A creative person is one who makes rich use of the relation between conscious and unconscious.[44] A commonly reported fact about a very creative person is that he is able to turn over problems in his unconscious. He works with intensity of consciousness until he meets with some block and turns to some other interest. Then, suddenly, while he is dreaming or thinking about something entirely different, the answer pops into his head.[45] This process has been noted throughout the centuries but only in a passing way. Recently, there has been a more detailed description of the process of scientific discovery, a process of dynamic interaction between conscious and unconscious.

I hope that the relevance of this material to the central theme of this book is evident. I am trying to indicate why the category of revelation may be one of the best words to describe reality. Sickness and creativeness signify something structural about all reality and not just about "sick people" or "creative people." When we turn to religion in the following chapter we will see that prophetic and mystical people raise the same kind of challenge to our understanding. The choice once more will be the

43. Erik Erikson, *Young Man Luther* (New York, 1958), p. 46.
44. See: Lawrence Kubie, *Neurotic Distortion of the Creative Process* (New York, 1961).
45. See: Bugental, *op. cit.*, p. 390.

same: to define some people as "religious people" and segregate them from normal humans or to challenge the limits of the human and allow the religious into every human life.

A world that does not understand the "sick person" will not understand the religious element in life. A society cannot accept revelation as a serious category in religion if it treats in cavalier fashion the revelational in the sick and the creative. Conversely, when society begins to find the sick and the creative a mirror for its own understanding, it may be ready to consider revelation as the fundamental category of life. Norman O. Brown's words provide a summary conclusion to this section:

Psychoanalysis began as a further advance of civilized (scientific) objectivity; to expose remnants of primitive participation, to eliminate them; studying the world of dreams, of primitive magic, of madness, but not participating in dreams or magic or madness. But the outcome of psychoanalysis is the discovery that magic and madness are everywhere, and dreams is what we are made of. The goal cannot be the elimination of magical thinking, or madness; the goal can only be conscious magic, or conscious madness; conscious mastery of these fires. And dreaming while awake.[46]

3. POWER

Another set of terms, which is related to conscious/unconscious, is the pair of words I have previously mentioned: active/passive. In this case, the terminology is more difficult to handle since the meanings of the two words keep shifting to the point of switching places. Nevertheless, what is expressed through these words is fundamental to human experience. As before, my thesis is that to the extent activity and passivity are considered to be separate elements, they will be destructive of human experience but to the extent that they are understood together they bring out the relational and revelational character of all experience.

46. Brown, Love's Body, p. 254.

Some of the ambiguity in the words active and passive can be seen by bringing in a third word: power. The word power is etymologically closer to words connected with passivity, although in ordinary speech today it would be much closer to activity. Thomas Aquinas, in his discussion of God as all powerful, notes the paradox of the words.[47] In Aristotle, as well as in medieval philosophy, power (*potens*) was the lowest rung on the scale of being, that is, not anything in itself but a capacity to receive being. The English word potential has retained this meaning. Aquinas thought that it made sense to use the same word at the other end of the scale. Thus, he can refer to a "passive" intellect and an "omnipotent" God. In the highest beings (spiritual beings) there is a process of generation which bears some similarity to the merely potential being that must receive actual form.

The language and approach of modern times differ considerably from the middle ages but the question of power remains as important as ever. It is probably impossible to re-establish the root meaning of power and to develop one consistent table of use. Current usage reflects the opposite meanings built into the word. Power in human affairs can refer to the capacity to overrun, to control or to dominate. Power as an external force against human beings is at the level of the most anti-human reality. On the other hand, power can refer to the highest human expression. It is only because of power that men can get together and accomplish anything.[48]

The ambiguity in the word power is not accidental; it is built into the word as a reflection of reality. The ambiguity cannot be resolved simply by defining that power *really* means ... Nor can one substitute two other words to replace the opposite meanings of the word. What we can do is use two closely

47. See: St. Thomas Aquinas, *Summa Theologica*, vol. 1 (New York, 1947), pp. 135–136; I, q. 25, a. 1.
48. See: Erich Fromm, *Escape from Freedom* (New York, 1965), p. 184.

related words to show the inner dynamism of human experience indicated by power. This is the reason for introducing the words active and passive. Both words express something about power but depending upon the interrelationship, the power can be an affirming or a negating of the human.

The first way of stating the relationship of these words is the following: At the bottom of the scale there is (helpless) passivity; at the middle of the scale there is activity; at the top there is (receptive) passivity. This typology, although clear, is not entirely adequate. At every point on the scale there is an interplay of passive and active. Therefore, we have to revise and extend the description in the following way. At the bottom of the scale there is almost total separation of activity and passivity; the two are simply juxtaposed. In this situation helpless passivity is most apparent. At the middle there is a growing together of the active and passive. An awareness of the values involved in activity is most evident. At the top of the scale of human experience there is an integration of the active and passive so that there is wholeness at any moment. The result is a peaceful attitude which comes from the "letting be" of everything or what can be called a receptive passivity.

In speaking of a scale with bottom and top I am presuming some criteria or standards of judging humanness. The full exposition of such criteria is what this whole part of the book deals with. The initial criterion I began with was diversity within organic unity. This principle can be filled out with a more extended description of the points along the continuum of human growth.

At the bottom of the scale there is no organic unity. A person here is both active and passive but he shifts erratically from one to the other. More often than not, he appears to be passive in the sense of getting stepped upon or pushed around. Many primitive religious forms join forces with political and military machines to make people submissive and even less than human.

When men submit to the fates or gods, freedom is hardly a factor at all and human experience can hardly be said to exist at all.

Occasionally, however, when the pressure lid is taken off, there appears to be a dramatic reversal. The "little man"[49] explodes in activity. Nothing has really changed in his personality; it is simply that the submerged part gets its chance to surface. The activity is not very human or humanizing because it comes in great, compulsive outbursts that are unrelated to any stillness and calm. Children during recess hour are often not at play; they are simply letting loose the energy which has been inhumanly submerged in a classroom. The lowly bureaucrat becomes a tyrant when he gets behind the wheel of his automobile. R. D. Laing catches the spirit of this split personality of modern times: "We are caught in a hell of frenetic passivity." The activity is frenetic because it does not issue from the human being as human. For all the show of might and force, what dominates such individuals is weak-kneed submissiveness.[50]

Farther up the scale, the activity of planned and logical reasoning comes to the forefront. In contemporary Western society, the word activity nearly always designates this application of reason to the world. The person who has made some progress but is still insecure judges himself and others by what they can do, how much money they make, and what kind of deference is paid to their status. The danger here is that activity in the form of aggressive conquest, which is obviously a good, can obliterate all other considerations. Any form of passivity may be looked upon with a degree of contempt.

The assumption that activity and strength constitute the highest ideal is related to the male domination of society. In this society certain characteristics are associated with the strong male

49. See: Wilhelm Reich, *Listen Little Man* (New York, 1948).
50. See: T. W. Adorno, *The Authoritarian Personality* (New York, 1950).

image and others go with the weak female type. A man is judged by whether he measures up to the qualities of *machismo*. The woman is supposed to accept the role of being taken care of by the kindly man. Any man who challenges this arrangement is suspected of being motivated by effeminate weakness. Any woman who opposes this stereotyping is dismissed as a failure in femininity. Unfortunately, many of the people who do resist the stereotyping get caught in the separation they should be fighting. Thus, many women, instead of urging the realization of a passive element in men, tend to deny the passive element in themselves. Instead of leading from the special strength of the passive element (even if distorted) they accept the falsehood that human strength is a matter of rational aggressivity.

The ideal at the top of the scale which ought to govern human progress is an organic interrelation of active/passive. At its best, human activity, without losing the careful, rational element, regains the passive as an integral element. There is intensity and accomplishment of purpose but there is reduction of the external activity pushing against the environment. What seems to be weakness at another level can become a point of strength when organically related to activity. Human freedom, at this point, comes to be understood not as "willfulness" but as readiness to respond to the unknown. People who are going through trouble are often told: "Pull yourself together." They could hardly be given worse advice. "Neurosis is precisely the disease of uncontrollable 'willfulness.' "[51] What they could use is the gift of another person's receptivity which would give testimony that the world can be trusted and one need not keep acting to create it.

The interpersonal relationship is the place where active passivity and passive activity become an evident necessity. If one is trying to understand mathematics, physics or geology, progress is possible without this proper mix of active/passive.

51. Fingarette, *op. cit.*, p. 58.

When it is a matter of human beings, there is no other way of making contact with the individual personality than by this difficult route. Anyone who thinks that there is nothing to this process or that it can be carried off by clever techniques simply does not understand the experience. Abraham Maslow has written on this topic with the greatest sensitivity:

> Slowly and painfully we psychologists have had to become good clinical or naturalistic observers, to wait and watch and listen patiently, to keep our hands off, to refrain from being too active and brusque, too interfering and controlling, and—most important of all in trying to understand another person—to keep our mouths shut and our eyes and ears wide open. This is different from the model ways in which we approach physical objects, i.e., manipulating them, poking at them, to see what happens, taking them apart, etc. If you do this to human beings you won't get to know them. They won't *want* you to know them. They won't let you know them.[52]

In interpersonal relations the active and passive interlock and transform each other. The active in one person meets the passive in another, but the coming forth of the passive is a kind of activity. The weakness of one calls forth the strength of another which makes the original weakness a kind of strength (that is, what calls forth strength is stronger than strength). In turn the original strength is revealed as weakness (that is, what has to be called forth by weakness is weaker than weakness). In the end, the only strength resides in seeing and accepting the fact that the active and passive are in each person and must be rhythmically and organically related. The greatest strength becomes the acceptance of weakness as the point at which persons meet.

It may be noted in passing that few religious traditions have ever grasped the complexity of the active/passive relation. The

52. Maslow, *Psychology of Science,* p. 13; see also: Marcel, *Philosophy of Existentialism,* p. 99; James Hillman, *Insearch: Psychology and Religion* (New York, 1967), p. 21.

head god has usually been very active in giving all the directions. The idea that divine strength might lie in a kind of passivity has not been entirely absent but has seldom taken center stage. The mother-earth symbols of many religions are intimations of this passiveness. The "crucified Lord" image of Christianity has been at the center but has been overlaid with all kinds of doctrines of justification and redemption. The main problem has been that the category of revelation has not been developed on the model of the most mature human relationships. Otherwise, the meaning of revelation would appear as a continuing process of interaction in which each party plays both an active and a passive role.

It may be helpful to transpose the description of active/passive into the terms dependent/independent. The former pair seems to center on attitude while the latter more directly denotes some social expression. As the word power embraces the relation of active/passive, so the word freedom will serve as meeting point for dependence and independence. In the contemporary West, freedom would most likely call up the word independence. However, to suppose that freedom means as much independence as possible and as little dependence as possible would be to misunderstand freedom and do violence to experience. Freedom is tied to a particular *kind* of dependence which derives from a particular relation of independence and dependence.

In a manner similar to passivity, the category of dependence is found at the lowest level of human experience and again at the very top. Among children, primitives and helpless people, there is a dependence which is a substitute for human autonomy. If a person is ever to come to full manhood, he has to initiate activity himself, take on responsibilities for his actions and be accountable to others. Freedom is therefore first experienced as a freeing oneself from shackles that bind externally. The freeing has to be done even when the shackler (e.g., a parent) has the best of intentions. Because of the first, intense struggle for free-

111

dom, freedom can easily be equated with "freedom from" some-thing, that is, freedom is identified with independence.

At some point when an individual has emerged from childish dependence he will raise the question of what things or people are going to interest him now that he has a choice. Although the question may not be phrased in this way, he is asking the question: "freedom for" what. At an early stage one's attention is dominated by the concern to break out of confinement and to cast off the slave master. It is frustrating to find that the problem of freedom is not resolved by this "liberation." Freedom can in fact be experienced as a burden so that some people even try to return to their old masters. What they find is that the process is irreversible and that the only alternatives are greater freedom or new slavery.

The only resolution, and it always remains a precarious resolu-tion, is to find someone or something worthy of love. But this fact means finding a new kind of dependence. For a person to be free he must find something to live for and someone to live with. This dependence does not originate from a personal de-ficiency but from the desire and ability to give of oneself. The word dependence is justified here because the person "needs" someone to give to and give with. Furthermore, even in the maturest and strongest human being it is never finally clear what is weak and what is strong. What is certain is that a relationship of independence/dependence structures human freedom and that for a man to be free he must accept dependence as an integral part of life. The alternative to an independent dependence on others is either to eliminate one's own independence in some masochistic form or else to attempt to live aloof from all relations. The latter is possible only at the cost of serving an idol of self-centeredness.[53]

When someone can grasp that a genuine *human* relationship does not diminish but increases a person, then he becomes a

53. See: Fromm, *Escape from Freedom.*

112

"being greater than his attributes" (Buber). He becomes secure enough to engage in a reciprocal movement with another person. From that moment onward, the meaning of being and freedom can never be the same again. "To discover that it is *not* devastating to accept the positive feeling from another, that it does not necessarily end in hurt, that it actually 'feels good' to have another person with you in your struggles to meet life— this may be one of the most profound learnings encountered by the individual whether in therapy or not."[54]

The reference to religious traditions on this point should be obvious. The emphasis on the virtue of obedience, particularly in modern Christianity, is enough to indicate an inadequate understanding of this point. If one were to take seriously the dependence/independence dialectic, then presumably obedience would be considered a virtue only in children. Or, the development of the word would have gone along another route and would have retained the meaning of "listening to" and "responding." The question of freedom is acutely evident in ecclesiastical matters but that is not the root problem. In back of a "hierarchy" and of exhortations to depend on holy mother church, there is an assumption about the meaning of revelation. Neither liberals nor conservatives will find solutions to church order unless the prior assumptions of anthropology and theology are first examined.

4. SUBJECT/OBJECT

The several foregoing discussions could be taken as concretizations of the main division in human experience, namely, the split of subject and object. When the question is approached philosophically these are the two categories most often used. The difficulty with talking about a subject/object dichotomy is

54. Rogers, *On Becoming a Person,* p. 85; see also: William Lynch, *Images of Hope* (New York, 1966), p. 206.

that it seems to many people to be an abstraction for which they have no feeling. That is why I have used conscious/unconscious, active/passive, dependent/independent as examples to fill out the relational character of experience. It should now be easier to take on this main theme of modern philosophy. In looking at the meaning of subject and object I am returning to the theme I began with: individual/being. Heidegger most emphatically among modern philosophers sees the split of subject and object at the heart of man's forgetfulness and misunderstanding of being.[55]

As in the previous examples, we can grapple with subjective/objective only by understanding the relational character of reality and by sorting out the several meanings of both subjective and objective. The underlying theme in the whole discussion is that reality is relational and, therefore, any perception of reality includes a subjective pole of understanding and an objective component toward which understanding is directed. The problem becomes one of determining both the quality and quantity of subjective involvement which are appropriate for the objective pole. Or, if one proceeds from the opposite direction, it is necessary to distinguish kinds and uses of objectivity.

We might first note the ambiguous meanings of subjective and objective. By this time it should not surprise us to find that each word has a very good meaning and a very bad meaning. I take up first the meanings of objectivity. Objectivity is usually used with a positive connotation in contemporary language. It is most highly praised in the mathematical-empirical science where a strict attention to facts is demanded. In these scientific judgments the individual person and his feelings should as far as possible be bracketed. If the judgment can be made by a machine rather than a person, so much the better.

The ideal of objectivity extends beyond the sciences. In a

55. See: Paul Achtemeier, *An Introduction to the New Hermeneutic* (Philadelphia, 1969), p. 45.

court of law, for example, attention is directed to facts which are measured against an external set of prescriptions. The judge must put aside all "pre-judices" and decide on the basis of law. This example indicates why objectivity is considered to be a virtue, that is, the word implies fairness, accuracy and clarity. A person's individual feelings and opinion have not got in the way of his judging upon the best evidence which is available.

This ideal of objectivity has been under challenge for a long time.[56] No one is really against fairness, accuracy and clarity; no one advocates that individual feelings should replace evidence. However, there are many people who maintain that in some areas of life a person's feelings are necessary for evidence to be revealed. In these instances a different *kind* of fairness, accuracy and clarity are at stake. They are saying that in the physical sciences, because of the particular object of study, it is helpful to measure by universal standards that are affected as little as possible by individual idiosyncrasies. Or, in the court of law, if the premise is the measurement of external actions against a body of law, then it is to everyone's advantage to eliminate passion and prejudice.

As the conditional clause of the last sentence indicates, some people today would include the courtroom in challenging objectivity because they reject the premise. Much soul searching is going on in the area of law regarding the restrictions built into the exercise of justice. The challenge has gone further in other areas. The psychology and sociology professions have undergone internal struggles on this point. When the "object" of study is human beings, it is arguable to what extent the subjective should enter the study, both the inner life of the one studied and the attitudes of the one studying. Historians are perhaps most affected by this question. Older historians spent years of rigorous discipline to come to factual conclusions that

56. See especially: Michael Polanyi, *Personal Knowledge* (New York, 1962), pp. 3–17; 249–268

would be free of the historian's own feelings. Some younger historians, to the chagrin of their elders, leave no doubt about their own attitude as they weave together interpretations. What to the older men is discipline to the younger men is desiccation. What to the younger men is involvement is to the older men bias.

The double meaning of objectivity is evident in this dispute. Very often in the midst of argument two quite different meanings of a word are assumed. On the one hand, objective can mean lack of bias; on the other hand, objective can mean lack of subjective involvement. These two meanings can be but are not necessarily co-extensive. While it is true that lack of subjective involvement can sometimes help one to avoid bias, it is also conceivable that there could be times when lack of subjective involvement could produce bias.

The correlative ambiguity of the word subjective should already be apparent. On the bad side, a judgment said to be "merely subjective" is one controlled by prejudice rather than evidence. A "subjectivistic" attitude is one that closes itself to the object of understanding, preferring instead unfounded opinions. On the good side, subjective and "subjectivity" can have very positive meanings in modern writing. The shortest statement of this is Kierkegaard's dictum: "Truth is subjectivity." What is meant to be affirmed here is the necessity of a person taking part in something to understand it. Truth has to be lived by the person before he can come to articulate an objective pole within the living relationship.

A step toward getting out of this maze of language is to notice that the positive meaning of subjective and the positive meaning of objective are not necessarily opposed to each other. Taken positively, objective means fair and accurate; taken positively, subjective means engagement of the person. If this much could be agreed upon, it could be seen that the subjective and objective do not have to vary inversely. The solution of the

116

problem would not be sought in the direction of getting a proper amount of subjective and objective. The presumption that this kind of problem can be resolved by a quantitative approach is itself a bias. The solution lies in living relationally and gradually coming to see the kind of objectivity and subjectivity demanded by various events of life.

The last sentence indicates why attempted solutions to this problem by philosophers, theologians or scientists always prove inadequate. It can be said repeatedly that the world does not consist of isolated subjects looking out at external objects; rather, that the universe is a set of relationships in which a subjective focus responds to an objective pole. But *saying* this does not accomplish the transformation because the very sentences are fitted into a world of subjects and objects. The transformation begins when one begins to *live* relationally; after that, one slowly and somewhat obliquely learns to speak relationally. The confusion of meanings described above is no accident nor can the confusion be eliminated by better definitions. The normal syntax of language breaks the relationship of the real and places us in a world of subjects and objects. No one should be surprised that the problem is not solved; to address it is to get caught in it. It is difficult to imagine a more difficult problem than one that is made impossible of solution because it is stated.[57]

The difficulty with the word revelation becomes evident in this context. A word like revelation which is grammatically a noun is presumed to be an object. To say the word revelation is to say that it is some *thing*. Christian theologians have said *ad*

57. On the philosophical problem of objective and subjective, see: Fontinell, *op. cit.*, pp. 61–66; Nicolas Berdyaev, *Solitude and Society* (New York, 1938), pp. 37–70; Gordon Kaufman, *Relativism, Knowledge and Faith* (Chicago, 1960), pp. 3–38; Abraham Maslow, *Psychology of Science*, pp. 45–66; on the inadequacy of subject-object as the starting point for philosophy, see: John Macmurray, *The Self as Agent* (London, 1957), pp. 39–83.

nauseam that Christian revelation is not a thing or object but their saying that does not overcome the problem. The premise which Christian theology works from is that Christian revelation has been given in the past. Such a "Christian revelation" must be either something or nothing. Despite some denials to the contrary it is assumed in Christian theology that "Christian revelation" is something. Because I am denying that revelation is an object I am saying therefore that "Christian revelation" is nothing.

The only way to preserve a meaning for the word revelation is to carry out an analysis of revelation as the relational structure of reality. There is no revelation given as a thing from the past. In this framework, revelation has a subjective element and an objective element but the word is not identical with either. Neither a subjective attitude nor an external object can be called revelation. There is a universal revelation which finds expression in lived relationships.

5. TEMPORALITY

The last consideration touched upon another relational aspect of experience, namely, temporality. Christian theologians have tried to overcome the subject/object split by using the category of history. It has been claimed repeatedly that history is central to Christianity and that what distinguishes Christianity from other religions is its attitude toward time.[58] This move may be a step in the right direction but the concepts of time and history

58. Jürgen Moltmann, *Theology of Hope* (New York, 1967), p. 50: "This cleavage into objectification and subjectivity is not to be escaped—nor can theology escape it in bringing the gospel to the modern world—by declaring one side of this kind of thinking to be vain, deficient, corrupt and decadent. Rather, theology will have to take the hardened antitheses and make them fluid once more, to mediate in the contradiction between them and reconcile them. That, however, is only possible when the category of history, which drops out in this dualism, is rediscovered in such a way that it does not deny the antithesis in question but spans it and understands it as an element in an advancing process."

cannot be used to solve a problem until they are examined in themselves.

The preceding discussion of this chapter should be helpful in examining the notion of time in human experience. The theme which runs throughout the following pages is a continuation of the theme of duality within unity, that is, that the organic unity of experience is constituted by complementary pairs. At first glance, this theme does not seem applicable to temporality because it is nearly always assumed that time has three components: past, present and future. However, I am going to deny this anthropological assumption that there are three kinds of time. I am going to defend the thesis that the unity of time is the present and that there are within the present two dimensions of time, the past and future. Man's choices are made in reference to how the two dimensions of time interrelate. Loren Eiseley, in writing on the ecological disaster facing mankind, writes: " 'When evil comes it is because two gods have disagreed' runs the proverb of an elder people. Perhaps it is another way of saying that the past and the future are at war in the heart of man."[59] This war between the past and the future in the heart of man may have no final armistice but it is some progress even to identify the combatants. The present is the battlefield where the war rages, not one of the combatants.

The most common image of time in modern Western society is the straight line. The present is imagined to be one point which constantly moves forward while the past consists of points to the left of the present and the future is made up of those points to the right of what is now present. This image of time runs deep in the Western psyche and it obviously has some strong basis in the experienced world. Aristotle had already defined time as a measure of motion conceived as before and after. Although challenging Aristotle on many fronts, modern science found this definition of time more than compatible with

59. Eiseley, *Invisible Pyramid,* p. 69.

119

its purpose and method. Science concentrated only on doing the job more precisely, producing for that purpose the mechanical apparatus called the clock. The seventeenth and eighteenth centuries' fascination with the clock seems to have put an indelible stamp on the mind of future generations, that is, that time is a matter of points accurately gauged by a mechanism in space outside man.[60]

This choice of definition may seem to be an obvious one. However, much of the human race does not view temporality in this way. I would contend that the choice to determine time by the mechanical motion of bodies in space is a subtle but definite reduction of the human meaning of time. The prescription that "time is nothing but..." is one of the primary cases of misplaced objectivity discussed above. If time consists of points on a line, then the past is simply behind us, the future is still to come and the present can only be called "fleeting." Where is the substance to human life? Time conceived of as linear exhausts life of any depth or breadth. It subsumes human life under a mechanical model. To choose linear time is eventually to choose against man and it matters very little if one talks about past or present or future as the important realm because all three are equally without humanity.

Christian theology in recent times has spoken of a linear concept of time as being at the heart of biblical religion.[61] This choice was a disaster from which Christian theology has not yet recovered. When Oscar Cullmann and others referred to this image as a unique contribution of the bible they were choosing linear (or a straight line of development) as opposed to cyclical. But instead of this being a new insight, the image of a linear time was what had been said on all sides for centuries

60. See: Mumford, *Pentagon of Power*, pp. 85–94.
61. The best-known work which helped to popularize the connection between Christianity and history was Oscar Cullmann, *Christ and Time* (Philadelphia, 1950).

120

in the West. The proposition that Christianity's concept of time is linear only gave approbation to some of the worst traits of our era which needed challenging rather than approving. Anyone who grew up in America with the slogan "progress is our most important product" had never for an instant doubted that time was linear and was directed to the future.

The trouble on the theologians' part was that they were taking as the two main choices: linear and cyclical. But both of these are only variations within the same mechanical model. In emphasizing the linear image they were approving a mechanical model which places man, god and nature subservient to the machine. The real choice for theologians and everyone else is between a mechanical model and an anthropological model. The latter which begins with the experience of relationship and community has room to include lines, spirals or circles but these are always within a larger human context.

When time is conceived of as mechanical, there is almost no *human* possibility to it. Men then conceive of time as separable elements outside themselves. Happiness is thought to be the right set of things which obviously does not exist at the present moment but might be found somewhere else. Sometimes the past is thought to be paradisiacal as in many primitive religions. Sometimes the future is seen as utopian, as in many technological societies. The differences between these two conceptions are not as great as one would first suppose. Both represent an escape from the human situation of freedom in limited form. When human freedom begins to emerge there is experienced a tension of sedimented actuality and precarious possibility. Time is not humanly understood until it is experienced as this relation between the world from which man emerges and the world which man can conceive as possible.

The key to understanding time humanly is the word present in all of its rich connotations. Man is the being who is present, who is not only there but aware that he is there. To be human

121

is to be present.[62] The word present in the English language can refer to a moment of time, a place in space, or a relationship to others. Only the last of these three is a comprehensive meaning of the word; the other two will surely be misleading unless they are set within the context of the third. Man can only identify a presence in space or time because he has found himself in relation to others. Temporal presence is an aspect of personal presence. "The present arises only in virtue of the fact that the *Thou* becomes present."[63]

Presence refers primarily to a way of life, to a particular way of relating the exterior/interior, the active/passive and the personal/non-personal. A good deal has been written in recent times of the relation of time to community. This writing has usually followed a line of thought which sees that community is not possible without time, that is, common memory of its past and hope for the future.[64] This line of development is helpful but it does not get down to the roots. There is a complementary and more basic relation of time and community, namely, time as human arises from community. Men can recover a past only as they experience a community; men can work to create a future only from within a community. Men come to awareness before the face of other men and it is only because of this that they can delve into what nature gives them as a past and what the possibilities are for a future.

The experience of the tension between past and future has reference not only to the interpersonal but the sub-personal as

62. William Ong, *In the Human Grain* (New York, 1966), p. 143: "For the present, in which alone man enjoys the interior sense of the *presence* of another (there is no *presence* in the *past*), is more directly personal and immediately interior than the past-as-past can ever be. The greater focus on the present in historical treatment thus represents not merely a shift from one 'point' in time to another 'point' (time really has no 'points') but an altered state of mind affecting the exterior-interior relationship."

63. Buber, *I and Thou*, p. 12.

64. See: Berdyaev, *Solitude and Society*, p. 69.

well. The devastating thing about a mechanical and linear notion of time is that it misses not only the humans but the subhumans as well. The choice is between the artificial and mechanical on one side and the organic and living on the other side. Another way of stating this is that an adequate anthropological model includes the sub-human as well as the human. The choice between linear and cyclical was easily translated into a choice between history and nature. In such a choice the human (and sub-human) lose with either alternative. Given these two options the choice for history is a choice of the artificial and mechanical; the choice for nature is a choice for a world without meaning and freedom. Christian theologians instead of rejecting the alternatives of history and nature eagerly grabbed for history, choosing against nature, against the organic and rhythmic growth of the universe. The result is not healthy for man, beast or plant, all of whom must grow in this universe. "The conception of time as the flux of organic continuity experienced as duration, as memory, as recorded history, as potentially and prospective achievement, stands in frontal opposition to the mechanistic notion of time simply as a function of the motion of bodies in space—along with its spurious imperative of 'saving time' by accelerating motion, and of making such acceleration in every possible department the highest triumph of the power complex."[65]

Probably the best example of presence as the human mode of being is the aesthetic experience. John Dewey, in *Art as Experience*, brilliantly analyzed the integration of the human in the realm of the aesthetic. "Art celebrates with peculiar intensity the moments in which the past reinforces the present and in which the future is a quickening of what now is."[66]

Nowhere is this aesthetic presence more dramatically illus-

65. Mumford, *Pentagon of Power*, p. 391; Eiseley, *Invisible Pyramid*, p. 115.
66. John Dewey, *Art as Experience* (New York, 1958), pp. 122.

trated than in play. When a person is at play he is alive to the present, i.e., to the people and things around him. He delights in the gift of being and uses what is available. One of the most intriguing and potentially fruitful interests of contemporary theology is its concern with play.[67] Some of the metaphysical and anthropological implications of man at play have been sketched by Hugo Rahner. "He is a man with an easy gaiety of spirit, one might also say a man of spiritual elegance, but he is also a man of tragedy, a man of laughter and tears, a man indeed of gentle irony, for he sees through the tragically ridiculous masks of the game of life and has taken the measure of the cramping boundaries of our earthly existence.[68]

Playful man in this context is not frivolous man. He neither grasps at life nor does he casually toss it away. He is a man who lives with passionate involvement but with awareness that life is given and can be taken away. Play is common among children; it is not by accident that it returns to adult life in two particular places: religion and making love. Maturity is best expressed in adult play which recognizes that pleasure and pain are never separable and that comedy and tragedy are present in all genuine human experience.

The fusion of these elements was studied at length by Abraham Maslow under the category of "peak experience".[69] In addition to playfulness, Maslow found characteristics of wholeness, aliveness, order, simplicity, richness and effortlessness in those experiences where the human being came to presence. No one lives at such a high degree of intensity all the time but Maslow gradually came to hypothesize that everyone can and should have experience of total presence. Delighting in the presence of being is not childish regression but a mature coming together of man's usually fragmented self. The moments when one is fully

67. See: Hugo Rahner, *Man at Play* (New York, 1967); Robert Neale, *In Praise of Play* (New York, 1969); Harvey Cox, *The Feast of Fools.*
68. Rahner, *Man at Play*, p. 27.
69. Maslow, *Religions, Values and Peak-Experiences*, pp. 92–94.

present to life may not be constant or even frequent but such moments reveal something about human life as a whole and make the rest of life worth living.[70]

In a mechanical concept of time the present is nothing; it is simply a hypothetical line between the past and future. In an anthropological notion of time the present is everything; it is the relation wherein past and future get their meaning. Admonitions to keep a balance among past, present and future make no sense. One must choose from the beginning: either the present is everything or it is nothing. The choice here is to make the present everything. The present exists and it is the only thing that exists. To be is to be present. The past and the future are those structural elements which are subsumed within the present. The opposite of present is neither past nor future; the opposite of present is absent. If one does not live in the present he is simply absent from human life. Likewise, if one does live in the present he comes to a greater appreciation of past and future.

The past is not a series of events that have happened but what is because it has been. The past is what is now solidified as accomplishment and remains the substratum of every human decision. The present is the relationship of men in community but any community is structured by some objective form. This form begins with man's flesh and blood and bones. The kind of body he has, and even that he is bodily, represents the element of the past in communal presence. Whatever man tries to do, it must come in response to and in gentle guidance of the millennia sedimented in his body and psyche.

Those people who try to efface time in the name of human

70. Buber, *I and Thou,* p. 34: "It is not possible to live in the bare present. Life would be quite consumed if precautions were not taken to subdue the present speedily and thoroughly. But it is possible to live in the bare past, indeed only in it may a life be organized. We only need to fill each moment with experiencing and using, and it ceases to burn. And in all seriousness of truth hear this: Without *It* man cannot live. But he who lives with *It* alone is not a man."

125

progress eventually undercut the human being. A hatred of the human race and a hatred of oneself are contained in the attempt to forget or escape from the past. The temptation runs extremely deep. It is especially a temptation for the man who does not recognize the earth as his brother. Memory and forgetfulness are at war in man. "There are those among us who wish, even in death, not a name or a memory to survive."[71]

In one sense the past is the surest and most stable way of being. Men may block the past by forgetfulness but their bodies do not forget. This past, however, can be expanded or changed in meaning. Psychoanalysis has been one form of changing the meaning of the past for an individual. Less dramatically, we are constantly engaged in "revisionism" at the individual, national, international and cosmic levels. So long as there is a future, the past will always be changing in meaning. A final statement about the past, which would embody the full meaning of the past, could only be made from outside time. There are undoubtedly false judgments that could be rendered about the past but there are innumerable true statements about the past that have not yet been rendered. Niels Bohr once said with reference to physics: "The opposite of a correct statement is a false statement. But the opposite of a profound truth may well be another profound truth."[72]

The study of the past beyond the memory of a few generations is a modern accomplishment. In one sense, therefore, the past is in a stage of rapid expansion. As the past comes to be better known and accepted as past, it ceases to determine us and becomes instead the material of our freedom. "Self-study in terms of our past is an enterprise which no other age of man has been able to undertake, for it did not have the requisite kind of possession of human antiquity. Moreover, our possession of

71. Eiseley, *Invisible Pyramid*, p. 97.
72. Quoted in Werner Heisenberg, *Physics and Beyond* (New York, 1971), p. 102.

the past is growing: the further we get from the beginnings of our universe itself, the more we know about them. We are constantly structuring more and more of the past into the present."[73]

In addition to structuring in the past, the present also includes the future. In some ways, of course, the future is an entirely different thing from the past. Everything the word past seems to imply in definiteness, the word future seems to lack. Indeed, considered in itself the future simply does not exist. The point of my discussion, however, is that neither the past nor the future should be considered in themselves. If the words are going to be helpful at all one must begin by setting them into the living relationship of presence. Here, the word future does designate a real aspect of life, namely, the quickening of life's possibilities.

Time considered as linear provides a past that is simply there, fatefully limiting where we are now; it also provides a future that simply is not here yet, distracting us by the thought of what may or may not happen. By contrast, time as humanly and organically understood frees us from the bondage of any fate and allows us to live as free men. "To the being fully alive, the future is not ominous but a promise: it surrounds the present as a halo. It consists of possibilities that are felt as a possession of what is now and here. In life that is truly life, everything overlaps and merges. But all too often we exist in apprehension of what the future may bring, and are divided within ourselves. Even when not overanxious, we do not enjoy the present because we subordinate it to that which is absent."[74] Dewey is contrasting in this passage the future experienced as promising and the future as ominous. The future does not become promising because someone tells us it is promising. Rather, when the future is experienced as integral to our human life it is promising; when the future weighs upon us externally it is ominous.

73. Ong, *In the Human Grain,* p. 12.
74. Dewey, *Art as Experience,* p. 18.

The promise of the future is whatever can be *experienced* as a human possibility of the present.

The category of revelation in both its religious and non-religious uses ought to be centered in presence. It is the present communal structure which includes the past and future. Revelation ought never to be spoken of as at some point of time. If a linear model of time is presumed it matters little whether one emphasizes the past, the present or the future. All three of them will be incapable of dealing with the category of revelation.

The most common way to speak about revelation in Christian circles is in reference to the past. This position is the most consistent one and one that is not really avoidable so long as the notion of a "Christian revelation" is retained. A "Christian revelation," no matter how it is defined or where it is located, is *something* and thereby belongs to that objective aspect of presence which is called past. Christian writing presumes that the "Christian revelation" was given to certain men in an age long ago.

It has become customary in recent years to talk of Christian revelation "continuing into the present." This is a manner of speaking which does not challenge the basic Christian premise that the past takes precedence. I would not speak of the present continuing the past revelation. The present does not *continue* the past; the present, if one is speaking humanly, *includes* the past. For the sake of the past itself the present must be the starting point of all inquiry. To use the past as the norm by which the present is measured is to choose things rather than man and a component of life above life itself. "Scorn of the past we hold to be as unwise as scorn of 'our wonderous Mother-age', but with whatever reverence and retrospective longing the Past is regarded, it should always be regarded as *past;* it should have historical and not absolute significance; it is our *ancestry,* not our *life.*"[75]

75. George Henry Lewis, *Leader,* Nov. 26, 1853.

As Christianity has experienced difficulty getting its message accepted it has tried to become "more relevant to the present." Unfortunately, this attempt has been made without challenging the inadequate meaning of "present" which is nearly always implied by this phrase. It is ironic that many so-called existential theologies are assumed to be concerned with the present while as a matter of fact it is they that are strikingly deficient in the sense of presence as communal structure.[76] Philosophy and theology which are wholly centered on the individual's moment of decision have gone the furthest in evacuating the presence of meaning and structure.

This unfortunate use of language is very widespread in our society. What sounds like a clear explanation may actually be an obscuring of the real issue. I would like to analyze the following statement as a typical explanation which thoroughly misunderstands the problem. A psychiatrist writes: "The hippy is a student who seeks an existence in which he is committed neither to past values nor future causes. With his focus on the present he is determined to experience everything he can. . . . Despairing of any hope for guidance from the past, pessimistic toward the possibility of altering the world in which he will live, he turns to himself. . . . As he turns more and more to the present, his behavior becomes more and more impulsive."[77]

The description may appear accurate enough but it is so only if the words past, present and future are understood serially. The psychiatrist is using the terms as commonly understood but he does not raise the question of whether this understanding of time is not a large part of the hippy's problem, and for that matter, the psychiatrist's problems as well. The practical conse-

76. The word "existential" is not very helpful in describing theological developments of this century. The word might have been helpful if it had led to a fuller analysis of human existence. Instead, existential came to be equated with "hearing the word preached and making a decision" which does violence to the full realm of human existence.
77. Seymour Halleck as quoted in Holmes, *op. cit.*, p. 55.

quences of a change of language might be considerable. Thus, a different rendering of the same problem would go: (1) the hippy is not committed to past *values* nor future *causes* but he is nonetheless thoroughly committed to the past and the future. He is held captive by his obsession with the past and future which weigh upon him. (2) His focus is not in the present because it is the present which is unbearable. (3) He may be determined to experience *everything* but certainly not *everyone;* things can be divided into a series of points but people are more resistant and demand an experience of the present. (4) Despair and pessimism rack his life so that the last thing he would do is turn to himself. He may go outside himself, inside himself or above himself but never to the person who is the meeting point of past and future and the responsible agent in a community. (5) The impulsive behavior is therefore the result of turning away from the present, that is, away from the living and organic action that always characterizes the present.

The student would be ill advised, therefore, to stop living so much in the present. He would be better advised to stop fighting the past and worrying about the future and to start finding the present. Of course, he will not be helped much by being *told* to live in the present; being told what his problem is is part of his problem. Living in the present means experiencing the presence of someone who cares. This fact gives hope because teachers, psychiatrists, parents and friends sometimes provide a presence despite their explanations and proposed solutions.

Revelation can be a helpful category for psychiatry, religion and elsewhere but only if it is a category of the present, that is, the relational structure of presence. Admonitions not to overemphasize the present are worthless. The choice is to live profoundly in the present or superficially in the present. The present can be misunderstood but it cannot be overemphasized. The penetration of the depth and meaning of the present can be inadequate and as a matter of fact it always is to some degree. But the present is all there is; the only alternative is the absent.

Christian theology's fleeting interest in the existential moment must become a full-fledged commitment to the present as the fullness of time. Before theology takes this step, however, it should be aware that it may get more than it is bargaining for. One does not grasp the present; one enters the present and is embraced by it. If theology wants to be present it cannot dictate to the present; it has to be ready to give up its restricted life and be ready for a transformation of all its meaning.

In recent years Christian theology has begun talking a great deal about the future.[78] This development heralds the possibility of a more open and more imaginative Christian position. At the same time, precisely because of the immediate attractiveness of the terminology, some caution must be expressed.

The interest in the category of the future in Christian circles accompanies a flow of conversation and writing on the topic in the wider society.[79] Very few people these days are ready to make a vigorous defense of the past or the present but almost no one attacks the future. To be concerned with the future seems to qualify one for the avant-garde by definition. The coining of the word "futurology" begins to arouse some suspicion. Can the future itself be the object of some science? Is it more likely that every science to the extent it studies existing things gives some understanding of what to expect and plan? Futurology, one could fairly well predict, would attract some keen minds who see further and deeper than everyone else; it would also attract some dull minds who, having neither the intelligence nor discipline to understand the real, place themselves beyond everyone else by talking about the non-existent future.

One's fears are not entirely allayed by much of the writing on the topic of the future. In one of the most popular books, writ-

---

78. In addition to Moltmann and Pannenberg previously referred to, see: Johannes Metz, *Theology of the World* (New York, 1969); Carl Braaten, *The Future of God* (New York, 1969); Kenneth Cauthen, *Christian Biopolitics* (New York, 1971).

79. See: Herman Kahn and Anthony Wiener, *The Year 2000* (New York, 1967); Daniel Bell, ed., *Toward the Year 2000* (New York, 1968).

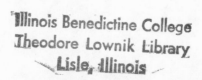

ten under the clever title of *Future Shock,* the author constantly speaks of time in a serial manner. Thus, of education he writes: "Just as the progressives of yesterday were accused of 'presentism,' it is likely that the education reformers of tomorrow will be accused of 'futurism.' For we shall find that a truly super-industrial education is only possible if we once more shift our time-bias forward."[80] One can doubt that education has ever progressed by shifting its "time-bias forward" and, more basically, one can object that this is not a helpful way to speak about time at all.

In this super-industrial society Christian theology finds a footing by its talk about the future. Christianity in the past was often taken to be an opponent of modern science and technology. Some of recent theology sounds as if a sudden conversion had taken place. The future-directed "Christian revelation" seems ready to join American or Russian machinery to save the rest of the world from its benighted past. Like all sudden conversions, however, the suspicion lurks that the reversal has either been too complete or else has not happened at all.

The first of these possibilities occurs if Christianity simply joins hands with contemporary industrial society at the lowest common denominator. A religious and/or Christian position should presumably offer a viewpoint other than what is said on all sides. Some criticism of our obsession with the future is surely needed. One critic, Loren Eiseley, writes: "In the extravagant pursuit of a future projected by science, we have left the present to shift for itself. We have regarded science as a kind of twentieth-century substitute for magic ... In short, the future has become our primary obsession. We constantly treat our scientists as soothsayers and project upon them questions involving the destiny of man over prospective millions of years."[81]

80. Alvin Toffler, *Future Shock* (New York, 1970), p. 345.
81. Eiseley, *Invisible Pyramid,* p. 105; see also: Erik Erikson, *Identity* (New York, 1968), p. 120.

The second possibility about the theological conversion is the one more likely to be true. Theology talks more about the future than it formerly did but underneath the surface theology's concern is the same as always: the deposit of the past. It was much easier for theology to switch from the past to the future than it would be to go from the past to present. The former merely requires a shift of emphasis; the latter would mean an opposite approach to theology. The choice, I must repeat once more, is not between the past and the future but between two kinds of presence. The choice is, on the one hand, the past and the future as separable segments of time and, on the other hand, the past and future as integral elements of communal experience.

It is evident that theology's choice is still for the past and future as separable elements. The promise of God, it is said, was given in the past but it will not be realized until the future. As for the living human being of today he is just as bad off as ever except that he is told he should have hope. For those who find it impossible to believe in some promise to an ancient people, all the talk about hope is spurious.[82]

It is not so much the future which is studied in theology as much as what a past document says about the future. Wherever future does become the central category of theology, the whole thing becomes rather hazy. For example, "the future coming to meet us" is an interesting use of language which may throw a different light on things. But the phrase cannot function as an opening statement for a metaphysics which works from the future back to the present. At the least, Christian theology could be more reticent in claiming to have found its proper object in the future.

The heart of talk about the future is the idea of promise. It is said that "God's words" were not factual information but words

82. For criticism of the theology of hope, see: Borowitz, *loc. cit.;* Langdon Gilkey, "The Contribution of Culture to the Reign of God," in *Future as the Presence of Shared Hope,* pp. 34–58.

of promise.[83] Man is encouraged to look to God rather than himself, that is, to the objects of past/future which purport to be divine rather than to the present where man is. There is no hope or promise in man, only in God. "The truth of the promise lies not in every demonstrable correspondence with the reality which was or which is. It lies not in the *adaequatio rei et intellectus*. The promise here proves its truth, on the contrary, in the specific *inadaequatio intellectus et rei* in which it places the hearer. It stands in a demonstrable contradiction to the historic reality."[84]

Many Christians, not to mention non-Christians, will find it difficult to see how the promise proves its truth by its demonstrable contradiction to the historic reality. If one can believe that a promise has been made by God, then one can accept all kinds of inherent difficulties with it. The difficult part is believing that any promises are God's. Theologians who insist that God's words are words of promise rather than words of information do not get to the problem many people have of supposing that any words are God's words.

Many years ago William James pointed out the centrality of promise in religion. He was not speaking of biblical exegesis but of a "positive experiential operation" for the concept of God. The concept of God, James said, "means the presence of 'promise' in the world. 'God or no God' means 'promise or no promise!' "[85] Unless promise is what man experiences as an essential element of his presence, no promises made to him will quicken him. Promises that come from outside the person's present experience are either ominous or irrelevant. The promise of man's life is found in man. Either human kind is promising or it is not. If in fact man is a promising possibility, then he can begin

83. See: J. B. Metz, "The Church and the World," in *The WORD in History*, ed., T. Patrick Burke (New York, 1966), p. 75.
84. Moltmann, *op. cit.*, p. 118.
85. Quoted in Fontinell, *Reconstruction of Religion*, p. 192.

134

to search diligently and to listen carefully for any further help in interpreting what his life is for.

6. LANGUAGE

In the context of the preceding sections of this chapter it will be helpful to say some things about the nature and function of language. Language is one of the key notions to demonstrate the relational character of experience. One could start with language itself as the way into experience. It has seemed preferable to me to postpone the consideration of language until other relations had been studied. A key theme of twentieth-century philosophy is that man is best understood as a being of language.[86] Although this path has proven fruitful, it can also lead to abstruseness and a new kind of impersonalism.

There is a naive presumption that knowledge is something possessed and something that can be deposited into words. This premise is attacked by everyone who tries to bring out the significance of language. What a man knows obviously determines the way he speaks, but in turn the way he speaks determines the way he thinks. In emphasizing the latter half of this statement some people seem to approach a kind of mysticism in which language is the creator of man. Thus, human existence and reality itself become a function of language.[87] It would seem that either a special meaning of the word "language" is being employed here or else an exaggeration is made in pushing the importance of language.

A distinction should first be made between language as the expression of being and language as discourse in oral and written signs. In the former sense each person not only has a language but is a language; his bodily being expresses who and what he is. There is popular discussion now about "body lan-

86. See: Heidegger, *Introduction to Metaphysics*, p. 69.
87. See: Achtemeier, *op. cit.*, pp. 85–100.

135

guage," a phrase that should be understood not just in the sense that the body can say some things in place of words but that bodiliness is a more basic form of communication. What is spoken by the mouth or written by the hand reflects only in part, and sometimes not very accurately, what the body says. The person's body may be speaking more truly than the statements he formulates.

Language as a universal structure of being is not dispensable or arbitrary whereas language, in the sense of one of the languages men speak, is historically conditioned and variable in form. Nonetheless, language in this latter sense is not quite so arbitrary an element in a culture as might be supposed. The history of a people is sedimented in their patterns of speech. How an individual will know and what thoughts are thinkable by him will be determined by the language that comes to him as a gift from his people. Language in this sense does not have a unilateral relationship to individual and social forms. Language arises from and is specified by other "artifacts" just as it in turn helps to determine their future. Likewise, an individual or group can also be a creative force for language just as language is (partly) creative of the individual.

Between language as co-extensive with being and language as a set of marks in one country, there are many intermediary aspects of language to consider. For example, language can be discussed in the context of the subjective/objective relation. Language at this level can be taken to mean the objectifying aspect of the human. Man is the being who comes to himself by objectifying himself; bodiliness is the way man is present to others and even to himself.[88] The externalizing of the human into the sphere of objectivity presents what is there and in presenting it fulfills what is there. The human being responds to what is objective, assimilates it to himself and then re-presents himself in a new cycle. The human being *is* this relation of interiority and

88. See: Berger, *Sacred Canopy*, pp. 3–28.

bodying forth. As with all the previous relations we have discussed, the conjunction "and" threatens to mislead. Human being is the bodying of interiority and the interiorizing of bodiliness. Even this circumlocution cannot avoid some of the spatial image which is not intended here.

If language for man is the bodying forth of his life, then attention should be directed to other forms of bodying besides formal discourse. Being, life and knowledge have an inner dynamism which push toward objective expression but one must beware of getting to the end too quickly. Because words are "ready at hand" it is easy to suppose that being, life and knowledge have come to fruition whereas in fact words have been appropriated as a substitute for the process of being, life and knowing. The danger is particularly great in many Western countries which have apotheosized a certain kind of language. This abstract, formal discourse seems to function without reference to the experience which gives it birth.

It must be emphasized, therefore, that language considered as a set of abstract meanings should not be isolated at center stage. Knowing arises in the experience of life. The primary question is not what shall we say but how shall we live. Man must answer to being in some objectified form but not necessarily in "words."[89] People for various historical reasons have various means of objectification. "Wisdom has alighted on three things: the brain of the Franks, the hands of the Chinese, and the tongue of the Arabs."[90] A Western man may think it obvious that if one knows something he will say it. In contrast, an Eastern man might say with Lao-tzu: "Those who don't know say, and those who say don't know." There may be truth in both the Western and Eastern beliefs depending upon the meaning of speech. In any case, Western man's problem is to become aware

89. See: Holmes, *op. cit.*, p. 120.
90. Adage quoted by Huston Smith, *The Religions of Man* (New York, 1958), p. 204.

of human life itself as the basic form of speech. Only this form of speech is a sufficiently comprehensive context for oral and written speaking.

In this regard, speech is an aspect of human action. The dichotomy between talking and doing in our world is disastrous for all forms of human activity. Much recent writing points out ancient man's belief that words are powerful and that the word "word" has a broader meaning in Hebrew scriptures or Greek philosophy than our translations can render.[91] Unfortunately, such comments often appear to be interesting folklore but not anything helpful to solving the sophisticated problems of today. The failure to understand even the significance of this question is symptomatic of a basic failure in anthropological understanding.

As with the preceding relational problems, the answer commonly given to the question of speech and action is to strike a balance, that is, some talk, some activity. However, the pendulum image does not work here, either. At almost every conference someone eventually stands up and says: "Talking is a waste of time; we ought to be acting." This remark, although understandable in the circumstances of many conferences, fails to appreciate the relation of speech and action. The remark accepts and perpetuates the split which is killing people.

One must make a basic choice of vocabulary here. If one is trying to prevent the juxtaposition of words and activity, then one must pick from the following: (1) action must include speaking (2) speaking must include action (3) a third word must include both. I take the first of these three to be the most workable, that is, speaking is a form of action. Much of recent theology has gone the second route and tried to make "word" all-inclusive. When this tended toward abstruseness, neologisms

91. See: Van der Leeuw, *op. cit.*, p. 403; John McKenzie, "The Word of God in the Old Testament," in *Theological Studies*, XXI (June, 1960), pp. 183–206.

like "word-event" have been introduced but to no avail. "Event" when joined with word does nothing to concretize or personalize what is at issue. Although the word "event" is popular in theological writing, it is a severely limited word.[92] People act, people love, people speak, people work but people do not event. An event simply happens and is there; all the rich dimensions of personal life have no particular relation to event. This peculiar character of event is the reason for its widespread use in one school of theology. I see no reason why other theological traditions should view it as a helpful word. It is doubtful that "Christ event," "event of salvation" or "word-event" are expressions that make sense to most people and it is just as doubtful that it makes sense trying to explain such terms. Neither word, event, nor word-event is a social and practical category that can comprehend personal life.

My preference, as I indicated above, is to work with the word action or activity as inclusive of speech.[93] "In the beginning was the action," relational, personal, communal, social, political, practical, verbal action. It is not stretching the meanings of words too far to make speaking a form of acting. Thus, there are verbal activities and non-verbal activities. Hannah Arendt has studied the rich, classical meaning of the word action.[94] I am not very sanguine about restoring the communal and political fabric of the word action but what Arendt says of speech and action has immediate practical import:

Action and speech are so closely related because the primordial and specifically human act must at the same time contain the answer to the question asked of every newcomer: Who are you? ... Speechless action would no longer be action because there would no longer be

92. On the inadequacy of the word "event" for philosophy and religion, see Macmurray, *The Self as Agent*, pp. 146–64, 203–222.
93. For "action" as the starting point in philosophy, see: *Ibid.*, pp. 84–103.
94. For Arendt's work on this point, see: *Human Condition*, pp. 79–174.

an actor, and the actor, the doer of deeds, is possible only if at the same time the speaker of words. The action he begins is humanly disclosed by the word, and though his deed can be perceived in its brute physical appearance without verbal accompaniment, it becomes relevant only through the spoken word in which he identifies himself as the actor, announcing what he does, has done, and intends to do.[95]

If this framework of speech and action were understood the role of speech would be much clearer. There would be fewer complaints about too much talking and not enough doing. The critical issue with regard to speech is not the amount of it but whether it is answering the questions "who are you?" and "what is the meaning of what you are doing?" Philosophers and theologians often sound as if language were a world of its own apart from where people struggle for life. Philosophers are not usually skilled in "thinking with their hands" but that should not preclude an appreciation of how truth emerges from human bodies in action.[96]

Another way to approach this total context of language is to point out the element of silence in language. The relationship of sound and silence has its roots in the previously discussed relation of the conscious/unconscious.[97] Silence is the test case for a world in which language can have multiple roles and functions. When language study is carried out by people who are themselves products of a rationalistic civilization their study might only further evacuate language of its non-rational possibilities. Challenge has to be raised to the presumption that language is a set of statements which can be verified as true or false

95. *Ibid.*, pp. 178–179.
96. Gregory Baum, *Man Becoming* (New York, 1970), p. 15: "Truth, Blondel said, is present in man's action. If we reflect on a man's action, we find implicit in it his values, his vision of life, his view of reality. Action incarnates man's grasp of reality and offers him the possibility of knowing it conceptually. The evaluation of life and the discernment of meaning take place in human action before they become concepts in the human mind."
97. Brown, *Love's Body*, p. 258.

by objective evidence. Silence paves the way for myth, symbol and dream.

If one begins with the actor, doer and speaker (i.e., a person) embodying his life in symbolic expression, then the examination of words eventually leads to silence, "a silence which is no longer the absence of the word but truly the word of the word itself."[98] Anyone who has been with a friend at a time of great joy or heavy sorrow will recognize this truth. Anyone who does not know how to speak in silence does not know how to use words. Language is a bodily rhythm with moments of sound and moments of silence that constitute the movement of human kind into expression.

Language is an aspect of the person/person relationship. Just as time emerges from community experience and in return becomes the binding force of community, so also language is possible because men act together and their speaking is what ratifies their communal bond. Aristotle's two designations of man as "speaking animal" and "political animal" are intimately related. Speaking together is the lighting up of the relationship which exists between humans. This illumination can create a structured relationship that is truly humanizing. Men can band together for labor and they can be related by violence, but when they speak there begins to be communion.

It is unfortunate that the English word "communication" has been flattened out so that for many people it means "giving out information." For example, in Susanne Langer's writing, communication is cited as one restricted purpose of language.[99] She looks to the aesthetic as a more comprehensive category to embrace the uses of language. In her use of the word communication, Langer is accepting the widespread meaning of the word and she is probably realistic. Nonetheless, the word communication may be worth fighting for insofar as it is connected to com-

98. Quoted in Monden, *op. cit.*, p. 112.
99. Langer, *op. cit.*, pp. 26–53.

munion. The word communion is a good one because it carries a rich sense of both unity and diversity while it also implies intelligence and freedom. Whether the specific purpose of language is political, social, religious or educational, its direction can be described as communion. Only if communication is separated from communion does it follow that language is "not merely for communication." When communication is rooted in communion, then language is not just for communication, it is communication, that is, the communion of expression and human life in verbal form.[100]

Speech is possible, therefore, only with the prerequisite of shared life. The life of a people and the involvement of an individual set the boundaries and rules for determining meaning and for deciding whether certain words are genuine human speech. In a strange country, said Wittgenstein, we may master the language and yet not understand the people. Not accidentally the words knowing and speaking are related to words for pregnancy and birth. A person has to "conceive" ideas and when he speaks genuinely he gives birth to new creation. "Only a man who is himself permeated with such language has the right to use it. It is authentic when spoken by a man who actually participates; it is inauthentic in a man who merely thinks it, or, worse yet, merely uses the word."[101]

Much of political and religious language that is "ready at hand" is a substitute for a person's living the truth. Language tacked on to oneself from the outside inhibits life. In contrast, the man of genius who speaks new thoughts is bound to have a painful birth; he is testing the limits of the community's agreed-

100. Dallas High, *Language, Persons and Belief* (New York, 1967), p. 102: "It is life—human life as historically conditioned and conditioning —that stands back of language. Language *qua* language is rooted in and receives accreditation from the human order. It is not rooted in and accredited by some sterilized or virgin logical order higher than the one which human beings are *responsible for* as well as *responsive to.*"
101. Karl Jaspers, *Myth and Christianity* (New York, 1958), p. 34.

upon boundaries. Changing the modes of discourse in a community is almost certain to be experienced as destruction of the community. Our deepest insights, wrote Nietzsche, will sound like follies or even crimes because most other people will not be ready to hear them.[102]

Language can also be understood as an aspect of the past/ future relationship which is our present. A community is a group of people who among other things have a common memory. The past, mainly in the form of artistic and written productions, is available as experienced within the present community. The future, that is, what men are thinking toward or imagining, is the other pole for what is documented from the past. But there is no place to read the past except in the present. "Without the voice of the present it is impossible to understand the past in its own distinctive—and hence different—quality."[103]

If this context functioned in the interpreting of texts, it would make sense of a few things otherwise difficult to explain. In particular, I refer to the fact that a text may say more than the author intended. There are obviously some limits and there can be violence done to a great thinker's statements. Nonetheless, Plato's philosophy could never have the same meaning after Plontinus, Augustine and Spinoza. The charge can be made that Aquinas distorted Aristotle or that Heidegger misinterpreted Kant. The charge may be true but it is also possible that the second thinker can now find more in the first than the first (directly) intended to put there. Plato could not say and could not even know all that Plato meant. John Ruskin wrote: "There is in every word set down by the imaginative mind an awful under-current of meaning, and evidence and shadow upon it of the deep place out of which it has come."[104]

102. Nietzsche, *Beyond Good and Evil*, p. 35.
103. Edward Schillebeeckx, *God the Future of Man* (New York, 1968), p. 23.
104. Quoted in Hart, *op. cit.*, pp. 253–254; see also: Franz Rosenzweig,

The image of a circle in discussions of textual interpretation can be very misleading. The image seems to spring from the linear concept of time criticized previously. One does not move from a point of the present back to a point of the past and return to the present. One begins with the experience of the present community and one attempts to understand a past document in this light. Community is the original context for interpretation and as a text is understood one's notion of community should expand. A text is distorted when it is taken to be an isolated piece of the past. One must set a text in the richest context possible precisely so that the text can speak for itself and in itself. As the text's meaning emerges, it will exercise a formative influence in the present community. There are cases when texts are obviously misunderstood, particularly when they are being "used" to support an opinion of today. There are other cases when the line is unclear as to whether a "retrieval" of meaning or a distortion of meaning has occurred.

Reality is not names but reality is not human and therefore not complete unless a person can name it. Each person's world emerges in language and his capacity to cope with life is in large part dependent upon his ability to speak about it. What he does not like in his life he has to reconstruct with words. It should be clear by this point that my reference to "naming" does not imply that language consists in individual words attached to individual things. Within the context of persons, the uses, forms and variety of language are unlimited. The attempt was made among some recent philosophers to reduce language to statements of fact verifiable at least in principle. Only empirical fact and tautology were allowed into the system. It is difficult to believe

---

Jewish Learning (New York, 1965), p. 73: "For a word does not remain its speaker's possession; he to whom it is addressed, he who hears it, or acquires it by chance—they all get a share of it; the word's fate, while in their possession, is more fate-ful than what its original speakers experienced when first uttering it."

that the project could have been intended as anything more than a logical exercise. In any case, its inadequacy quickly became apparent.[105]

It is now widely accepted that there is no single set of rules for the use of language. Wittgenstein compares words and statements to tools in a tool box or pieces in a chess game.[106] The meaning of one of the pieces of language can only be understood within a "language game." The later Wittgenstein popularized this image of "game" as the best way to understand language. Game has the advantage of indicating that one must get inside the game and understand what is going on before speaking of truth and falsity. For example, if one wishes to understand football, one has to understand how all the rules of football interrelate and what each part of football reality means in relation to the rest. Likewise, a poem or an epic myth has meaning or significance that must first be discovered before any judgments of truth can be made on the writing. Or, in therapy, one can consider the patient as being given a number of possible games to play. When he finds a game that he can play and one that enables him to put together assorted pieces of his life, he can begin to make some progress.[107]

It must not be forgotten that games are devised by people

105. See: A. J. Ayer, *Language, Truth and Logic* (New York, 1953). For the development of logical positivism in the direction of "use" as well as "verifiability," see: R. B. Braithwaite, "An Empiricist's View of the Nature of Religious Belief," in *The Philosophy of Religion,* ed., Basil Mitchell (New York, 1971), pp. 72–91.

106. Ludwig Wittgenstein, *Philosophical Investigations* (New York, 1953), no. 11, p. 6; see also: Justus Hartnack, *Wittgenstein and Modern Philosophy* (Garden City, 1965), pp. 61–103.

107. Fingarette, *op. cit.,* p. 25: "A therapeutic interpretation given to the patient is, as has been said, a suggestion that a new conception of one's life may be worth trying, a new 'game' played. But it is more than a suggestion about a 'conception,' it is the dynamic (existential) offering of the conception at the appropriate moment of dramatic involvement. It is more than the suggestion of a new way of talking about one's life descriptively; it is the proposal to *experience* genuinely and *see* one's life in terms of the meaning-scheme suggested by the words."

145

and, thus, games do not have an autonomous life of their own. As statements have meaning only in concrete contexts and these contexts have meaning only as part of a larger language game, so the language games have meaning only within human life as a whole. Language is, in Wittgenstein's term, one of the "forms of life."[108] But it is a form of life that is not juxtaposed to other activities. Language is intrinsic to doing and acting of all kinds, a fact which causes a particular complication with language games. The games overlap and can never be entirely sorted out as if all the sporting events of Madison Square Garden were happening in the place simultaneously.[109] Each language game develops its own technical apparatus but each game is rooted in a more immediate and more primitive language. Each game draws upon the fund of words in ordinary speech where innumerable games intersect. Dallas High catches the sense of language in the following summary:

Language when working, not idling, is a happily complicated but unified network of uses and speech-environs, overlapping, overcrossing, spilling over, by virtue of its being given life by the ability and action of persons doing something with it. The unification of language-games and thus of language occurs with players or users who stand in and behind speech and move about freely with all forms and mixtures of speech.[110]

The way is open in such reflection for the place of poetic and mythical speech.[111] These can now be seen as valid ways of speaking that reveal the human. I shall say more later about the bias against myth that still operates in Christian theology. I

108. Wittgenstein, *op. cit.*, no. 23, p. 11.
109. See: D. Z. Phillips, "Religious Beliefs and Language Games," in *The Philosophy of Religion*, ed., Basil Mitchell (New York, 1971), pp. 121–142.
110. High, *op. cit.*, p. 92: see also Luis Aloso Schökel, *The Inspired Word* (New York, 1965), pp. 134–173.
111. See: Flannery O'Connor, *Mystery and Manners* (New York, 1969), p. 97.

146

would only note here that mythical ways of speaking are, as far as can be determined, as old as the human race. Myths continue to exercise an important role. It is not sufficient to dismiss them or to interpret them out of existence. They are liable to return in all kinds of devious and distorted forms.[112]

Revelation, used as one of the main categories for describing reality, always has a linguistic element but is never identical with words. Because Christian theologians use revelation to refer to something in the past, revelation is nearly always identified with words, primarily the biblical text. In modern times there has been some attempt to separate revelation and the Bible but it has been in the wrong direction. Revelation has been identified with "events" that *preceded* the texts. Both conceptions, revelation as event and revelation as word, fail to grasp the place of language in human experience. Language must be situated in the context of a present community that constructs and reconstructs its life.

Christian theologians jump quickly from language as revelatory to the Christian Bible as the revelatory texts. There are many intermediary steps one must travel. What I have tried to set out here is the foundation for a religious use of language. A "religious language" is not a language used in religion or a set of words denoting religious things. No religion has a set of truths which describe God. It is probably true that nothing can be *stated about* God because that would be to make God into one *object* within the universe. The alternative, however, is not a series of *bliks* unrelated to man's intelligent awareness. There are many aspects of experience which are difficult to get at directly. There are classes of statements (including ones with the word "I") which are not in principle verifiable but which are

112. Guilford Dudley, *The Recovery of Christian Myth* (Philadelphia, 1967), p. 14: "In point of fact, our American culture is mythic to the core. We feed upon paltry myths that delude and betray us, leaving us victims of famine which only a myth with the staple of truth can relieve.

meaningful.[113] Any attempt to speak about God would and should be a puzzling, odd and strange way; however, such speaking makes sense when one's context is that of being born, living and dying.

113. See: Carlo Huber, "We can Still Speak About God," in *Gregorianum*, XLIX (1968), 667–693; Ian Ramsey, *Religious Language* (New York, 1963).

Chapter Three : Divine Aspects

1. EXPERIENCE AS RELIGIOUS

THE premise of this book is that unless the word revelation has currency and solidity outside the religious area, then discussions of religious matters will always rest upon very insecure foundations. Technical words have to be developed by professional students of religion and these words need not have an obvious correlate in daily experience. But religious issues will be unintelligible unless there are foundational words which arise from the immediate and ordinary experience of mankind. I have been trying up to this point to show that the word revelation could be an appropriate and fruitful term for comprehending the relational, social and practical aspects of human experience.

In the previous chapter, discussion of religious matters was kept to a minimum. This does not mean that the last chapter was about man and this chapter is about God; both chapters are about experience. In this chapter, however, I am extending the analysis of human experience to uncover, if possible, more than what is immediately apparent. In this chapter I will bring in more explicitly the experience of religious traditions and studies of the religious phenomena.

It could be said that I am asking whether revelation is more than human. It should first be recalled that my use of the word experience includes the human by definition. Thus, the phrase "human experience" would usually be a redundancy. Every experience is human insofar as the subject experiencing is a human subject. Furthermore, experience is participated in by more than one person. "We experience our world" even if I am sitting alone in a corner deep in meditation. At least indirectly and by implication, experience is always social in that it arises from men's experience of a common world.

Experience is always human but is it always or sometimes more than human? There are two possible meanings of "more than human." If "more" means "other," that is, something in addition to the human, then the answer is surely in the affirmative. If "more" means "greater," that is, something or someone superior to the human, the question is not immediately answerable. However, the distinction between these two meanings of "more than human" allows us to proceed with our inquiry into revelation without first answering a question like "Does God exist?"[1]

I am presuming, therefore, that human experience does include more than the human. This is true in the obvious sense that human experiences always contains elements of a non-human world. Furthermore, human experience does have a "more" than human in the sense of "superior," at least according to some criteria. For example, the sea has a certain superiority to man: the sea gave birth to the human, the human constantly depends upon the sea for survival and in any battle the sea can easily destroy man. Of course, by the way men usually rank things, man comes out on top of oceans, trees and ants. The judgment that "reason" or "consciousness" is the decisive power that places man at the top may be accurate. It should be noted, nevertheless, that this judgment is a somewhat recent one

1. I leave open the question of whether one can speak of the "experience of God." The titles of many recent books seem to be assured that you can; for example, John Smith, *Experience and God* (New York, 1968); Joseph Whalen, ed., *The God Experience* (New York, 1971). On the other hand, Louis Dupré, "Meditations on Secular Theology," *Christian Century,* Nov. 20, 1968, 1469–1472, maintains that a "positive experience" of transcendence is a self-contradiction. In any case, the introduction of the word God to explain experience is liable to block further consideration of the complexity of experience.

and some of the assumptions on which it is based are questionable.

The use of the word "divine" in this chapter does not imply
a whole set of assumptions about God and religion; it simply refers to the "more" than human, in the sense of superior. I am
starting from what people have experienced all through the centuries and continue to experience today. The word "divine" is
freighted with connotations but, most basically, it simply places
the discussion of "more than human" into the realm of the religious. There is no doubt that a religious realm does exist, that
is, gestures, attitudes and questions which pertain to the more
than human. It could be, for example, that the most divine thing
in experience is the ocean or the earth although few if any people have stopped with these things. It may be that the divine is
the totality of the universe. If that is asserted, however, one
must then inquire further about the meaning of human.

Some people will suppose that this kind of inquiry necessarily
leads to what they call atheism, pantheism or agnosticism. I do
not think any of these words should be immediately excluded.
On the other hand, each of them carries overtones which are
liable to hinder further inquiry if they are adopted as battle
cries. For example, atheism is a negative word; it has meaning
only in opposition to theism. Suppose one does not like the historical connotations of the word theism? Must one be defined
by atheism? Or, if one refuses to be classified as theist or atheist,
must one be called an agnostic with all of the nineteenth-century overtones of that word.

The most common and most general classification has been
one of "believers" and "non-believers." It has often seemed that
if a person was a believer it did not matter much what he believed, in whom he believed or how he believed. In reaction to
this, some religious writers today are trying to re-establish the
word believer by pointing out that everyone believes in something and there really are no non-believers. I have some sym-

151

pathy for this attempt to redefine the word and I might at times participate in the attempt. But one should not be surprised that the people who have been condemned as "unbelievers" are not impressed by this neat switch which makes them all into "believers." They can hardly be faulted for distrusting their erstwhile condemners who kindly but still imperiously are going to define them into belief. In any case, I am not presupposing here any set categories of belief and unbelief.

The problem of terminology is reflected in the phrase "religious experience." There is a strong tendency to refer with this phrase to a small set of experiences that are bizarre or private. A religious experience is presumed to be something like the speaking in tongues of a pentecostal group or the mystic flights of an individual. While I would not wish to dismiss either of these experiences, neither should "religious experience" be restricted to such esoteric instances. This restriction would eliminate many other experiences that might be found to be religious to some degree. It also puts the most unusual experiences into a defensive and irrational posture.

The tendency to narrow the meaning of "religious experience" is evident in many works by "religious psychologists." If religious elements are integral to human experience then they are subject to psychological study. This study should be of human experience to the extent that it is religious. In carrying out this inquiry it may be found that some experiences are more religious than others or that some experiences seem to be so lacking in religiousness as not to be of interest to a student of the subject. Thus, at some point one might designate some individual experiences as religious compared to other experiences which are not. But in doing this, one is using a shorthand way of reporting a complex situation. If the term religious experience is to be retained at all, it must never be lost sight of that we are talking about experience, that is, the social matrix in which we all participate.

152

A similar warning can be given about the term "religious language." That term may suggest a set of words and sentences arranged in one part of life or one group of books. It might then be assumed that "religious experiences" are reported in "religious language." There are important questions about the use of language in a religious context but this is different from trying to justify a set of words and sentences that would constitute a "religious language."

A distinction should be noted between a theological language and a use of language for religious purposes. Theology is a reflective and technical study which develops a specific terminology for its constructs. Where one passes the line from the religious into the theological is difficult to determine or get agreement on. For example, if theology designates any reflective articulation, then the Christian scriptures are already a theology. If, however, theology means a logically structured and coherently ordered system, then Christian scripture is pre-theological. In any case, the statements in the Christian scripture are a stage of development in a process that both precedes and includes them.

Much of what purports to be a study of "religious language" by Christian writers turns out to be a study of the statements of Christian theology. It is then assumed that one has reached the bedrock problem when one analyzes biblical texts. Although the Christian scriptures have religious meaning and value, the statements of the bible are not the primary models or exhaustive content of a "religious language." Such an assumption would be narrow-minded and it would also do violence to the *literature* which stands at the origin of Christianity. As literature, rather than as a set of statements comprising a religious language, the Christian scriptures are significant in a religious quest. Despite all the talk about literary criticism of the bible it is doubtful that the literary character of the bible has been widely accepted.

There is a general failure here to approach understandingly

153

great masterpieces of religious literature. There is a modern reductionism which opposes religion because it does not fit into a monodimensional world. Such a position assumes that the only valid knowledge is in the form of falsifiable scientific hypotheses. The consequent procedure is to discard unverifiable propositions and to strip away the metaphorical guise of those which might be valid.[2] Religious literature does not fare well under the scrutiny of this kind of analysis.

The failure of imagination represented by this approach is not surprising. What is surprising is the acceptance of the same premises by those who are spokesmen for the religious traditions. Christian theologians, instead of defending religious literature, go almost inevitably to the bible for the religious truths still defensible in the modern world. Under the guise of great reverence for biblical tradition, this tactic is destructive of the bible itself.

The reason for trying to fight the war on the opponent's battlefield is the unreconstructed notion of revelation. Christian theology assumes that a "Christian revelation" has been given in the Christian scriptures. Theology then consists in stringing out other statements which are defended on the basis that they can be extrapolated from the bible. A fundamentalist who refuses to have much to do with theology is being consistent. If one already has the revealed truth, "God's word," then why add anything to it? All that "God's word" needs is "application" to contemporary problems. It should not be surprising, therefore, that many people consider theology to be a usually harmful but probably necessary game played by a handful of churchmen.

The alternative to a consistent fundamentalism ought to be equally consistent. A "liberal" theology would, in the first place, not be a Christian theology. A theologian could be a Christian but his attention would not immediately be restricted to Chris-

2. Robert Bellah, *Beyond Belief* (New York, 1970), p. 251.

tian documents. He or she would begin with life as it is experienced by people today. A theologian's main interest would be the nature or quality of the divine which is manifest in the revelation participated in by all people. The historical tradition of the Christian church(es) has much to offer in this theological inquiry. What the Christian church does not have to offer is a "Christian revelation." The retention of that term and that category of thought stands in the way of developing a truly ecumenical theology.

In summary, there is a problem of "religious language" but biblical exegesis is only a small part of the issue. Like a man speaking prose, people may be speaking religiously every day of their lives without realizing it. The bible is certainly a book which uses language in a religious context. The Christian scriptures contain religious testimony but so do all the pieces of great religious literature in the world. Furthermore, "religious language" is to be sought in much of the poetry, painting and architecture of the world and in the gasps of joy, the cries of sorrow and the sighs of tedium of the unheralded masses of the world's population.

It is with some skepticism that I view Christian theology's recent discovery that God is the problem in theology. There is something banal, if not blasphemous, in phrases like "God talk" or "the God problem." Christian theologians, working on the same shaky ground and with the same inadequate tools, seem intent on wrapping up this remaining problem, viz., God. It is difficult at first sight to see what could be meant by saying that God has become the central problem in Christian theology. What has been going on for centuries past? Theology by definition would seem to be an inquiry concerned with God. Saying that Christian theologians are interested again in the question of God might simply be an admission that, having formerly wandered from their main job, the theologians have sheepishly come home. If this were the case, however, one would not

155

expect elaborate announcements that Christian theology has discovered that God is an issue.

The rhetoric about a "God problem" more likely reflects an attitude that is still narrow and fragmented. After theology exhausted grace, sin, sacrament, Christ, Virgin, church, etc., it occurred to some people that God, too, could use analysis. This move results in the demand that God must also conform to our canons or else he too must be eliminated. One cannot be very sanguine about God measuring up to standards.

The bind in which Christian theologians found themselves was in having cut off all forms of mediation between God and man except that form of statement found in the bible and approved by modern analysts. "It needed only the cutting of this one narrow channel of mediation, though, to open the floodgates of secularization. In other words, with nothing remaining 'in between' a radically transcendent God and a radically immanent world except this one channel, the sinking of the latter into implausibility left an empirical reality in which, indeed, 'God is dead.' "[3] A school of Christian theology which proclaimed that "God is dead" was a phenomenon of only a few months duration but its repercussions were powerful. That such a phenomenon could exist was symptomatic of a deep-seated problem in any Christian theology. Many Christian theologians became aware that God was a name bandied about in their books. The one who is supposed to be the ultimate support of theology was himself in trouble within theology. Thus, God has been given center stage so that we can all get straight to the heart of the matter.

This attempt to solve the "problem of God" by pursuing the topic directly and relentlessly could be a most unfortunate tactic. The religious traditions of the past and many great religious men of the present sound an entirely different note. They have not sent for God and spoken of him as a problem. On the

3. Berger, *Sacred Canopy*, p. 112.

156

contrary, they have been extremely reticent to speak about God at all. When the religious quality of human life begins to be lost, then men begin to ask whether meaningful statements can be made about God. "To the man who is no longer able to meet yet is as able as ever to think, the only possible religious question is whether man can ascertain the existence of the gods. This question, in the absence of any experience, must be answered in the negative."[4]

A study of "religious language" is an important venture. But if the question is taken to mean whether statements can be made of God that are comparable to the statements made of objects in the world, it takes no lengthy analysis to come up with a negative answer. One cannot experience God in the same way that one can experience a tree. One may come back to the phrase "experience of God" but, if so, it cannot be a statement isomorphic with "experience of tree" or "experience of Mr. Smith."[5] The fact that men cannot directly take hold of God is hardly a discovery of twentieth-century theologians. However, it has been a rude awakening for theologians who had come to believe that they possessed a revelation which told them straight out what God is like and what his will is. "The religious man, on the other hand, even the most uncultivated, knows very well that all the thousand and one images he bestows on God are 'only' names and images, and that all their purpose is to clarify, or perhaps awaken in others, the one and undivided substance of the intentional object which is inadequately present to him in the religious act itself."[6]

Theology, if there is to be such a thing, should arise from the religious life of mankind. The only adequate instrument of reflection for this is the life of all men. If one were to reflect on how people live, pray, struggle and die, then theology might

4. Martin Buber, *Eclipse of God* (New York, 1957), p. 44.
5. See: Fontinell, *loc. cit.,* p. 178.
6. Max Scheler, *On the Eternal in Man* (New York, 1960), p. 179.

157

in many indirect ways convey some understanding of the one whom in their prayers men address as God.[7] Pronouncements that we need a "whole new language" to speak about God are a little naive. All words about God are inadequate and a logically purified set of sentences is a move in the direction of greater inadequacy. This fact does not mean that nothing can be said about God but it does mean that the best speech about God has always been in the form of richly variegated poetic images interspersed with plenty of silence.[8]

This book is about revelation. Indirectly and by implication it is about God although God is not spoken about much in these pages. It is sometimes said these days that the first question is not revelation but God and that one must first put together a God doctrine. I deny the possibility of that venture. Of course, God is the issue throughout theology but God is not one of the doctrinal problems to be tackled by a frontal assault. The closest one can come to the "God question" is in the religious experience of mankind as it is gathered together but not replaced by some reflection.

The category of revelation is as far as one can go in bringing the topic of God into direct focus. For some religious people that is already going too far and possibly they are right. But for those who feel some responsibility for reflecting in this area, revelation should be the category to bind together an immediately experienced religious life and a consciously articulated theology. The term revelation is not the first word that has come to the lips of men as they met their gods. On the other hand, it is not too far removed from that experience. Although the word revelation is a theological word it is intended to gather into some unity the rich imagery of divine-human intercourse. In pursuing the divine aspect of revelation I am not trying to

7. See Barth's comments on Anselm's use of the direct address in theology: Karl Barth, *Fides Quaerens Intellectum* (Richmond, 1960), p. 39.
8. W. C. Smith, *The Meaning and End of Religion,* p. 64.

uncover God behind the data. I am merely trying to understand the non-human other which men from earliest days have encountered in their religious acts.

RELIGION

It will help at this point to say something explicit about the word religion. In the above sections I have used the adjective religious rather than the noun religion. There is a reason for this choice although it is probably not possible to avoid entirely the word religion. The failure to achieve an acceptable definition of religion is indicative of the fact that there is something basically wrong about the use of the term in modern times.

The various uses of the word religion are classified by W. Cantwell Smith into the following four: 1) personal piety 2) an individual system of belief and practice as it exists in the ideal 3) the individual system of belief and value as an actual historical phenomenon 4) the generic summation of religions. "The first sense discriminates religion in a man's life from indifference (or rebellion). The second and third (possibly intermingled) discriminate one religion from another. The fourth discriminates religion from other aspects of life, such as art or economics."[9] Smith goes on to say that the term religion is confusing and unnecessary in the first and fourth senses while it is distorting in the second and third senses. His own preference, if the word is to be used at all, is for the first sense, that is, personal piety. This meaning would be the most closely related to Augustine, Aquinas or Calvin in their understanding of religio.[10] My preference for the adjective over the noun pushes the meaning in this direction (religious attitude, religious acts, religious person) and away from the generic meaning (the study of religion) most common today. At the least, these dis-

9. *Ibid.*, pp. 47–48.
10. *Ibid.*, pp. 30–38.

159

tinctions should make one wary of setting forth the "essence of religion."

The confusion built into the word religion went unrecognized in attacks launched on religion in the nineteenth century as well as in responses to the attacks in twentieth-century Christianity. The crisis of nineteenth- and twentieth-century religion had been prepared by the framework that had developed in the seventeenth and eighteenth centuries. Assumptions about the nature of experience came to be accepted both by the new scientist and the traditional theologian.

The new perspective which came with the mathematical-empirical sciences assumed or implied certain splits in human experience. The split was brought on by the desire to preserve religious belief from the corrosive effect of the new sciences. The founders of modernity, contrary to popular belief, were not iconoclasts who challenged religious doctrines; nearly all of these men were theological conservatives. Understandably but unfortunately, Pascal, Newton or Faraday avoided trying to reconceptualize religious and theological belief. What seemed safer in the short run proved disastrous over the long haul. Lewis Mumford makes this harsh indictment of Galileo: "Actually, Galileo committed a crime far graver than any of the dignitaries of the Church accused him of; for his real crime was that of trading the totality of human experience, not merely the accumulated dogmas and doctrines of the Church, for that minute portion which can be observed within a limited time-span and interpreted in terms of mass and motion, while denying importance to the unmediated realities of human experience, from which science itself is only a refined ideological derivative."[11] The limited area which Galileo and his successors did investigate proved to be incredibly fascinating, mysterious and fruitful of consequence. Science came to be a religion in itself with its own myths, priesthood and hope for salvation.

11. Mumford, *Pentagon of Power*, p. 57.

Science took all of observable nature as its domain but it was willing to respect religious beliefs by not touching them. The implication of such "reverence" was that religious belief was in some other realm than natural and observable experience. A bifurcation of the human being and the human sources of knowledge was thereby established. The religious spokesmen of the time eagerly and gratefully accepted the deal. From the seventeenth century onward, the religious question was posed in the terms which Bishop Butler chose: natural religion and revealed religion.[12] The choice of terms could hardly have been worse and yet religious discussion down to this day is haunted by the assumption involved in the opposition of natural and revealed religion.

In one sweep the fatal decisions had been made. Henceforth, it could be assumed that a religion is a scheme of belief and practice possessed by various groups. Presumably one religion can be compared to another religion. In addition, it was assumed that the two ways in which religions originate are from nature and from revelation. If the first way is "natural" the only other way available is "unnatural," a fact which Christian theology accepted but did not admit in its term "supernatural." The maneuver was successful in removing from criticism the re vealed or supernatural religion but the victory was a pyrrhic one. The removal of historic religious traditions to heights above the natural experience of the human race exposed these tradi tions to desiccation. At the same time this move approved the use of the word natural as equivalent to scientifically verifiable, thereby placing undue limitations upon what is naturally experienced by human beings.

For several centuries the Christian church was strong enough to convince many people that they must accept the superstructure of a "revealed religion." It should hardly surprise us, however, that during this period men began shifting their interest

12. Bishop Joseph Butler, *Analogy of Religion*, 1736.

161

to "natural religion" as the better source for the actual support of their lives. "As the eighteenth century debates about the use or uselessness of revelation show, for not a few the knowledge of God through nature had become the only relevant source of our knowledge of his power, and even of his benevolence."[13]

By the nineteenth century the "revealed religion" of Christianity could be sufficiently separated from nature to be put into a logical scheme and compared to other religions. These "other religions," it was assumed, were also "revealed religions" of the same general kind as Christianity. None of these "revealed religions" had a leg to stand on when it came to the cross-examination. The reason for this fact is not difficult to trace. For the two centuries preceding, both the foes and friends of "revealed religion" had been performing the amputation.

Up to the nineteenth century many people had held on to Christianity because it did seem to have a set of data uniquely accessible in its unique revelation. However, when the comparisons began many Christians began to suspect that their religion was not that unique and very likely not all revealed. As soon as "revealed religions" were put in comparison to each other the concept of "revealed religion" crumbled. This disintegration of the concept might have been progress. But instead of challenging whether "revealed religion" was from the start a meaningful category, people who were both scholarly and religious went for the only other option available, namely, natural religion.

The concept "natural religion," as the seventeenth through nineteenth centuries understood it, was the pale counter image of "revealed religion." Men wished to be religious but in the nineteenth century they felt obliged to exclude the concrete, historical ways that men had lived religiously. The result was a drift toward vague syncretism in which the distinctiveness of a

13. Langdon Gilkey, *Religion and the Scientific Future* (New York, 1970), p. 10.

religious tradition was played down for the sake of a general belief about the fatherhood of God and the brotherhood of man.

The period has come to be known as theological liberalism but it is doubtful how liberal the whole process was. Much of this modern position was an abstraction living off the patrimony of a Christian past. There was no vital nerve binding men together; only minds constructing, comparing and devising for themselves a religion.[14] In reference to my earlier remarks about the noun and the adjective, one could say that the decline in religious experience and religious life is likely to be accompanied by an increasing interest in religion.

Since Christianity as a "revealed religion" seemed increasingly indefensible, many thoughtful Christians gradually slid toward the generalized, naturalized religion which seemed to be the best alternative. Theological liberalism, however, could not be a final resting place. When the political liberalism with which it was allied underwent the trauma of World War I, the time was ripe for a realignment of forces. From within the Christian church a counterattack was launched against the reduction of the Christian life to one religion in the general category of religion.

Karl Barth led the charge to be followed by several generations of theologians who in one way or another took their lead from Barth. It would be unfair to denigrate Barth's work; he did more than his share in awakening men to the great issues confronting them. Criticism would more accurately be leveled at those who have since then accepted Barth's terms of argument. In hindsight it should have become clear that Barth's regrounding of Christian faith was a powerful but narrow one. The presumptions about Christian faith in the Barthian wake have become dangerously and embarrassingly unecumenical.

The inadequacy of the twentieth-century Christian reaction has been its failure to get in back of the split between "revealed

14. See: Van der Leeuw, *op. cit.*, pp. 269–272.

163

religion" and "natural religion." Barth sensed the impossibility of making any sense out of (a) revealed religion and the inadequacy of a natural religion. But this led him to blast away at both forms of religion with something supposedly purer. He did not re-establish the ground on which Christian and non-Christian could meet each other. He was not concerned with a meeting ground but with reasserting the vital center of a Christian faith. Barth's reaction was understandable; but the last half century should have taught Christians that the line dividing the human race is not between the good Christians and everybody else, and that the Christian church's distinctiveness of the future cannot be maintained by separation from others but only in close relationship.

Barth's tactic was to challenge the assumption that Christian faith could be subsumed under the general category of religion(s).[15] The word of God revealed in Jesus Christ simply cannot be treated as a religion with dogmatic belief and elaborate ritual. The call was to life instead of system, to faith in God rather than the holding of doctrines. The intent was correct but it was carried out within a Christian church and a concept of revelation not sufficiently in touch with the best of life around it. The reaffirmation of Christian faith could have been carried out in a way that did not imply condemnation of sincere, intelligent and faithful men. Barth's position tends to pit (Christian) faith against (other) religions. He might have better posed the question as believing and/or religious people as over against generalities and/or rigid systems.

Religion, as I have previously described, can function either positively or negatively in relation to faith. Religion can be negative in an individual's life, in the Christian church or in other religious groups. Nonetheless, religious attitudes, beliefs, rituals and practices are necessary and good; the embodiment of

15. See: Karl Barth, *Protestant Thought from Rousseau to Ritschl* (New York, 1959); *Humanity of God* (London, 1967).

a believing direction to human life will always be inadequate but that is not grounds for disparagement, let alone condemnation. The simple opposition of faith and religion lifts the problem out of its complex human setting, conveying the impression that there is a simple solution. When religion in this context slides between a general anthropological category and concrete religious groups (e.g. Islam) we have an unfortunate and untenable imperialism.

It is amazing how writers since Barth could perpetuate this posture. For example, in what would pretend to be an ecumenical book, Daniel Niles can write: "Through long ages religion has been man's attempt to question the universe and wrest an answer from it as to its meaning.... When you study the Christian faith, however, you will find that basically the position is reversed."[16] If the author of this book were fair, he would admit that Buddhism is not reducible to his negative concept of religion. Faith as positively conceived exists within Buddhism as well as within Christianity just as religion negatively conceived applies to both Christianity and Buddhism. Apologists for one group tend to compare an ideal form of their own faith with an empirical form of their opponents. "We return, then, to the Christian's flat assertion: 'The Christian faith is not one of the religions of the world.' Students of comparative religion have been wont to decry such sentiments, even dismissing them as ridiculous. I, in contrast, would argue vigorously that the Christian who says this—for instance, Brunner—is profoundly and critically right. Only, I would go on to assert with equal vigour: *Neither is the faith of any other people.*"[17]

In this context, the aggressive move against the concept of religion in the 1960's was not the beginning but the end of an era. Dietrich Bonhoeffer, with a twenty-year time lag, pro-

16. Niles, *op. cit.*, p. 28.
17. W. C. Smith, *The Meaning and End of Religion,* p. 126; see also: Young, *op. cit.,* p. 41.

vided the impetus to this anti-religion movement within Christianity. Writing notes in a prison cell, Bonhoeffer was struck by the conflict between men who lived by faith and men inside of religion who accepted an encrusted system. In regard to the prophecy of his prison notes, Bonhoeffer was inaccurate in the formulation he chose: "The time when men could be told everything by means of words, whether theological or simply pious, is over, and so is the time of inwardness and conscience, which is to say the time of religion as such. We are proceeding toward a time of no religion at all: men as they are now simply cannot be religious anymore."[18]

The most accurate part of this statement is the claim that men cannot be told everything by means of theological words. This is certainly true but I wonder whether this has not always been the case. As for proceeding toward a time of no religion, this can be true only if religion is given a wholly negative meaning. The identification he makes between religion and men being religious is unfortunate. If religion as negative, world denying and inhuman is to be overcome, it will be because religious men break through the rigid forms and express faith anew. Bonhoeffer seemed to assume that the "religious premise" was a kind of slot into which religion fitted. As the slot was filled up, religion (including Christianity as a religion) was being eliminated. This peculiar assumption about religious man derives from a narrow Western tradition which assumes it understands the whole religious life of mankind.[19]

Before leaving this historical sketch of the vicissitudes of natural and revealed religion, I would like to reiterate a point made in chapter one. In all this discussion of faith and religion there is no serious attempt to re-examine the meaning of the

18. Dietrich Bonhoeffer, *Letters and Papers from Prison*, rev. ed. (New York, 1967), p. 139.
19. *Ibid.*, p. 168; see also Gabriel Vahanian, *No Other God* (New York, 1966), p. 30.

word revelation. The word, of course, is widely used. Indeed, Barth is often referred to as the theologian of revelation which only obscures the problem more. Barth did not return to the question of revelation; he turned to the Christian scriptures. Although a re-emphasis of the gospel may have been laudable it was nevertheless a way of avoiding the question of revelation. The subsequent description of Barth's achievement as a new concern with "the Christian revelation" demonstrates that the issue was not clarified.

The assumption in Barth and in Christian theology is that faith is correlated to some given, that is, a revelation preserved in the gospel. Whether or not this word of God is identified with the empirical written gospel is often not clear but there is never left any doubt that there is a divinely bestowed "Christian revelation." Faith as man's acceptance of that revelation is therefore entirely good while religion as an external casing of the revelation is almost of necessity bad. The unrealism and imperialism of recent Christian usage of the word religion follow from these premises.[20]

The categories of faith and religion are inadequate to carry through a reconstruction of the area. The concept of revelation

20. Young, *op. cit.*, p. 41 writes: "When Kraemer writes of the Christian religion (the empirical religion) that 'the revelation . . . has in the course of history engendered many ideas, concepts and experiences that are subject to the vicissitudes of ordinary human development; but they are never adequate or to be equated with the revelation from which they flow' —we would have to agree. But, using the same word, 'revelation,' we would have to add: Neither are other expressions in other religions to be identified with their revelation." Young does not seem to realize that the question cannot be discussed with the words Kraemer has chosen. The narrowness of Kraemer's position follows from his supposition that there is a "Christian revelation" from which a Christian religion flows. As soon as one accepts the framework of "our revelation" and "their revelation" one is faced with a choice between intolerance and indifference. A dialectic of *faith* and religion, although open to confusion and ambiguity, is immeasurably better than *revelation* and religion, Whereas it is quite proper to speak of one's own personal faith being embodied in religion, it is disastrous to think that one has a personal or group revelation from God that is expressed in religion.

167

floats vaguely between faith and religion. If revelation functioned well it could unite the two but when revelation is disregarded it has a deleterious effect on both. When it is presumed that there is some "revelation" which is purer than the religious experience of human beings, religion will be a hard shell that is shucked off in one's own life and is open to denigration in the lives of others. Similarly, when it is presumed that there is a "revelation" to be accepted by faith, then faith is not quite as open as we would like it to be. In fact, it is a somewhat irrational subjective movement that claims to recognize some words as God's.

The word religion has made a remarkable comeback in recent Christian theology. It is not clear whether the shift away from the flat opposition of faith and religion represents genuine progress or whether it is just another swing of the pendulum. The main pressure for re-evaluating the word religion did not come from within Christian theology but from psychologists, sociologists, historians, ecologists and others.[21] If Christian theology has simply given in to this pressure it would be a case of begrudgingly admitting that a little religion is not so bad and in any case seems to be ineradicable. In contrast, the shift in meaning of religion could mean that theologians are becoming aware of the intricate relationship of faith and religion, and the need to understand faith within a developmental process.

The word religion has ambivalence built into it. The ambiguity of the word springs from the ambiguity of life. Definition can eliminate some of the confusion of the word but it should not be at the expense of the genuine complexity of the subject. Religion can function either as a positive value in the development of human life or as a negative value inhibiting life.[22] There

21. See: Moran, *The New Community*, pp. 16–34; David Martin, "Toward Eliminating the Concept of Secularization," in *Penguin Survey of Social Sciences 1965*, ed., Julius Gould (Baltimore, 1965), pp. 161–182.
22. See: Allport, *Person in Psychology*, pp. 148–149 and the same author's *The Individual and His Religion* (New York, 1960)· see also:

are not two things under the name religion, one good and one bad. Rather, religion designates a way of living; what makes religion negative is that a form of expression proper to one people or one time functions improperly for other people or other times. A child's mythical understanding of the universe is appropriate for him while he is a child but when he is grown up and has his Ph.D. the same religious life would be of negative value. The child's mythical and spontaneous gestures are not bad and should not be eliminated. They simply need to be critically examined, progressively developed and healthfully integrated into the life of an adult.

Because the childlike should re-emerge in an adult life, then religion is a word that can span a whole set of children's activities and at the same time the most profound understanding of human life. Thus, life at the most integrated level is likely to find expression in a religious form. However, it should not be surprising that life in disintegration or life at its most barbarous will often take a religious form. "Religion can be, and has been, the main instrument for progress," wrote Alfred North Whitehead, but in the same passage he notes somberly: "Religion is the last refuge of human savagery."[23]

Religion can be understood, therefore, on the one hand as a pre-logical, pre-rational, pre-reflective style of life which is proper to human life at primitive stages of development and, on the other hand, as a post-logical, post-rational, post-reflective style of life which is proper to human life at advanced stages of development. This distinction implies that there is a second stage of growth in between these two where logic reigns and where religion is practically excluded. In fact, of course, these three stages of development are not clearcut, either in the historical development of civilization or in the life of an individual. The

Henri Bergson, *The Two Sources of Morality and Religion* (Garden City, 1935), p. 205.

23. Whitehead, *Religion in the Making,* p. 36.

169

distinction is a helpful one, nonetheless, despite the blurring and overlapping of stages. The struggle of a second stage of civilization against a primitive or childish attitude is probably unending, just as the emergence of a third stage is always tentative and incomplete. The most important thing to recognize here is that tentatively achieved adulthood comes from a synthesis of stages that precedes it. This framework is more helpful than the Comtian sequence of myth, metaphysics, and positive science, both because of the flattened meaning of each word in this sequence and because it is sequence rather than synthesis.

If religion were understood as a developing way of life, then probably no religion would be written off as world denying. Certainly, none of the great religious traditions of the world can be dismissed that easily. There is a theme of denial and negation built into religious activity. However, negation can be part of a process of affirmation if one adverts to the temporal and finite character of human life. Religion as a static collection of beliefs and rituals is almost inevitably a negation of life. But wherever there is a religious life or a religious community, a static collection of things does not stand at the center. What functions at the center of life for such a community is a growing enlightenment about what is worthwhile and in which direction lies genuine life.

The charge that religion is a negation of the world has been made by many opponents of religion. Unfortunately, it is also a charge still commonly made by Christian apologists against the great religions of the East. The accusation is not accurate. The attempt to secure Christianity's position by contrasting (Christian) faith as world affirming and (Eastern) religion as world negating has not been a well-advised or successful tactic. It leaves unresolved both the meaning of "world" and of affirming/negating. At the same time it shows an ignorance of what Eastern religions have attempted throughout the centuries. There are certain differences between Hindu and Christian but

170

the cannot be reduced to a simplistic choice of affirmation or negation.

It has been fairly easy for Christian apologists to score points against the East for its attitude toward the universe. For example, the Hindu doctrine of *máyà* is often interpreted in the West to mean that the world is bad or unreal, a veil of deception to be torn aside. The "failure" of the East to measure up to Western standards of technology and morality is often connected to the religious denial of the material universe. A far more intelligible picture is painted by Radharkrishnan:

It is urged often that belief in the illusory character of the world associated with the Hindu religion conflicts with ethical seriousness: It is wrong to interpret the meaning of the doctrine of *máyà* in a way that affects the urgency of the ethical demand. The doctrine of *máyà* declares that the world is dependent on and derived from the ultimate reality. It has the character of perpetual passing away, while the real is exempt from change. It has therefore a lower status than the Supreme itself. In no case is its existence to be confused with illusory being or non-existence.[24]

When such a doctrine is lifted from its context it can take on a different meaning. No religious doctrine can make much sense except as an interpretation of a stage of development. Twentieth-century psychology is fascinated by the developmental process but this notion had long been embedded in Hindu tradition. A rather elaborate charting has been made of the wants and desires of man. "Hinduism regards the objects of the Path of Desire as if they were toys. If we ask ourselves whether there is anything wrong with toys our answer must be: on the contrary, there is something tragic in the picture of children deprived of them. Even sadder, however, is that of adults who fail to move on to interests more significant than dolls and electric trains."[25]

24. *Radhakrishnan,* ed., Robert McDermott (New York, 1970), p. 42.
25. Smith, *Religions of Man,* p. 20.

171

Pleasure, success and duty are what lie along the Path of Desire. So long as men are content with these things they should enjoy them. When these wants no longer satisfy it is then that Hinduism encourages men to look for a more ultimate goal in life. It is at this point that the Hindu enters one of the four paths to the goal, i.e., through knowledge, love, work or exercise one advances across the stages toward the supreme goal.[26]

My intention here is not to show that the Hindu way is the best way or even a good way but simply to insist that it is a *way,* i.e., a searching, striving, affirming attitude that finds expression in life. The best kind of understanding, and probably the only adequate form of understanding, comes through traveling that way and discovering stages of growth for oneself. Some limited understanding can undoubtedly be achieved across religious boundaries. However, the person who approaches this complex phenomenon confident that he has the capacity to render final judgment upon it is perhaps the one most subject to illusion.

There is no denying that religion has been experiencing traumatic upheaval and that more of the same can be expected. Religion has undergone a fundamental dislocation in recent times, a fact that Eastern groups with their longer ranged vision also have to admit. The TV set, the bulldozer and the jet plane have touched every village at least indirectly. For better or worse, technology is coming into immediate presence everywhere. The ramifications upon the religious life of mankind are beyond measurement. Hans Urs von Balthasar, after describing the crisis of a cosmological form of religion, continues: "This is the point in history when the consciousness of mankind (comprising that of every individual) has reached an immediate relation to the religious question."[27]

26. See: *Ibid.,* pp. 32–61.
27. Hans Urs von Balthasar, *The God Question and Modern Man* (New York 1967), p. 71.

172

The religious spirit of man has not only survived the technological era but has raised the religious question in a more urgent
way. The religious question comes back partly as a result of and
partly as a reaction to technology. In one sense the "game" has
changed so much that a continuity from old religious questions
to new is doubtful but the spirit of man with his search for
ultimacy has survived the change.

The emergence of "modern man" in the last few centuries of
the West has showed that the enemies of human development
are many and subtle. Although religion can play the role of
enemy, it is by no means the only threat. Twentieth-century
political movements have demonstrated what is perhaps a worse
danger, namely, the promethean urge toward power. The struggle of man against the gods for power, as embodied in the
myth of Prometheus, is no longer an adequate myth for our day.
Jean-Paul Sartre's presentation of this myth in *The Flies* may
still inspire individuals to storm heaven for a power denied to
man. But looking at the social situation, one can only conclude
that men have more power than they know what to do with.
The needs today are to find means to prevent some men from
making slaves of other men, to use power to improve rather
than destroy the earth and to find some reason for living at all.
These problems are not at all resolved by the heroic act of
taking fire from the gods. In fact, the promethean attitude becomes part of the problem unless it finds a larger context to
direct it.[28]

Irrevocable forces have been unleashed by Western technology. There is no hope of putting the genie back into the bottle.
But it is urgently necessary to keep these forces from being
clothed in religious myth and ritual. The only way that this can
be done is by re-examining once more the impetus toward religion that has characterized the past. In that way we can rec-

28. See: William Lynch, *Christ and Prometheus* (Notre Dame, 1970),
p. 65

173

ognize the distorted expressions of the religious which appear with dictatorial leaders and technological obsession.[29]

2. A RELIGIOUS DESCRIPTION

My intention in the following pages is not "comparative religion" nor a summary of non-Christian religions. I am trying to describe religious experience borrowing from some specific religious traditions. I began with the premise that the term revelation can function as a helpful description of all human experience. Within this revelational structure I wish to explore certain mysterious elements that have found expression in religious activity. These elements challenge man's tendency to settle down into the ordinariness of things. The pole in experience toward which the religious activity is directed is what I have called the divine in revelation. There is no method by which one could prove that there is a "divine revelation," but by probing some aspects of revelation one might awaken some awareness of the divine which has always been present in the revelational pattern of experience.

In trying to understand the religious activity of mankind one does not have the choice of starting either with God or with man. The operative choice is between things and man as a starting point on the way to God.[30] Of course, the choice for man does not exclude things but the choice does decisively affirm that things are to be understood through understanding man and not vice versa.

In religion as elsewhere one must achieve a total framework of things and people. The task is to understand the whole but

29. See: Kenneth Boulding, *Beyond Economics* (Ann Arbor, 1968), p. 196; Loren Eiseley, *The Unexpected Universe* (New York, 1969), p. 39; Hartshorne, *op. cit.,* 147–155.

30. On man as the key to understanding the universe, see: Teilhard de Chardin, *Christianity and Evolution* (New York, 1971), pp. 103–108.

the whole cannot be wholly understood all at once. In relating persons and things, there are two opposing ways to proceed. One can start with things and consider them to be the norm of existence. With such an assumption, person becomes an unusual thing which breaks through the pattern of things as a kind of "sport." In contrast, one can start with person as the norm, that is, as the central and most significant reality. Things then become lesser realities whose greatness consists in pointing toward the personal.

There is a strong conviction today that the second way, in which the personal is primary, is the better way. Its great advantage is that it is a more comprehensive approach. The disadvantage of this second way is that it leads to a more difficult mode of understanding. If the personal is taken as primary, then categories like history, society and freedom will be at the center of inquiry. The inquirer finds that his conceptual tools cannot entirely embrace this reality but for that very reason he may feel that he is getting closer to the lived truth. For example, no one who experiences freedom can believe that non-freedom is a better way to comprehend the truth. Freedom experienced not only as the choice among alternatives but as the capacity to create new alternatives establishes itself as a more comprehensive truth than non-freedom.

A study of religion as a quest for God must therefore look to the phenomena of history, society and freedom. At the same time it must be understood that freedom includes elements of non-freedom, history includes nature, and society includes the individual. This sense of inclusion must be stressed since there is a danger of trying to choose person *instead* of things. The precise reason for choosing the personal is that it can include things whereas if one starts with things persons will not be included within things. To choose the personal in an exclusive way is inadvertently to do just what one is trying to avoid, that is, one has reduced the personal to one of the things to be chosen to the exclusion of the other things. The adjective personal is more flexible than the noun person and less likely to mislead.

I would agree with Mircea Eliade that we are at the beginning of a new era of exaltation of *les choses*. In the popularity of Teilhard de Chardin and Levi-Strauss, Eliade sees a rejection of existentialism and of history in the narrow meanings those two words had. Eliade sees a reabsorption of man back into nature.[31]

I would only point out that this move is not a reversion to a pre-twentieth-century method which did not recognize the distinctiveness of the personal. What we have instead is a re-emphasis of the link between the personal and the non-personal, a resituating of the personal in the total environment of nature. (It is debatable, of course, whether placing man back into nature should be called a new understanding of history or a subordination of history.) In the great enthusiasm for the personal, the non-personal may have been implicitly denigrated. The crucial task now is to reassert the total sense of nature without overwhelming the precarious position of the personal.

This methodological point may seem to be an obvious and simple one but it is often a stumbling stone. Conclusions depend very heavily upon the first question that is asked. And the real significance of the first question is not so much what is asked as what is presupposed by the question. If the first religious question pertains to the study of religion rather than the study of religious men, the way may already be lost. If one studies religious men one can find out something about their religion but one could study a religion and never gain more than a suspicion about the life of religious people.

This problem of method is particularly acute in religious study. Every religious tradition (as the word tradition itself shows) seems tied to ancient documents and to ideas coming down from the past. There are religious people today but there

31. Mircea Eliade, "Cultural Fashions and the History of Religions," in *History of Religions*, ed., Joseph Kitagawa (Chicago, 1967), pp. 21–38

seems to be a preponderant influence of the past in any actual religious body. Can one study the past and not put things above people? Is not the past the realm of things as opposed to the present which is the realm of persons?

In answer to these questions one must admit that the personal is not fully recoverable from the past. The past, as it exists today, is the things men have bequeathed to us. Nonetheless, one can struggle against the final failure and before one admits that the personal is not wholly recoverable from the past, one can experience some solidarity with a figure of the past, some glimpse of his inward self, some feel for a world that has been. One needs not only scholarly apparatus to understand the past on its own terms but also a kind of reverence which Gabriel Marcel refers to as "intellectual piety."[32]

The student of religion thus encounters the problem of the historian. For religious understanding one cannot choose between history and something else (e.g., experience). It would be most preferable if history could be developed in an all-embracing way; or at least as a necessary part of experience. History, in the common sense of a study of the past, is not the origin, source and norm of religious understanding. Even though history plays a massive role in religious inquiry it is the religious person today who is the point from which and to which the religious search leads.

This methodological change would allow us to escape from an odious comparison of religions. Statements of truth can be compared and, if the statements contradict each other, one must be judged true and one false. Two things can be compared and one thing is almost certain to emerge as bigger or better. Thus, one can compare the idea of God in Christianity with the idea of God in Hinduism and the study is not without value. But these ideas are abstractions as indeed Christianity and Hinduism are themselves abstractions.

32. Gabriel Marcel, *Decline of Wisdom* (London, 1954), p. 48.

177

Abstractions and ideas have a place but their limitation should not be overlooked. The question "Is Christianity the true religion?" is not only unanswerable; it is a question that should not be asked. The question only arises because of false presuppositions brought to the first religious question. It would be more to the point to ask: Does this religious question make sense to me? Does any religious tradition throw light upon my life? Is one religious tradition the best one for me? To the person who asks this kind of question it is unthinkable that he could judge his own religion right and other religions wrong.[33]

For the purpose of studying religious life in a more fair and open manner, the development of a phenomenological method has been very helpful. Edmund Husserl is usually credited with giving the main impetus to this movement.[34] His dictum of "back to the things themselves" might seem incompatible with much of what I have said above. His reference to "things," however, was not in contrast to persons but in opposition to conceptual constructs. The *phenomenon* toward which Husserl was redirecting attention was precisely that full range of human experience that is so easily overlooked in a narrow rationalistic

33. Stephen Neill, *Christian Faith and Other Faiths*, 2nd ed. (New York, 1970), p. 4: "It has to be recognized that those things which are experienced as wholes are in fact not commensurable with one another, any more than one scent is really comparable with any other. Genetic or historical connections may be traced; it is just the fact that a certain knowledge of the Bible and of Christian faith underlies certain parts of the Qur'an. An understanding of such connections is useful in the study of religion as it is in the study of music. But, when we have said that the young Beethoven was at certain points influenced by Mozart, we have not really said anything important about either of them; the music of each has to be felt and appreciated in terms of itself and nothing else. Even when, as can happen, one musician has actually stolen a phrase or a melody from another, what he does with it is so idiosyncratic that the connection has little more importance than that of a historic accident. The greater the composer, the less it is possible to think or speak of him in terms other than those of his own achievement."

34. Husserl, *op. cit.;* for the change from "scientific" to phenomenological approach in religion, see: Frederick Streng, *Understanding Religious Man* (Belmont, 1969), pp. 13–45.

178

approach. Intrinsic to the method is some degree of suspension of judgment. Before one can judge whether something is true or false one must know what is meant. Before one can judge that an activity is good or bad, one must understand what the activity is. There may be much more to reality than what our conceptual scheme is filtering through. One must spend a little time with the phenomenon, get a feel for it from the inside, and participate in its flow of life.

Phenomenology in this general sense is no longer a strict method but a general attitude which characterizes much of twentieth-century study. For example, the "temporary suspension judgment" is an integral part of many therapeutic techniques. The religious field stood to gain the most from this attitude. Religion becomes quickly embroiled in polemics for or against it. The appearance of works like William James's *Varieties of Religious Experience* and Rudolph Otto's *The Idea of the Holy* was a breath of fresh air in that these works attempted to start from peoples' religious experience without judging the case before they started.[35]

During the last fifty years much phenomenological and psychological study of religion has occurred. Unfortunately, in the Western church such study still seems at the periphery of the main business, namely, the preservation and transmission of the church's revelation. Psychological studies of religious experience have had little effect on the church's notion of revelation. The psychologists, for their part, have generally abided by this judgment. Thus, "religious experience" and "Christian revelation" seem incapable of any real intercourse.

There are instances today, however, when psychology does grow very close to religion on this question. It is fascinating to trace through the last fifteen years of Abraham Maslow's writing. He had a growing suspicion that his psychological studies of

35. James, *op. cit.;* Rudolf Otto, *The Idea of the Holy* (New York, 1958).

"peak experience" brought him very close to the religious claim to revelation. He gradually recognized that his own attitude toward religious phenomena had been biased by the organized religions of the day. He began to look forward to the time when new coalitions could be formed of people who respected and appreciated an open humanism. Concerning the relation of an open humanism and a religious community, he concluded:

It's quite possible that there wouldn't be much difference between them in the long run, if both groups accepted the primary importance and reality of the basic personal revelations (and their consequences) and if they could agree on regarding everything else as secondary, peripheral, and not necessary, not essentially defining characteristics of religion, they then could focus upon the examination of the personal revelations—the mystic experience, the peak-experience, the personal illumination—and of the B-cognitions when they ensue.[36]

This agreement has not been reached and probably cannot be reached by religions as they now stand. To shift the primary meaning of revelation to the personal experience of people today would involve a traumatic upheaval for any organized religious body. If it is founded upon a message revealed by God to an ancient prophet, then its authority is undermined by locating revelation in the experience of all men alive today. But what is felt to be a threat to religious organization, and indeed is a threat, also holds the promise of establishing religious authority on a sounder base than ever before. Humanistic psychology could show that the basis for religion is not first the testimony of an ancient prophet conveyed to us through questionable documents but, rather, the experience of each person who opens himself to the possibility of the divine and joins with other men in examining the human and the divine in revelation.

Another interesting example of a psychological notion which has strong religious overtones is the use of the word "transcendence." The word transcendence had fallen upon hard times in

36. Maslow, *Religions, Values and Peak-Experiences*, p. 47.

Christian theology to the extent that many theologians advocated giving up the term. Taken by itself the word does have an air of abstraction and lifelessness. Over the years it had become more and more of a problem theologically. Transcendence was seldom explained but simply joined to another word, immanence, for a description of God.

The word immanence seemed to be less of a problem. It came to mean that God could be met within this world and as part of human experience. Transcendence then came to mean that God was outside this world, above and beyond experience. What seemed to properly define God was not immanence but transcendence. God qualified as God because he was a transcendent being.

The difficulty with this conception is how to get in touch with a transcendent being. How can one know about a being above or beyond our experience? The answer seemed to be that he had sent a message (or in Christian terms had sent his Son, the Word). This premise becomes increasingly difficult to believe because there seems to be no way one can validate a message from a transcendent being. Like Vladimir and Estragon in *Waiting for Godot,* men may cling to the cryptic messages and keep hoping that someday he will appear, but the world itself is experienced as bleak, empty and godless.

Christian theology reached the end of the road in the use of the words transcendence and immanence. More subtlety of definition could not recoup the losses. The most logical thing seems to be to drop the words and try to use others. This move has been advocated by some people, that is, not to drop transcendence and speak of an immanent God but to drop transcendence/immanence as an adequate way to approach the subject.[37]

37. Fontinell, *op. cit.,* p. 204 suggests otherness/presence as an alternative to discussing transcendence/immanence. Kee, *op. cit.* p. 224, seems to be going in the opposite direction: "Everything that has been said about God can be interpreted in terms of transcendence." This may be true but it is doubtful whether this represents any progress. Presumably the word

It may be, however, that the word transcendence will re-emerge in theology not from within theology but as a result of the urgings of psychology. The meaning will be quite different from the past because it will have a rich, experiential meaning which theology could not find.

The first prerequisite would not be to defend God as transcendent but to establish a viable meaning for the word transcendence in human experience. For this purpose no artificial constructions are necessary; the word is helpful to describe a realm of experience for which there is a paucity of language. Eugene Fontinell writes: "I find great significance in the fact that at a moment in man's history when the notion of a transcendent divinity is severely criticized by a majority of the reflective members of the society—that at this moment man is conceived as an essentially self-creative and self-transcending being."[38]

The phrases "self-creative" and "self-realization" are somewhat ambiguous. They could mean, and occasionally have meant, a supreme individualism in which self functions as all-sufficient agent. The reason for introducing the word transcendence is to indicate the relationship of the self to all that is other. Paradoxically, self-affirmation means a letting go of the self, a going beyond one's ego. Transcendence is a word that philosophically, psychologically, and socially expresses the universal phenomenon of the self being formed in the going beyond itself.[39]

---

transcendence has for Kee the rich, experiential meaning I advert to in the following pages. But far more work will have to be done with the word before its substitution for God can be hailed as a great victory.

38. Fontinell, *op. cit.*, p. 202.

39. Erich Fromm, *The Revolution of Hope* (New York, 1968), p. 89. In a more social vein: Thomas Luckmann, *The Invisible Religion* (New York, 1967), p. 49: "We may, therefore, regard the social processes that lead to the formation of Self as fundamentally religious. This view, incidentally, does no violence to the etymology of the term. It may be objected from a theological and 'substantivist' position on religion that in this view

J. F. T. Bugental, drawing upon the work of Thomas Hora, lists eleven different functions of the word transcendence.[40] Similar to peak experience in Maslow, Bugental finds a way to overcome dichotomies of subject/object, mind/body, temporal/spatial, etc., by using transcendence as his most encompassing notion. He does not shy away from religious overtones of the word, believing as he does that a humanistic psychology should be open to a religious interpretation of experience. As a possible definition of the word, Bugental writes: "Transcendence is a broadened state of consciousness enabling man to cognize reality in dimensions which are above and beyond dualities and multiplicities."[41] One cannot easily transpose this definition to a religious use that refers the word to God. Nevertheless, the implications for religious study may be profound as psychology investigates the transcending and transcendent character of human experience.

These examples from psychology indicate a new willingness to take seriously some phenomena that were once dismissed by "right thinking" people. The phenomenological attitude embraces the non-rational in life along with the rational side of things. Not only must the non-rational be allowed a hearing; in many ways it has priority. William James wrote concerning the inadequacy of rationalism: "Your whole subconscious life, your impulses, your faiths, your needs, your divinizations, have prepared the premises of which your consciousness now feels the weight of the result; and something in you absolutely *knows* that the result must be truer than any logic-chopping rationalistic talk, however clever, that may contradict it."[42]

The plea here is not for an irrationalism which overthrows

---

religion becomes an all-encompassing phenomenon. We suggest that this is not a valid objection. The transcendence of biological nature *is* a universal phenomenon of mankind."

40. Bugental, *op. cit.,* p. 278.
41. *Ibid.;* p. 277.
42. James, *op. cit.,* p. 72.

the power of rational thought but for a willingness to appreciate what cannot be thought. Thinking, at least when used as equivalent to the rational and discursive act, is not adequate to comprehend life. The irrepressible religious phenomenon is evidence of this fact. A society that will not allow in the nonrational has no place for religious men although it may not only allow but support an establishment of religion.

A genuine religious life cannot long subsist without some sense of the mystical and prophetic. Whatever divergences there are in defining these two words, there is no doubt that both of them stand somewhere outside the logical, planned patterns of a rational world. Allowance is usually made for accepting prophets and mystics of the past; dead prophets become explainable and ultimately acceptable. Even religious people have a tendency to honor only the ancient prophet while overlooking the religious eruptions all about them. For example, the artist is often dismissed as irreligious or immoral at the very moment that he is trying to make contact with the realm that religions often glibly describe. Martin Esslin has described absurdist drama as "a symptom of what probably comes nearest to being a genuine religious quest in our age: an effort, however timid and tentative, to sing, to laugh, to weep—and to growl—if not in praise of God . . . at least in search of a dimension of the Ineffable."[43]

A search for the ineffable requires unlimited amounts of patience, a willingness both to look and to listen, and a realization that even if one finds one must still seek. Finding the divine in revelation does not mean that everything will become translucent and manageable. The more someone is revealed the less clear they become insofar as revelation is an immersion into a reality that has no bottom. For this reason is the paradox true: to reveal is to conceal. What is possessed as knowledge is not revelation even though revelation includes the most intense kind

43. Martin Esslin, *The Theatre of the Absurd* (Garden City, 1961), p. 271.

of knowing. "In revelation something is disclosed to me that no eye has ever seen—not even mine! I hear something that no ear has ever heard—not even my ear! Something is prepared for me which has entered no human heart—not even my own heart!"[44]

I would like to refer at this point to Rudolph Otto's *Das Heilige,* a book that I have previously mentioned as a groundbreaking work. It has always seemed to me ironic that the English title of the book is *The Idea of the Holy.* One way of stating the theme of the book would be to say that "the holy," whatever else it is, is not an idea.

Otto dealt with the limitations of language in the same way as many other great thinkers, that is, he created his own language or at least he broke through the old language by coining his own key words. One cannot summarize poetry or translate it into prose. However, Otto's book is well known and I shall therefore presume some acquaintance with it. I shall restrict myself to a few points concerning his method and his conclusions.

Otto begins his work by paying tribute to the rational side of religion, suggesting that a highly developed religion will always have a high degree of rationality. His own interest, however, is expressly in the non-rational side which he sees as the wellspring of every religion.[45] Religious activity at base is an immediate experience of the universe and a realization of a quality of the universe often lost in our ordinary dealings. This "experience" should not be equated with "feeling" if the word feeling is the opposite of knowing. One does not know about science and feel about religion, a distinction which would be advocated by many opponents of religion and accepted by many of its supporters. Otto searches for a more comprehensive starting point than thinking, willing, feeling or knowing.

Otto locates the basic religious act in the experience of "the holy." At this originating point the total person encounters the

44. Van der Leeuw, *op. cit.,* p. 565.
45. Otto, *op. cit.,* p. 6.

universe as an all-encompassing power. The word holy does not originally refer to what is ethical and rational; it refers to a more primitive and more complete involvement of the person. Although the holy cannot be defined, "there is no religion in which it does not live as the real innermost core."[46] Since definitions are impossible, Otto is forced into an elaborate description and into a variety of images which he hopes can evoke some awareness of the presence of the holy. For describing the non-rational elements of the holy he reinstated the term *numinous* and for the object of the numinous he originated the phrase *mysterium tremendum*.

From my earlier comments on phenomenological approach, it should be obvious why Otto does not begin by talking about God and divinely revealed truths. Otto is examining data of immediate consciousness while suspending judgment on the truth or validity of religious claims. He is not, however, inside the mind and faced with the problem of bridging the chasm to the outside world. From the very begining his attention is directed to an experience which is intrinsically relational. The numinous is never experienced as "merely subjective" and which may or may not be "objective." The basic religious act is one of being enveloped by an "other" in a way which involves the subject while leaving no doubt that there is some power that confronts the subject.

The sense of power seems to be the basic element that founds religions, not just any power but an awe-inspiring power which works with mysterious and extraordinary effectiveness.[47] The first religious act, therefore, has never consisted in arguing to the existence of the gods or specifying the character of being. Rather, the religious man is the one who has experienced overwhelming power that seemed to reduce everything to nothingness. On looking again he grasps that he is not utterly nothing,

46. *Ibid.*
47. See: Van der Leeuw, *op. cit.*, pp. 23–28.

186

that he is of some significance, but only in relation to and in responding to the "all," the "other," the "ultimately real."[48]

The mysterious character of this power is the reason for its ambiguity. This ambiguity cannot be resolved by conceptual distinctions because the experience precedes concepts and will be distorted if reduced to clear ideas. There are two aspects of this ambiguity that I wish to comment upon: (1) whether the power which is experienced is good or bad (2) whether this power is personal or non-personal. The two questions are to some degree interconnected.

In contemporary language the word holy is presumed to refer not only to what is good but to what is morally good and ethically proper. A reductionism has crept in here even from the time of earlier western words for holy. *Sacer* had an element of what we would call "cursed"; *hagios* carried the double meaning of pure and polluted. In the development of western religion God came to be called good in the sense of acting in accord with the nature of things. If God is good he will then act properly, not doing violence to the things he has created, not playing tricks on man, but bearing all things to their fulfillment. The Jewish scriptures, most strikingly in the Book of Job, were not quite that sure of God's goodness or at least what God's goodness might mean for man. Even more so, other religious traditions have not assumed that the gods are good and clearly on man's side. Men would like to believe that God is on their side but the evidence does not all go in that direction.

The fundamental religious experience is an ambivalent one in the precise meaning of that term. The experience is not of something good and of something bad, nor is it an experience in which one is not sure whether the thing is good or bad. Instead, it is an experience of some ultimate which precedes or transcends our normal divisions into good and bad; the good/bad is experienced as one. Otto tries to dig down into the double mean-

48. See: Scheler, *op. cit.*, pp. 166–167.

ing sedimented in words like awe, fascination, majesty, stupor and dread, although each of these words has been flattened out in the course of ordinary speech. One must therefore use round-about descriptions to convey the ambivalence and to keep insisting on both sides of the experience. G. Van der Leeuw writes: "Power awakens a profound feeling of awe which manifests itself both as fear and as being attracted. There is no religion whatever without terror but equally none without love, or that *nuance* of being attracted which corresponds to the prevailing ethical level."[49]

The aspect of terror is not difficult to trace. Overwhelming power poses a threat simply because it is overwhelming. Is the small and insignificant human being to be entirely swallowed? If the other is totally other, then is there any chance of coping with it or does it simply overpower and obliterate? If the totally other is not a thing, is it not no-thing? The last question is more than a trick of speech. There is a close connection in the history of religion between All and Nothing. If one goes beyond things to encounter the ultimate principal at the origin of things, it is not clear whether this should be called All or Nothing or both of those terms.

In any case, terror arises from this confronting of the human with what is beyond all grasp. Kierkegaard, Heidegger and modern psychology gave to popular speech the word *anxiety*.[50] Whereas fear is directed toward one thing or another and fear can be resolved, anxiety is directed toward the unnamable and is intrinsic to the structure of life. The human being born into a world not of his own choosing, and living for a finite length of time, faces the possibility of death at any moment. None of the things in his immediate experience seems to be of permanent value. The alternative is to turn toward the All/Nothing, but, whether this is done consciously or unconsciously, it exposes the person in all his vulnerability to the overturning of his life.

49. Van der Leeuw, *op. cit.,* p. 48.
50. See Kierkegaard, *op. cit.,* pp. 155–161.

Despite the presence of terror, anxiety and dread, there is always another side to the religious act. The religious man experiences the world as one in which he is not alone and one in which there is effective power. Here there appears a crucial difference between philosophy and religion; the religious man experiences a power which he knows is not nothing. The no-thing may be experienced as an abyss which threatens the existence of everything finite but it is at the same time a real force which seizes men and establishes a ground to existence. The religious man embodies this experience in gestures and material forms which, however ambiguous their meaning, have an indubitable reality to them. He does not create them alone nor does he have to create them moment by moment.

Commenting on the numinous experience, Carl Jung writes that it is "a dynamic existence or effect, not caused by an arbitrary act of will. On the contrary, it seizes and controls the human subject which is always rather its victim than its creator."[51] The valid point here is the reality of being "seized." I think, however, that the word "victim" carries an inappropriately negative meaning. Creator and victim are not the only two possible alternatives. Man neither creates nor controls the numinous but he does receive and respond to it. A victim simply suffers harm at the hands of an oppressor. The religious man does not think of himself as victim so much as caught up into the frightening but fascinating ultimate. St. Augustine's description was more accurate: "Who shall understand this? Who shall relate it? What is that light which shines upon me but not continuously, and strikes upon my heart with no wounding? I draw back in terror: I am on fire with longing: terror insofar as I am different from it, longing in the degree of my likeness to it."[52]

If both aspects of this experience were kept in sight, it would clear up some of the argument about "dependence" in the religious act. Friedrich Schleiermacher originated much of this dis-

51. Carl Jung, *Psychology and Religion* (New Haven, 1938), p. 4.
52. St. Augustine, *Confessions*, XI, 9.

cussion by defining religious experience in relation to dependence: "The self-consciousness which accompanies all our activity ... is itself precisely a consciousness of absolute dependence; for it is the consciousness that the whole of our spontaneous activity comes from a source outside of us ... To feel oneself absolutely dependent and to be conscious of being in relation with God are one and the same thing."[53] Schleiermacher was perhaps clear in his own mind what he meant by this statement but words like "dependence" and "outside" created confusion. Unless dependence is placed in the context of ambivalence, it is almost certain to be misunderstood. The stereotyped image of Western religion is that God is like a banker or policeman while man is an obedient functionary. Schleiermacher's stress on absolute dependence could unfortunately reinforce this image.

Criticizing this recent emphasis, Nicolas Berdyaev has written: "Schleiermacher is wrong when he says that the religious sense is a sense of dependence. Dependence is an earthly thing. There are more grounds for saying that it is a sense of independence."[54] There may be more grounds for speaking of independence but to speak of independence *alone* would also be misleading. What I tried to show in the second chapter is that to be *humanly* understood dependence and independence must be related to each other. What I am adding here is that it is *religiously* that the two are most completely and mysteriously interrelated. Religion can never be simply reduced to an unquestioning obedience to a God on whom we depend. The relation is not like that of a dog depending on its master. The religious act always establishes the independence of the religious man who, though acutely aware of his own frailties and failings, can still muster the courage to address his god. In the Book of Job, the dialogue is by no means an even exchange. Job, nevertheless, still challenges

53. Friedrich Schleiermacher, *The Christian Faith,* ed., H. R. MacKintosh and J. S. Stewart (Edinburgh, 1928), pp. 16–17.
54. Berdyaev, *Truth and Revelation,* p. 59.

God, and, if Job's questions do not get him the answers to resolve his problems, they do seem to give him help to live with
his problems.

No religious tradition can come up with a complete explanation of what is bad or wrong with the universe. The immediate
identification of the holy and the good is an attempt to give a
premature answer. Some religions have imagined a good deity
and a bad deity, a solution which does not in the long run
satisfy. Other religions, including Christianity, have developed
the notion of a being who personifies evil but is subordinate to
the good God. The projection of evil onto a devil has not been
a very healthy development.[55] It prematurely separates the good
and the bad in human experience and particularly in the human
experience of the holy.

The human race can be very mistaken about what is good
and what is bad. For example, before deciding that certain feelings connected with sexuality or aggressiveness are bad, perhaps
people would be better off living with ambiguity and trying to
understand what is happening. The tendency to suppress part of
human experience, and sometimes part of the human race, is related to the drive to conceive of a good, reasonable god instead
of an ambiguous numinous mystery. The use of the word good
with the word God is not necessarily to be excluded, but if faith
arrives there it must be careful not to short-circuit the process
which brings it there. There must be a continual challenge as
to how the word good is to be used in a religious context.

The second ambiguity on which I wish to comment is the personal and non-personal character of the holy. I say non-personal
rather than impersonal because the latter word carries the note
of sub-personal. When one inquires whether the religious experience has for its object the non-personal, this could mean that
the holy is either supra-personal or infra-personal. In other
words, religious traditions which say that God is personal may

55. See: Henry A. Kelly, *Toward the Death of Satan* (London, 1968).

not be sufficiently exaltive of the divine. The statement that God is personal may be true but not adequately so. The use of the adjective personal rather than the noun person is significant here. If one asks whether God is a person, one is locked into a framework in which the only answers are yes and no. If, on the other hand, one asks whether the numinous is personal, the answer may be: That is one way of describing the Ineffable but there are other non-personal ways that are legitimate and helpful.

In western religion the question "Is there a personal God?" still functions as a touchstone of orthodoxy. In most people's minds the question of a personal god is identical to the question: Is God a person? On the basis of its doctrine of the Trinity the Christian response to the latter question would seem to be: No. In strange language that never seemed to function very practically in Christian life, Christian doctrine spoke of three persons in God. Whatever else this was to signify, it surely says that God is not a person. In practice, however, God has never been called "they" or "it," but always "he," the masculine singular pronoun. The picture is of a god who is someone like us only much better at being a good person.

The chief reason why God is conceived of as a person seems to be that this is the only way in which he can be better than us. Since Western man is totally convinced that he is the best or highest thing on earth, anything not a person is necessarily lower on the scale. Saying that God is not a person seems to be saying that God is less than man which is equivalent to saying that there is no God at all. Thus, the phrase personal God becomes a redundancy; God is a person or he is not at all.

Within the given framework, this position is a consistent one. If the best things are persons, the name God cannot but designate a person because he is the best one of all. John Robinson, in his best-selling *Honest to God*, tried to slide out from this framework but without much success. He tried to maintain that

192

God is not a person but that he is personal.[56] Reactions to that book indicated that many readers saw a kind of vaporization of God in passing from noun to adjective. Can one pray to an adjective or hope in salvation from an adjective? Many critics decided that Robinson had gone atheist but was keeping up the pretense of belief in God by identifying God with the love between two persons.

What Robinson had sought to do was not to dissolve God but to enrich the religious realm by exploring a wider spectrum of experience and relationships. Before one can answer the question of a personal God, one has to ask whether the word personal is clear and whether the attribution of the term personal is not also a limitation. It may be that personal images are the best ones we have but even then they would only be images and they would only be the best, not the only, images.

The most basic religious experience of overwhelming power does not at first sight have much connection to the personal. However, neither does this power necessarily exclude a personal character. The evolution of religion in the West, both in Greek and Hebrew traditions, led to speaking of God in personal terms. Specific factors which led to this will be discussed later. Here I only point out that even if the movement toward the personal represents genuine progress, it does not occur without limitations and dangers. When the personal comes to be neat and defined, sufficient unto itself, then a distortion has occurred and the total context has been lost.

In recent Christian theology there was a turning away from the bizarre, the mystical and the cosmic toward the personal, the free and the historical. Emphasis on a personal god led to what Jung referred to as an "unbearably refined 'I-Thou' relationship to God."[57] For this reason studies like Otto's have not been

56. See John A. T. Robinson, *Honest to God* (Philadelphia, 1963), pp. 48–49; and more developed by the same author, *Exploration in God* (Stanford, 1967), pp. 142–161.
57. Quoted in Young, *op. cit.*, p. 118.

held in high favor. To a religious tradition centered on a "personal God revealed in Christ," the fascinating and frightening power of the holy seemed irrelevant if not incompatible. There is no denying strong differences here. In *Mysticism East and West,* Otto claimed that mysticism always conceives of God other than in relation between an I and Thou.[58] Without abandoning its tradition of speaking of God personally, the West might consider whether this is the only way and whether the use of a personal mode of speaking itself demands a nonpersonal language as well. At the least, Christians could be more hesitant about judging Eastern groups whose language moves back and forth between personal and non-personal images of God.[59]

For a more concrete and particular description of religious activity I would like to turn now to the work of Mircea Eliade. His descriptions and interpretations of religious symbols are extraordinarily helpful in understanding the problems of religious man and the range of answers to these problems. Eliade's writing is like a great symphony with a few simple, major themes running through a rich variety of detail.

Eliade placed himself in direct descendence from Otto's work. After describing Otto's investigation into the non-rational side of the religious act, Eliade writes: "We propose to present the phenomenon of the sacred in all its complexity, and not only insofar as it is *irrational.* What will concern us is not the relation between the rational and the nonrational elements of religion but the sacred in its entirety."[60] What he apparently means by

---

58. Rudolf Otto, *Mysticism East and West* (New York, 1970).

59. See: Wach, *op. cit.,* p. 83; Ewert Cousins, "The Trinity and World Religions," in *Journal of Ecumenical Studies VII* (1970), p. 481: "(The Christian) may not know his own mystery of the Trinity until he has opened himself to and responded in depth to the Trinitarian dimension of other traditions."

60. Mircea Eliade, *Sacred and Profane* (New York, 1961), p. 10; this work and his *Cosmos and History* (New York, 1959), are the most ready summaries of his work.

investigating the sacred in its entirety is that he will carefully examine the individual religious rites and symbols from all over the world. From this base he is in a position to elaborate a kind of "metaphysics" that religious activity implies. Embodied in religious rites and symbols is a world picture which is consistent on its own terms. This picture cannot be judged or dismissed until it is understood, and one should not quickly presume that he has grasped the logic of this world view.

We may note here that Eliade's work, like Otto's, has been exposed lately to criticism by some Christian theologians.[61] Eliade generally deals with primitive and ancient forms of religious expression. He investigates in copious detail the place of religion in pre-industrial civilizations. At the same time he uses the term *homo religiosus* in a way which implies that man is by nature a religious being. Thus, he refers to rituals and attitudes of the contemporary scene as manifestations of the fact that man is still a religious being. "To acquire a world of his own, he has desacralized the world in which his ancestors lived; but to do so he has been obliged to adopt the opposite of an earlier type of behavior, and that behavior is still emotionally present to him, in one form or another, ready to be reactualized in his deepest being."[62]

It should not be difficult to surmise what the objection of some theologians has been. As we have seen, the word religion had taken on a peculiarly negative meaning in Christian theology. Largely through the influence of Bonhoeffer, religion was viewed as an historical and temporary form of human expression which was now at an end.[63] If this were the primary meaning of religion, then *homo religiosus* would be a term applicable to men of primitive civilizations and perhaps to a small class of

61. For example, Kenneth Hamilton, "Homo Religiosus and Historical Faith," in *New Theology, no. 3,* ed., Martin Marty and Dean Peerman (New York, 1966), pp. 53–68.
62. Eliade, *Sacred and Profane,* p. 10.
63. Bonhoeffer, *op. cit.,* pp. 168–172.

unenlightened people today who will soon be extinct. Studies like those of Eliade would then be of interest to people curious about their ancestors but such study would throw little light on the truly modern man.

The recognition of negative elements in the word religion represents an important step, particularly when the admission is made by people who have been involved in religion. However, the attempt to suppress the word religion by making it incompatible with modernity has been a clear case of overkill. The attempt to save Christian faith by extricating it from religion has been disingenuous.

The positive elements built into religious activity must be considered before the rendering of any sweeping judgments. A quite different kind of judgment might then emerge. For example, Van der Leeuw writes that "the most probable derivation of the word is from *relegere*—to observe or pay attention; *homo religiosus,* therefore, is the antithesis to *homo negligens.*"[64] Obviously, Christian theologians who have joined faith and secularity in opposition to religion do not suppose that the opposite of *religiosus* is *negligens.* Van der Leeuw's point is not the final one but it is a valid one not lightly to be brushed aside.

The word religious has many nuances that some Christian theologians were not attentive to. This failure is caused in part by their abstracting the word from its actual historical development. The more basic reason for the misuse of the word religion is Christian theology's unwillingness to reconstruct the category of revelation. So long as it is presumed that there is a "Christian revelation" and that it is the true revelation, then the religions of the world are bound to have either negligible or negative value. Why laboriously plow through the religious rites of ancient people if one already knows the truth? Or, if one does pursue the subject and discovers that ancient men were interested in

64. Van der Leeuw, *op. cit.,* p. 50.

nature, law, fear, place and past, then are these religions not false compared to Christianity which talks about person, freedom, love, history and the future?

Before one renders such judgments, he should first understand how and why religious activity originates, and the ways men have embraced life in the past. It is possible, for example, that precisely because Christianity *talks* so much about person, freedom, etc., that it does not represent progress but is instead a desiccated verbal form of some more vital religious experience. The particular qualities of revelation as understood in the history of religion must be appreciated before any Christian claim to have something better. To Christians the non-Christian religions may seem to have little to say about revelation. The deficiency may lie with the Christian who wants to get more data. For a religious man the meaning of revelation is not discursive; it is expressed in the way he lives and the symbols in which he participates.

For the moment, therefore, we can say that *homo religiosus* is an open term. It is not necessarily incompatible with modernity. The movement from pre-modern into modern times has caused grave upheavals in all religious traditions. There is no going backward into a simpler era although it may be possible to go forward to something simpler. Many rituals and symbols have no doubt suffered mortal wounds. Deeply rooted human gestures do not come and go lightly but it is possible for some of them to die. It is also possible to have new forms arise not through being created *ex nihilo* by man but by being drawn from the depths of human life. These facts do not resolve the question of whether man is by nature religious, or, better expressed, whether religious is a word that can span both pre-modern and modern man. The question is not decided by debating what the word religious *really* means. We must examine the origin and intent of religious activity and the change that has occurred in contemporary ways of dealing with these problems.

197

We would then be in a better position to judge the effectiveness of using the word religious to describe contemporary man.

In Otto's perspective, as we have seen, the central problem of religious man is the confrontation with the frightening but fascinating "other." Eliade provides far more detail on how individual groups understand this problem and the meaning of religious symbols which emerges in the process. The great variety of myths and symbols indicate "man's deep dissatisfaction with his actual situation, with what is called the human condition. Man feels himself torn and separate. He often finds it difficult properly to explain to himself the nature of the separation, for sometimes he feels himself to be cut off from 'something' *powerful,* 'something' wholly *other* than himself and at other times from an indefinable, timeless 'state,' of which he has no precise memory, but which he does however remember in the depth of his being: a primordial state which he enjoyed before Time, before History. This separation has taken the form of a fissure, both in himself and in the World."[65] In this passage one can find most of the themes of Eliade's writing, and the one which is most dominant, viz., religious man's attitude toward time.

The human beings find themselves in the midst of temporal flux. Not only does nature around them change continuously but their own bodies are subject to a process of constant change. For the adult human being, change is not neutral; it involves decay, suffering and eventually death. The inexorable law which governs human existence seems to condemn every person without exception to non-existence. The activity of the religious man acts as a counter to this process and resists the conclusion that life is nothing but a prelude to death. The main way to deal with suffering and death is to deny that they really exist, that is, to deny that they are really real. There would be no suffering and death if time and change did not exist. Thus the means to do

65. Mircea Eliade, *The Two and the One* (New York, 1965), p. 122.

away with suffering and death is to deny that time has meaning. There is obviously some shade of reality to the ordinary flux of experience but this hold on reality is said to be so slight that time can be said to have no meaning.

The real and meaningful are to be found, therefore, in a permanent and unchanging realm called the sacred. Eliade's use of the word time in reference to the sacred can be a little misleading. The sacred, as a series of eternities, precedes time or is above time. The really real is found in eternal archetypes which are paradigmatic gestures fixed by the gods. Religious activity, which establishes contact with these eternal archetypes, represents a desperate clinging to reality.[66]

The religious rite is the most important datum to reflect upon in coming to understand the ancient world. Men did not speculate about the gods; they performed the rituals which the gods had handed down at the beginning of time. The narrative which accompanies such rites is called myth. So long as the myth remains an interpretation of the rite, it has a restricted and subsidiary role. If the religious life of a people disintegrates, myth is liable to expand and to include within itself numerous bizarre details. The rational element is not likely to improve myth but to corrupt it, that is, to change it into mythology.

Religious rites manifest an attitude of reverence for and acceptance of the nature in which man finds himself immersed. Trees, rivers, rocks and crops of the earth play key roles in man's attitude toward the gods. Probably no one simply identified trees with god but the woods are often considered to be sacred places for meeting the gods. The tree can be the medium of the revelatory relationship between god and the religious group. In this sense a tree or rock can have a "divine" quality, that is, it can be part of a divine hierophany.[67]

66. Eliade, *Cosmos and History*, p. 92.
67. Eliade, *Sacred and Profane*, p. 12: "A *sacred* stone remains a *stone;* apparently (or, more precisely, from the profane point of view), nothing

Because of this belief that nature is medium of the divine, religious man's attitude toward nature is a reverent one. It might have been supposed that since he sees no meaning to the flow of time he would rebuff nature or exploit the things of this world. But religious man does not try to negate time; he tries simply to escape from it. "He is living in the perpetual light of a past dream time which still enfolds him. He is at peace with the seasons and, through decreed ritual, even with the animals he hunts."[68] Thus, the ideal is to adjust to the cosmic rhythm so far as that is possible and then at specified moments to make contact with the realm of permanent archetypes. The cycle of the seasons dictates a large part of the framework for religious activity as does the struggle of life against death.

Each great event of the group's life can take on the character of this cosmic struggle against death. Marriage, birth and initiation are steps along the path to the realization of life. Agriculture, law, war and the establishment of a city are crucial factors in a people's life. For example, the development of agriculture is intimately related to religious expression. "The discovery of agriculture basically transforms not only primitive man's economy but also and especially his *economy of the sacred.* Other religious forces come into play—sexuality, fertility, the mythology of women and of the earth, and so on. Religious experience becomes more concrete, that is, more intimately connected with life. The great mother-goddesses and the strong gods or the spirits of fertility are markedly more dynamic and more accessible to men than was the Creator God."[69]

The new year's feast originally corresponded with the agri-

distinguishes it from all other stones. But for those to whom a stone reveals itself as sacred, its immediate reality is transmitted into a supernatural reality. In other words, for those who have a religious experience all nature is capable of revealing itself as cosmic sacrality. The cosmos in its entirety can become a hierophany."

68. Eiseley, *op. cit.,* p. 113.
69. Mircea Eliade, *Sacred and Profane,* p. 126.

cultural new year. The celebration of the new year has special significance. The greatest divine work is understood to be the creation of the world. Furthermore, man nostalgically desires the pure world that came from the hand of the creator. Thus, the new year rite is a ritual commemoration of the cosmogony. Intoxication as a way of forgetting the past and resolutions as a way of facing the future are both integral elements of this ancient religious ritual. New year's ritual is the most dramatic attempt to escape from the contamination of time and start over again.

Religion has from ancient times been associated with the establishing of a native place and a human settlement. The defense of one's city in war was a religious act: a re-enactment of the victory of the gods over the dragon of chaos. The sacred is connected to this world through a fixed point at the center of the world; there is a kind of umbilical cord which gives direction to everything else. The closer one's city is to the center of the world the more sacred it is. The temple was thought to be at the exact center of the world. It is possible to avoid the motion of a wheel by finding the exact center. At that point which is perfectly motionless, communication with the gods becomes possible. One common image has a rope at the center of the world and certain holy men can climb to heaven by means of this rope.[70]

The other way to escape the wheel of change is by getting outside of it, presumably through death. However, the biological fact of death does not carry a sure guarantee that the problem of change and decay is solved through dying. In fact, there is some evidence against this release. Death is from one point of view an escape from suffering but it is a journey into the unknown. It is also an experience which leaves the remaining members of the community bewildered and frightened. If all nature is taken as

70. See: Mircea Eliade's essay on "Ropes and Puppets" in *Two in One*, especially p. 167.

the model of understanding, then death seems to be part of a larger cycle of growth and decay. To the extent that man experiences brotherhood with non-human nature, he seems to participate in the cycle of birth and death. This fact cuts both ways. On the one hand, man's solidarity with nature means that death is not annihilation; *life* follows death. On the other hand, since man is part of the cycle, death is not of itself entrance into being; only *impure life* follows death.

Although death of itself seems neutral in value, it becomes in a human life the critical moment of gain or loss. For the individual it represents the conclusion of a movement toward greater or lesser life. If the person did well enough in this particular existence, it can be hoped that he totally escapes time and can rest in peace. For the society, death is a severe testing time to see whether the world holds together before the terror of this unknown. "Every human society is, in the last resort, men banded together in the face of death. The power of religion depends, in the last resort, upon the credibility of the banners it puts in the hands of men as they stand before death, or more accurately, as they walk, inevitably, toward it."[71]

As one might therefore expect, all societies develop a rather elaborate funeral ritual. Death lets loose instincts and impulses: to run away in horror, to abandon the village, to destroy the belongings of the dead man. The cohesion and solidarity of a people as well as the stability and continuity of civilization are threatened by death. "The ceremonial of death which ties the survivors to the body and rivets them to the place of death, the belief in the existence of the spirit, in its benevolent influences or malevolent intentions, in the duties of a series of commemorative or sacrificial ceremonies—in all this religion counteracts the centrifugal forces of fear, dismay, demoralization, and provides the most powerful means of re-integration of the group's shaken solidarity and the reestablishment of its morale. In short,

71. Berger, *Sacred Canopy*, p. 51.

religion here assures the victory of tradition and culture over the more negative response of thwarted instinct."[72]

3. CONTEMPORARY RELIGIOUS PHENOMENA

The preceding considerations about time and death lead to a few tentative conclusions about religious attitudes and rites. Religion throughout the centuries has had a conserving role in human society. The appropriate word in this context ought to be "conservative." Unfortunately, the word conservative has picked up political overtones that are not part of the attitude I wish to describe. As I will use the word the opposite of conservative is not liberal; the opposite is squandering, destructive or disorienting. We must carefully distinguish the two meanings that have become intertwined in the word conservative.

In the first place, the older and more logical meaning of conservative is a movement to preserve and stabilize. Human society is a precarious form that must be held together in the face of chaos. Religion has been one of the elements that has functioned as glue for society. Nature as a whole is a precarious balance which needs careful preservation. The "conservation" movement is a recovery of this first meaning of conservative although many conservationists seem confused on how to integrate nature and man.

The second meaning of conservative is more political and more recent. Since the French Revolution became installed as the prototype of change, the word conservative came to have the meaning of *status quo ante*. This attitude works from the premise that the ideal resides in the past and that change is all downhill. The conservative movement then becomes one of restoration, or if one cannot move backward, one can at least drag one's feet going forward.

72. Bronislaw Malinowski, *Magic, Science and Religion* (Garden City, 1954), p. 53.

The opposite of this political conservatism is assumed to be political liberalism. In this framework liberalism conceives of the ideal as being in the future and all change as running upward. The liberalism which attempts to program the future utopia is the counter image of a conservatism which tries by arguments to prove that the past was better. As has become clearer in recent decades, conservatism and liberalism are more closely related than they would like to believe. A typology of conservative versus liberal is no longer adequate as a description of the political scene; in fact, it is downright misleading. Yet, the terms continue to be used as the accepted political language because there is either an unwillingness to face the new situation or else an incapacity to understand it.

New positions may eventually crystallize around the words radical and revolutionary but the meaning of these words remains in flux. The etymologies of radical and revolution are sometimes appealed to but etymology will probably not determine how the words come to be used. Just as liberal and conservative came to their positions by attitudes toward previous movements, so a new set of terms has to arise from attitudes toward today's movements. What is confusing today is that conservatives, liberals, and radicals often accept the same basic model of historical change, that is, a linear model in which the present is a moment between past and future.

This brief excursion into the confusions of political language is not irrelevant to my interest in establishing the significance of religion. Religion has usually been a conservative force in the first sense of the word described above. It is doubtful that it can give up that role and it is doubtful that it should wish to give up that role. If people agree that nature and society are worth saving, then it is difficult to understand why the conserving role should not be an exalted one.

The reason, of course, why so many people would shy away from describing religion as conservative is because of the second meaning described above. Religion has often aligned itself with reactionary political forces on the mistaken assumption that to conserve means to resist change.

Some further points must be made here about the religious man's attitude toward time. It is often said that religious man looks backward to some ideal past for his revelation; that conception is not exactly true. Rather, he looks outside time or before time but the past does not interest him much. In ancient times men had little access to the past. A myth is a sketchy report of some critical happening which is not so much remembered as it is sedimented in the life of a people. Myths often embody something of past events but what is important and expressed in myth is a timeless truth about the gods and man.[73]

The basic religious movement is not a glorification of the past but a striving for permanence, not a going backward but a going toward God. This point must be stressed because of the mistaken impression that the primitive religious man strove to restore the past. The corresponding misunderstanding is that a sophisticated religious faith like Christianity must be centered on the future. The thesis put forward here is that religious man, to the extent he is religious, lives in the present. The present person subsumes the artifacts of the past and the seeds of the future but he discovers life in the only place it is: the present. A person attentive to the full experience of the present lives with constant change but this fact is compatible with the fact that a plumbing of the depths of the present leads to a state that seems timeless. This point of total togetherness is testified to by mystics of all ages. Mysticism is a temptation which can seduce attention away from aspects of life but it is probably no worse a temptation than the belief that change of any kind is the ideal, and that stability and permanence of any kind must be overthrown.

Religious man lives in the present. No one fully lives the

73. Mircea Eliade, *Cosmos and History*, p. 43.

205

intensity of the present but the present is where anyone who cares for life must be. The alternative to the human present is not the past or future. If one is not present one is absent; thus Van der Leeuw's contrast of *religiosus* and *negligens*. When one is absent from the human, one may be in the vicinity of other people but one is not with people. Such a person is cut off from mutual relations with non-human things and he is even a stranger to himself, located inside his own skin but not living in and with his bodiliness.

If one is consistently absent from the trees, the animals, one's neighbor and oneself, then one will cease to be religious. When one ceases to be religious one is likely to acquire a religion. A religion as a thing externally fitted to a person is almost by definition oriented to the past. As the vital religious life of a people falters, magic and mythology emerge. At this stage there is likely to be an expansion of details from a real or presumed past. Men of primitive times were vulnerable to an absorption into magic and mythology. Literate man gets protection from change because he is able to construct compartments of the mind. The ancients were constantly in danger of being overwhelmed by the forces of life. They therefore constructed dikes which could easily become magical and superstitious.[74]

The supposition that modern man has finally done away with magic and superstition is very questionable.[75] Magic takes many forms and it lives within the most "modern" society. It cannot be eliminated except to the extent that people are

74. Ong, *op. cit.*, p. 8.
75. See: Emmanuel Mounier, *Personalism* (London, 1952), p. 122; Carl Jung, *The Undiscovered Self* (Boston, 1957), p. 26: "Magic has above all a psychological effect whose importance should not be underestimated. The performance of a 'magical' action gives the person concerned a feeling of security which is absolutely essential for carrying out a decision, because a decision is inevitably somewhat one-sided and is therefore rightly felt to be a risk. Even a dictator thinks it necessary not only to accompany his acts of State with threats but to stage them with all manner of solemnities."

capable of facing the mysteriousness and unpredictability of life. Mystery and magic are opposed to one another. A mono-dimensional attitude which tries to reduce reality to a series of technical problems produces as a side effect some pseudo-religious and magical activity.

The religious traditions are evidence that the mystery of life cannot be dissolved. Anxiety before death cannot be cured, and more basically, is not a problem to be cured. The mysterious presence of evil in the world is not a technical or mechanical matter to be eliminated by better processing techniques. Evil, suffering and death can neither be cured nor ignored because "the skull will grin at the banquet" (William James). Men in earlier times coped with the mystery through religious rites which at least dealt with life and the great struggle of life against death. Life did not consist in piling up data to solve problems but of experiencing revelation that touched the depths of life. Concerning the key religious rite of initiation, Eliade writes: "Initiation usually comprises a threefold revelation: revelation of the sacred, of death, and of sexuality. The child knows nothing of these experiences; the initiate knows and assumes them, and incorporates them into his personality. We must add that if the novice dies to his infantile, profane, non-regenerate life to be reborn to a new, sanctified existence, he is also reborn to a mode of being that makes learning, *knowledge*, possible. The initiate is not only newborn or resuscitated; he is a man who *knows*, who has learned the mysteries, who has had revelations that are metaphysical in nature."[76]

The rites of expression used by ancient peoples may be un-usable today but their attitudes toward birth, sexuality, nature, time and death might still teach us something. We might find that people are still engaged in a quest for life and for a mean-ing of life. Religions have a tendency toward denial of the

76. Mircea Eliade, *Sacred and Profane*, p. 188.

world or parts of the world, but there are other forms of denial which accompany a non-religious attitude.[77] The question is not whether one accepts the world but whether one accepts it in its unexplored depths and unguessed possibilities. "If we accept the whole, shall we do so as if stunned into submission —as Carlyle would have us—'Gad! we'd better!'—or shall we do so with enthusiastic assent?"[78]

The difficulty in "accepting the universe" is the apparent meaninglessness of death. The quest for permanence continues in our day and with it the search for some kind of "immortality." One of the people who has investigated this phenomenon is Robert Jay Lifton. He has tried to show that men cannot live without belief in some symbolic immortality. If one way is blocked they will look to another, sometimes to caricatured forms of immortality. Lifton sees many people today turning to what he calls "experiential transcendence,"[79] a kind of desperate fling at a state outside time. This desperation can manifest itself in two ways that seem opposites, viz., dropping out from society or else revolutionary activism within society. Both actions are attempts at total and permanent commitment to an ideal which transcends the flux of time. The search for permanence is one that cannot lightly be dismissed as a peculiarity of ancient people. A breakthrough could occur if it were recognized that permanence and change are not

77. Dewey, *op. cit.*, p. 53, attacks militant atheism for its lack of "natural piety." "The ties binding man to nature that poets have always celebrated are passed over lightly. The attitude taken is often that of man living in an indifferent and hostile world and issuing blasts of defiance." The lack of appreciation of nature can come from the opposite direction of religion; Watts, *op. cit.*, p. 152: "The general trend of Indian thought was to fall into the very trap which it should have avoided: it confused the abstract world of *Maya* with the concrete world of nature, of direct experience, and then sought liberation from nature in terms of a state of consciousness bereft of all sense experience. It interpreted *Maya* as an illusion of the senses rather than of thought projecting itself through the senses."

78. James, *op. cit.*, p. 49.

79. Lifton, *Boundaries*, p. 26.

contradictories. What has been sought in the past and is still confusedly sought is a "permanent revolution."[80]

The forces which gave rise to religion in ancient times are still with us today. Most globally, this force can be called a search after meaning. The religious part of this search is not the meaning of one thing or another but the meaning of all. A fantastic increase of means to end production makes more acute the haunting question about the end of it all. What is the use of use? This question assumes practical importance for people who have harnessed great energy but have lost sense of the direction in which to move. The "secular age" which looks for meaning on earth rather than behind the clouds does not do away with the issue of ultimacy. The rightful appreciation of the beauties of this world and the urgent struggle to ameliorate the injustices of this world still leave the question: What is the point of it all? The question of ultimacy is not one of the data in experience; it is the total context in which particular meanings subsist.[81]

The context of meaning has undergone shifts for modern men. Some of the descriptions of Otto, Eliade or Van der Leeuw sound irrelevant because they seem to suppose an un-civilized man crouching before an incomprehensible world that he cannot cope with. The inexplicable "sacred" seems to have retreated with the advance of education and technology. This picture is a little deceiving, however. The realm of the sacred, which was identified with untouchable things outside man, has steadily diminished. This disappearance has been accompanied by the appearance elsewhere of mystery, that is,

80. *Ibid.*, pp. 97–98.
81. L. Gilkey, *Naming the Whirlwind,* p. 296: "The ultimate or uncon-ditioned element in experience is not so much the seen but the basis of seeing; not what is known as an object so much as the basis of knowing; not an object of value, but the ground of valuing; not the thing before us, but the source of things; not the particular meanings that generate our life in the world, but the ultimate context in which these meanings neces-sarily subsist."

a realm beyond control and comprehension. The religious question has shifted to the relation between persons and the relations which constitute each person. Thus, Huston Smith locates the sacred of contemporary experience in the unconscious, interpersonal relations and the edge of evolutionary development.[82]

Each person is called upon today to find the meaning of his own life. It is evident that he cannot find that meaning unaided. Ancient man went "outside" himself to make contact with the sacred. People today are more likely to find their aid in those relational structures which affirm life. To discover the meaning of life in relation, there has to be a "letting go," a taking one's feet off the bottom of the lake. Some highly rational people would see this move as an inhuman one. The religious traditions have always recognized that letting go of one's reason can be human and more. Reason is at the service of man and to immerse oneself in the ground of reason (which by definition is not rational) is a positive act which affirms man and his world.[83]

Two examples of things that escape rational explanation and thereby point beyond themselves are humor and love. Each of these phenomena provides both a starting point for inquiry and some indications about the quality of divine-human relationship. Humor is not a trivial matter, peripheral to the serious matters of the human race. The most profound understanding of human life is embodied in the light touch which fully appreciates every detail of the universe. "The man who plays after this fashion is one who is earnest about life, because he knows two things and holds them both together: he knows that his life has meaning and that his existence in creation is not the product of necessity."[84]

82. See Huston Smith, "Secularization and the Sacred: The Contemporary Scene," in *The Religious Situation*, ed., Donald Cutler (Boston, 1968), pp. 583–600.

83. Ernest Becker, *Angel in Armor* (New York, 1969), pp. 97, 130.

84. Rahner, *Man at Play*, p. 26; Neale, *op cit.*, p. 41.

210

The order which religion has discerned in the world is not a matter of causal sequence but a sense that being is trustworthy and will not play tricks. The divine humor which sets order to the universe is wry but not cruel. The religious man, even in the midst of great sorrow, is playful man who makes contact with the gods through celebration and artistry. Nietzsche wrote: "I would believe only in a god who could dance," expressing an insight that would have been obvious to ancient religious peoples but was foreign to Nietzsche's nineteenth-century contemporaries.[85] The sense of the divine and its relation to the human are best exemplified in the humor by which life is made bearable. "By laughing at the imprisonment of the human spirit, humor implies that this imprisonment is not final but will be overcome, and by this implication provides yet another signal of transcendence—in this instance in the form of an intimation of redemption."[86]

Another example of the irrepressible religious quality of life is the experience of human love. It also serves both to indicate the existence of the divine and some of the characteristics of a divine pole to experience.

Love is a much abused word in the English language; it covers a multitude of sins in a way that the New Testament did not mean. Much of what passes for love is a parody of the ideal; much of what is supposed to be love is eventually exposed as a fake.[87] Nonetheless, from a religious point of view even the failures are significant. Human love seems to promise more than it can deliver. But the existence of an ideal of love and the fleeting realization of genuine love are sufficient to prove that life is made known through love.

The nature of the divine in revelation is intimated by the experience of love. This is true because love conveys a sense

85. See: Sam Keen, "Manifesto for a Dionysian Theology," in *New Theology, no. 7*, eds., Martin Marty and Dean Peerman (New York, 1970), p. 93.
86. Berger, *Rumor of Angels*, p. 88.
87. See: Greer, *op. cit.*, pp. 135–142.

211

of mutuality, individuality and immortality. Each of these three can bear discussion. Mutuality is a quality that has become better understood in recent times. The second quality, individuality, follows from the first and needs further development. If both of them were better understood, it would help to throw light on the third issue, immortality. The question of immortality will always be clouded in obscurity but it should be possible to show that immortality is not an outdated issue unworthy of discussion.

By mutuality I refer to the fact that love is a bilateral relationship in which each member both gives and receives. Love can only be counterfeit if one person dominates and controls the other. Even if one party's intention is benevolent, a relationship which does not go in both directions turns one party into an object and the other party into a possessor of objects. Mutuality does not mean equality; as a matter of fact, in practice mutuality probably excludes equality. If two persons contribute their own unique qualities to a continuing relationship, the notion of equality is not central. Equality has a reductionist character built into it. In some areas of life equality is a valid and necessary concern. For example, people ought to have equal protection of basic human rights, that is, there ought to be no discrimination of people before the law. However, in nearly all other aspects of life there should be rich diversity and much inequality. The human relationship of love, therefore, works not on the basis of equality but by the mutual sharing of life. Each person makes a significant contribution to the relationship and is in turn supported by it. Who makes what contribution is a question that seldom arises in practice.

It is obvious that the relationship of love implies continuous change on the part of each person. Some *kinds* of change are excluded; for example, a fickleness of taste that at one moment goes one way and in the next moment goes in the opposite direction. Thus, one must distinguish two kinds of consistency:

212

one is of value in relationships, one is not. A mechanical same-
ness or a programed connection between concepts is not
especially human. On the other hand, a consistency of fidelity to
another person is one of the highest activities of the person.
The attitude of fidelity supposes not that the other person
has not changed nor that one can be faithful *despite* change.
Rather, fidelity is a positive attitude toward change: an affirma
tion of the person to become whatever person he or she is
called to be.

The problem of being and change is not thereby resolved but
it takes on a different outlook when one takes the relationship
of love as the primary model of understanding. Change is not
incompatible with stability and permanence. Immutability cannot be held up as the ideal since our richest experience is one
of relationship.[88] A feeling of permanence can arise in relationships but not from a negation of movement. Permanence
arises at the point where the rhythm of change is synchronized
with the person and where no violent wrenching disturbs the
free flow of experience.

The point I am making here is a simple one but one that
the main religious traditions have not come to terms with. The
religious man of ancient times, overwhelmed by the terrors of
the environment, could conceive the divine only in the form
of immutable archetypes. For an isolated individual or for a
group under threat, goodness appears in the form of protection
against change. The main lines of both Eastern and Western
traditions have dealt with this problem but they have not
adequately met it.

The East has not emerged from a collective form of civilization. Each individual is not distinct and unique. The mutuality
of persons could not become the model of religious understanding. In Hinduism the *ātman* as principle of individual
consciousness can merge with *brahman* as super-personal ground

88. See: Fontinell, *op. cit.,* p. 196.

of the cosmos. Such an understanding is an all-embracing movement. What does not happen is an understanding of the divine
through the model of a partnership or a small group. The
Hindu can understand "the flight of the alone to the alone"
and he can also understand the divine in a given social structure
which is determined by custom. What is foreign to him is the
establishing of new communities in which persons freely attach
themselves to a group to create in the interchange what has
not existed before.[89]

In western tradition the sense of relation to the divine did
arise from the experience of a small group. The implications
of this profound experience were always richer than the instru-
ments of understanding used upon the experience. Medieval
Christianity faltered on the question of change. It gave priority to a strain of Greek thought which can be traced to
primitive religion, that is, the belief that non-change is good
and change is bad. Theology had to engage in some subtle
maneuvering to reconcile that principle with the biblical tradition.

At the beginning of modern times Martin Luther made a
valiant effort to restore the sense of a living God. Much of
Christian theology since the Reformation has unfortunately
perpetuated the alternatives of the late middle ages. Thus, we
have discussions of Greek and Hebrew mentalities. Worse still
is the opposition between philosophy and the "word of God."
The vital question of how the divine is experienced today
was left to the so-called non-believers. Working from the
premise that an unchangeable God has left us a revealed
message, theology could not avoid coming up with a dead
god whether the message was stated in Greek or Hebrew.

The other road open in the West for those who wanted a
living, breathing God was to reduce God to the image of a
lover. Religion has had an interpersonal side in Christianity

89. See: Neill, *op. cit.*, p. 95.

214

built around a Jesus piety. Unfortunately, this attitude easily led into a sentimental romanticism in which God could function as the hoped for prince charming. The Jewish and Christian bibles had almost never spoken of "loving God" as if he were one more neighbor to which one might give some affection.

My reference to the love relationship as a key to understanding the divine must be distinguished from this tendency. I did not say that the basic religious experience is one of loving God. In fact, it is difficult to see what the words "love God" can mean. Perhaps after one has lived with human love long enough one can glimpse how the word applies to the divine. After ninety years' experience St. John presumably knew what he was summarizing with the word love. However, it may be misleading to put the word into the mouths of people who do not know what it means to experience the divine. "First," wrote Rilke, "you must find God somewhere, experience him as infinitely, prodigiously, stupendously present—then whether it be fear or astonishment or breathlessness, whether it be in the end Love with which you comprehend him, it hardly matters at all."[90]

The love of other human beings is one of, if not the best, models for understanding the divine pole of experience. Intrinsic to love is exchange, that is, mutual change. Relationship to God cannot exclude this factor. "If God permits us every privilege, but not that of enriching his life by contributing the unique quality of our experience to the more inclusive quality of his, by virtue of his sympathetic interest in us, then he does less for us than the poorest of human creatures. What we ask above all is the chance to contribute to the being of others."[91]

This fact does not imply that God is an equal partner, a

90. Quoted in Marcel, *Homo Viator*, p. 222.

91. Hartshorne, *op. cit.*, p. 55; see also Max Scheler, *Man's Place in Nature* (New York, 1961), pp. 94–95.

mere co-worker of man's. There is a power at work in the universe before which man is puny and helpless. The supposition that man is king of the universe is ridiculous in the face of the evidence. The crucial question is the nature of the force that envelops the human. Is it a unilateral power which men can placate or escape for a while but a power which eventually overcomes and destroys the human? Or, is it possible that this power is the most related of all, working toward a harmonization that sustains individual freedom? In this latter case, "he is the poet of the world, with tender patience leading it by his vision of truth, beauty, and goodness."[92]

The above comments on mutuality lead directly into the second quality connected to love: individuality. If love were used as the main model of understanding, then individuality and freedom would be less of a problem. They would remain mysterious but they would not be denied as impossible or disregarded as insignificant. Genuine mutuality affirms the right of the other to be and to choose. Relationship does not minimize the individual partners in relation; on the contrary, it sustains and cultivates the individuality of each person. Love differentiates as it unites. A person who loves influences the other by awakening in him possibilities he had been unaware of. One person provides another with a ground of confidence, that is, with the feeling that it is all right to choose and that there is more than one right way to follow.[93]

The religious traditions could have avoided much misunderstanding if they had seriously considered this individualizing process. Much of nineteenth-century theology operated on the premise that "individuality is sin." The greatness and absoluteness of the divine seemed to require the reduction of everything else. This was a myopic vision projected by men who

92. Alfred North Whitehead, *Process and Reality* (New York, 1969), p. 408.
93. Lynch, *Images of Hope,* p. 149.

seem not to have had experience of mutual relationships. The lack of individuality in ancient times is understandable but once the process of individuation had occurred there was no going back. People who have experienced the full force of individuality can never believe that it is simply bad and that mass collectivity is preferable. Individuality is often distorted and misdirected; "individualism" is the bane of human institutions. Nevertheless, the only solution to the aberration is to situate the individual in relationships that are both supportive and corrective. Opposing egoism to altruism and then preaching altruism is a disastrous policy. The policy cannot ultimately work and even to the extent it does work it is illusory and unhealthful.[94]

The language which stresses selflessness, self-sacrifice and freedom from self has a dangerously misleading side to it. The reason for the need to be freed from a false, isolated self is so that one can affirm a true, related self. Bugental can write that "to be freed of the *Self* would be to meet our lives with 'new innocence' (Maslow), to choose in terms of the intrinsic properties of the alternatives, to enter into dialogue with another person without pretense and with genuine contact with him."[95] Bugental, in citing Maslow within this passage, obviously sees no contradiction between Maslow's writing on "self-realization" and Bugental's own chapter called "emancipation from the Self." Underneath the apparent opposition of aim, the two authors do converge on the concept of self.

The ambiguity around the word self is not the result of carelessness in modern psychology. Since earliest times, the religious traditions have sensed the two-sidedness of the issue. The paradox of self is summed up by the saying: he that loses his life will save it. Westerners often see Eastern religion as

94. See: Frankl, *Will to Meaning*, p. 97; see also: John Dewey, *Individualism Old and New* (New York, 1962), p. 143.
95. Bugental, *op. cit.*, p. 323.

a denial of the individual and an absorption of everything into a pantheistic absolute. Much of the imagery does point in that direction. However, there is a whole other way of looking at the situation: yoga is a method of purifying the self through freeing the individual from illusion. Whether the last step in the process is the elimination of self or the fulfillment of self is perhaps not answerable in our language. The language which mystics have used has usually been in the direction of eliminating the self. They are led this way by the force of what they are trying to convey and by the limitations of ordinary speech. Meister Eckhardt wrote: "If therefore I am changed into God and he makes me one with himself, then, by the living God there is no distinction between us.... Some people imagine that they are going to see God, that they are going to see God as if he were standing yonder, and they here, but it is not to be so. God and I: we are one. By knowing God I take him to myself. By loving God I penetrate him."[96] In this passage the strongest possible affirmation is made: there is no distinction between God and man. Nonetheless, in the last two sentences, at least grammatically, there remains a difference. God has not wholly swallowed the I.

The above passage comes from Western tradition but it is closer in spirit to the East. The apparent denial of the self in mysticism is much more characteristic of East than West. In Western tradition a negation of self-hood is usually the result not of mystic flights but of asceticism. Religion in the West has often been centered on the perfection of the individual. Within a complicated system of piety, morality and asceticism, God seemed to be the desired object and the supplier of the means. Even this kind of mechanical religion could not avoid the dialectic of affirming/negating the self. Here it was not

96. Quoted in Erich Fromm, *Art of Loving* (New York, 1956), p. 68; for Eckhart's ideas on creator and creature, see: Otto, *Mysticism East and West,* pp. 105–115.

the false, isolated self that was negated for the sake of the "all" (including the true, relational self). Instead, almost the reverse was the case. The empirical self related to the world was denied in favor of an inner self (or soul) that was to be saved by God. At its best such religion could bring out a peaceful, contemplative side to life. At its worst it was a masochism which left the world unattended.

The attitude toward the individual self is a crucial issue on which East and West do differ. Each tradition has a lot to learn from the other. A great advance would be signaled if people would see that the individual and the all are not incompatible. More positively stated, individuality is a good, but precisely insofar as it is in relation to the all. The Eastern sense of contemplating the whole is an attitude that has been sorely lacking in the West. What the West did have was a sense of the unique, irreplaceable value of each person. Unfortunately, the affirmation of the self has never been worked out in cooperation with all of the other: self has opposed self, nation has fought nation, manhood has dominated nature.[97] Yet, the irreducible value of the individual person survives such distortions.

If religious analysis were attendant to the relationship of love and if revelation were grounded in a community experience, then the place of the individual would become clear.[98]

97. Ernest Becker, *Beyond Alienation* (New York, 1967), p. 206: "The whole history of religion testifies to the tragedy: Men band together to support each other's meanings, but they band together against groups of other men; they try for freedom in opposition to tyranny, and so they themselves tyrannize. . . . Freedom itself becomes fetishized, and love itself feeds on a scapegoat. . . . But men must continue to try for God as the pinnacle of meaning for a society of free and equal men." With reference to the last sentence of Becker's see: Robert Johann, *The Pragmatic Meaning of God* (Milwaukee, 1966), pp. 40–66.

98. See: Joseph Sittler, *The Structure of Christian Ethics* (Baton Rouge, 1958), p. 13: "If God is sought in order to integrate the personality, the actual God is not God but the integrated personality, and when men are urged to renovate their religious values in order that the Republic may be

The person, as initiator of free and intelligent activity which reaches out to all, is not in opposition to the whole. Consequently, the principle of individualization does not have to be denied to exalt the divine. At the same time, the self as relational and active does not exclude a contemplative interiority. A. N. Whitehead once defined religion as what a man does with his solitariness.[99] The definition is not complete but it touches upon an essential component, an inner side to relational activity. As one is immersed in the relations of the universe the sense of interiority increases. The alternatives therefore are either an illusion of self propped up by obsessive activity and alienated loneliness or else a self that engages the world in intense, organic activity which includes an interior realization that everything is a gift including the self.

The last note on the significance of love as the model of understanding is the sense of immortality. The question of immortality emerges from individuality as a positive value. The quest for meaning through the experience of love is the demand for something permanent, that is, for a lasting value. The affirmation of the individual as unmistakably valuable asserts that love is stronger than death. If love is real, then the apparent dissolution of every individual cannot be the last word.

The first thing to be noted is that the word *immortality* is not well suited to this discussion. The biological organism, which each person experiences as his own, does die. Nothing is more obvious than the fact that men and women are mortal. Arguments for immortality start from a hopeless position posed against all of the evidence. The word immortality came to prominence not in reference to men and women but in con-

more firmly glued together, this covert idolatry reaches a peculiarly pernicious and untruthful pitch. There is a relation between a people who are blessed because their God is the Lord, but one does not find it recorded that God the Lord consents to be compounded into political glue."

99. Whitehead, *Religion in the Making,* p. 19.

nection with the soul. Until recently great stock was placed in arguments which purported to show the immortality of the soul. Roman Catholic tradition had held tenaciously to this element of Aristotelian-Thomistic philosophy. The belief in an immortal soul is probably still widespread among Catholics but vast numbers of Catholics find it increasingly difficult to maintain this belief. Protestant tradition did not rest its case on a particular philosophical doctrine of an immortal soul but some remnant of this philosophy was never absent. Protestants did not have the elaborate system of help for the "souls of the faithful departed" but there was hope for the soul resting in eternal peace.

The underpinning for this whole belief in immortality grew perilously thin in modern times. Many Catholics and Protestants welcomed new scriptural studies which provided a new basis of belief. The "resurrection of the body" which had been peripheral in Christian belief was invigorated by the biblical movement. A new freedom seemed to be provided by the fact that the guarantee of immortality was not philosophy but the words of the New Testament and the example of Jesus.[100] Shaky foundations in Greek philosophy were to be replaced by confidence in the "word of God." If one can believe that the bible is the word of God, the assurance would indeed run high. However, that is just what the problem is. The string connecting human experience and the bible as God's word is not as sturdy as biblical scholars would like to think.

The presumption that the alternatives are the Greek concept of immortal soul and the Hebrew concept of resurrected body is what must be challenged. Neither immortal nor resurrected, neither body nor soul, are the right terms to begin discussion. Many people can no longer live with belief in an immortal

100. For example, see: Oscar Cullmann, "Immortality of the Soul or Resurrection of the Dead?" in *Immortality and Resurrection*, ed., Krister Stendahl (New York, Macmillan, 1965), pp. 9–53.

soul and they are not likely to find more compelling a doctrine about resurrection. However, this fact does not mean, as some theologians suggest by their silence, that the whole issue is a naive and irrelevant concern. The peculiarly inadequate language in which discussion is carried on cannot be corrected by changing a few words. The words reflect a wrong starting place and a narrow breadth of experience. I cannot propose an entirely new terminology. What I can suggest is where the right starting point is from which would eventually issue a new language.

This starting point, I have indicated, is the personal, relational, social and practical experience of people today. The human person examined in relationship is found to be in quest of a wholeness that would include a personal, creative center and an all-embracing other. The human being in relation to others experiences an intimation that the end of his search is not an intrinsic impossibility. As experience is plumbed in all its depth there emerges a conviction that being is better than non-being, that life is more real than non-life and that human kind with a growing individuality is not an alien, temporary intrusion but a true and genuine value that affirms the world. A study of human freedom, for example, can lead to the conclusion that the person is not a passing phenomenon. In a study of freedom which does get to this depth, Karl Rahner writes: "Freedom is not the capacity of being always able to do the opposite, of infinite revision. It is the capacity to do something for good and all, the capacity to do something which is valid forever precisely because it is done in freedom. Freedom is the capacity for the eternal. Natural processes can always be revised again and altered; this is why they are indifferent. The result of freedom is the true necessity which remains forever."[101] One could challenge Rahner's use of the word eternal here, and, even more so, his opposition of free and natural processes. But his thesis that freedom is the ca-

101. Rahner, *"Theology of Freedom,"* p. 211.

222

pacity to affirm forever strikes deep into the roots of human experience. Lovers go immediately into the language of forever and this fact cannot be dismissed as accident or illusion. Love affirms in the face of death that we shall live forever. Where men and women deny that death is final it is almost certainly based upon the experience that the reality of love demands that the loved one cannot cease.

Religious traditions have constantly expressed in varying degrees of mythical elaboration this intimation of a life beyond life. Religion has always been the refusal to accept the universal death sentence.[102] Any of the higher religions, including Christianity, ought to express themselves in reference to this drive of all people. The question which a religion can never decide in detail is the nature of individual survival vis-à-vis the whole. But that the whole and the personal are permanent values is the basic experience which religions ought to sustain and cultivate. In the following chapter I will return to the particular contribution of Christian tradition.

The material in the preceding part of this chapter gives an indication of what is appearing in the religious life of mankind. People who declared that religious issues are no longer relevant and that God is dead have not proved to be the far-sighted visionaries. It is conceivable that some long-standing religious institutions are at an end. But a person has to carefully distinguish the particular institutions he has grown up in from the vast sweep of human history which surrounds us all. Human history as a whole does not seem to move toward

102. See: Teilhard de Chardin, *Christianity and Evolution*, pp. 109–111; see also Alexander Skutch, *The Golden Core of Religion* (New York, 1971), p. 171: "Of all human aspirations, that for immortal life has been the most widespread, persistent, and intensely cherished. There have been religions that recognized no God, but none which taught that the soul which perishes with the body has ever won a wide following or endured for long. ... The whole purpose of religion can be summarized in one sentence: To prepare us for eternal life; to teach us to live as though the best and most intimate part of ourselves will endure for ever."

the elimination of the religious. "The modern world is as alive with religious possibility as any epoch in human history. It is no longer possible to divide mankind into believers and non-believers. All believe something, and the lukewarm and those of little faith are to be found inside as well as outside the churches. The spirit bloweth where it listeth and men of passionate integrity are found in strange places. If we have outgrown the ideas of mission, we have probably also to outgrow the idea of dialogue, as though separated human groups must talk across a chasm."[103]

A religion of the future has to presume that a unity already exists. The unity is not one to be created as a kind of "esperanto religion" in which elements of existing religions would be pieced together.[104] A construction made up of abstractions by a scholarly elite will never satisfy the religious life of mankind. The notion of a single, universal religion which avoids all conflicts is a tempting vision but religion has to grow organically out of peoples' lives.

The unity which already does exist does not yet have a unified expression. Perhaps a United Nations flag is all that can be mustered for the moment. There is some movement to break down barriers between people and the individual religious traditions must be understood within this process. The religions could contribute to the unification but they have to do so on their own terms. "The price of existence must be paid," wrote W. E. Hocking; "we shall not arrive at the world faith by omitting the particulars."[105] It is a common failing of the intellectual class that they disregard the concrete symbols in which a religion embodies itself. Answers to religious questions cannot

103. Bellah, *op. cit.*, p. 228; see also: Kenneth Boulding, *The Meaning of the Twentieth Century* (New York, 1964), p. 155.

104. See H. Robert Schlette, *Toward a Theology of Religions* (New York, 1966), pp. 111–112.

105. Quoted in E. L. Allen, *Christianity among the Religions* (London, 1960), p. 145.

usually be said but they can be expressed in the rich imagery and particular character of a culture.

A comparative study of religion has the purpose not of abstracting truth from falsity but of providing a perspective of understanding for each religious tradition. Some religious groups consider such study a breeding ground of indifference or a temptation against faith. What is more likely to be the case is that the study of another person's religion will confirm one in a greater appreciation of one's own. In any case, we are arriving at that point in history where a person to be Muslim, Christian or Buddhist must intelligently relate it to the other religious and non-religious options of his society.[106]

Great differences and misunderstandings still infect the relationships between these various traditions. The religious differences have always been intertwined with the political and cultural differences. Differences between East and West remain severe. No successful ecumenical movement can occur while the political scene remains one of terrible conflict. Nonetheless, a growing religious understanding might be one way of easing political and cultural conflict. There have been some beginning steps here with the influx of Eastern forms of religion into the West. The "new religions" often take a bizarre form and are still only the taste of a small minority. Their direct and indirect effects, however, cannot be discounted.[107] The study and practice of Eastern religions is a live issue in universities and among people in centers of cultural diversity like San Francisco and New York.

The growth of interest in Eastern religions stems from the realization that Western knowledge is incomplete and that

106. See: Ninian Smart, *The Religious Experience of Mankind* (New York, 1969), 683; also Joseph Campbell, *The Masks of God* (New York, 1970), p. 33.
107. See: Jacob Needleman, *The New Religions* (Garden City, 1970); for the growth of new "spiritual communities," see: Robert Houriet, *Getting Back Together* (New York, 1971), pp. 329–378.

Western churches are a replica of this limited form of knowledge rather than the complement of this form. Western religions, besides incorporating the scientific element, have to discover an intuitive and mystical side which is not in contradiction to science. F. S. C. Northrop called the difference between East and West the split of the theoretic and the aesthetic. The difference is not intellect versus feeling, activity versus contemplation or this worldly versus other worldly. Instead, the West has developed one form of knowing which is theoretical abstraction, highly efficient in practice; the East has developed another form of knowing which is an immediate, artistic, ineffable immersion in experience. Eastern mysticism is the opposite of an abstract and isolated speculation; it is a deep feeling for what is immediately apprehended in experience.[108]

The basic differences between East and West are not irreconcilable. The complementary religious attitudes should be demonstrating the possibility and the need for cultural cooperation. Unless the science and technology of the West can be used to improve conditions of the East, then the aesthetic appreciation of life will not be available to the great masses of population and may eventually be strangled for all. In contrast, unless the aesthetic attitude of the East humanizes the technology of the West, then Western culture may act as a cancerous growth on the body of mankind.[109]

108. See: Northrop, *op. cit.*, p. 304; D. T. Suzuki, *An Introduction to Zen Buddhism* (New York, 1964), p. 35.
109. See: Tagore, *op. cit.*, p. 177; also: Northrop, *op. cit.*, p. 463: "There will be no religion nor culture which adequately meets the spiritual as well as the intellectual needs of men until the traditional Western theism, after being reformed to bring it abreast of contemporary knowledge of the theoretic component in things upon which it rests, is also supplemented with the primitive traditional Oriental religion of intuition and contemplation with its cultivation of the aesthetic component. And before this is possible there must be an art in the West, like that of the Orient, but our own, in which the female aesthetic intuitive principle in things speaks in its purity, conveying itself for its own sake. Only if such an art is created can the West break itself of the habit of regarding feelings

The reconciliation of religious traditions is not a matter for scholars poking around in ancient documents. Living religious communities must come together to experience the religious life of others. Once we accept the fact that there is one universal revelation which is the context of continuing and diverse interpretations today, a situation of tolerance and ecumenical understanding is already established.

Nearly every religious tradition has sacred scriptures which have been preserved from ancient times. Such writings are an invaluable source of inspiration and illumination for lives today. Nothing I have said here is in the direction of denigrating these documents. Nevertheless, I insist in the strongest possible way that the word revelation must be carefully distinguished from any ancient writing. There is some tendency to do that but there has to be a clean break with a traditional use of the word revelation as a synonym for sacred scriptures. A decision is needed to use the word revelation to refer primarily to the worldwide religious experience of living people.

I shall come back later to the Christian practice of referring to the bible as revelation but the problem is larger than that. There is a common misunderstanding of the origin and transmission of all religions. The identification of revelation with ancient documents epitomizes the failure at understanding religion. The misunderstanding is pinpointed in this passage from Maslow: "The very beginning, the intrinsic core, the essence, the universal nucleus of every known high religion (unless Confucianism is also called a religion) has been the private, lonely, personal illumination, revelation, or ecstasy of some acutely sensitive prophet or seer. The high religions call themselves revealed religions and each of them tends to rest its validity, its function, and its right to exist on the codification

---

and emotions and the immediately given portion of man's nature and the nature of all things as mere superficial appearance, or mere symbol of the theoretic component beyond."

and the communication of this original mystic experience or revelation from the lonely prophet to the masses of human beings in general."[110] It is possible to read the history of religion this way but, as Maslow himself gradually came to sense, it is a disastrously false reading. To the extent that a religious tradition bases its validity on the codification of a revelation to an ancient prophet, it is no longer a living religion but an archeological curiosity.

A prophet does not tell people revelations; instead, he awakens the revelatory character of their own lives. Revelation is not what prophets have, it is what communities experience. Far from being isolated from the community, the prophet is the one most deeply in touch with the roots of the community's life. Like the artist he will not conveniently fit into the ordinary framework of the community. He will be strongly opposed by part of the community. This is the test of true prophets who persist in trying to awaken the whole community to its undreamt possibilities. The only final test of the prophet is whether he does eventually succeed, that is, whether his words and actions resonate in the experience of mankind.[111]

The widespread presumption that religion is founded on revelation to lonely prophets is bound to lead to narrowness and intolerance. Neither faith, nor religion, nor revelation can be communicated to the masses by preachers of religion. What the masses need is a realization that they are all prophets who must speak their convictions with passion and must test their wisdom in the community. What they could use for help is neither imperialism nor condescension but a helping hand. They can come to discern the meaning of their own lives with interpretive help from the religious traditions.

It seems certain that if Budda, Jeremiah or Jesus were alive today they would not be saying: Exegete these ancient

110 Maslow, *Religions, Values and Peak-Experiences*, p. 19.
111. See: Tagore, *op. cit.*, p. 139.

texts and you will know the truth. More likely they would be saying: Look what is happening. Don't trust my pronouncements but listen to what your flesh and blood whisper. It is ecstatically attractive and agonizingly fearful but do not pull away. You are not alone; nature including human kind envelop you. And the one who sent me still lives in the body of man.

Chapter Four : Jewish and Christian Experience

1. A Concrete Embodiment

THE discussion of religious concepts in the preceding chapter is endangered by the tendency toward abstraction and generality. Religions have never existed as theoretical constructs about the gods but as ways of living with the gods. An intellectual elite speculating on divinity can produce philosophy but not a religion. The religious life of a people lives in concretely embodied form. At first sight, this concreteness seems to destroy the universal truth value of a religion. If it is true of all human life that one must pay the price of existence, it is especially true of the religious aspects of life. "Where people eat and drink, and even where they worship," said Nietzsche, "it usually stinks."[1]

The above principle is a difficult one for many people to accept. The principle has not been accepted as a basis for discussion about religion. Otherwise, the first question would not concern whether one has the "true religion."[2] A person's religious life is surely not separate from his search for truth. To share in the religious life of a community one must believe there is some truth or some truths in it. But religions do not originate because men think they are true. In the intricate web of action and expression the issue of whether the whole complex is true cannot really be raised. The refusal to raise

1. Nietzsche, *op. cit.,* p. 36.
2. See: Wilfred Cantwell Smith, "Can Religions Be True or False?" in *Questions of Religious Truth* (New York, 1967), pp. 65–95.

the question of whether a religion is true is not indicative of a religious indifferentism. Indeed, the emphasis on a religion being true is likely to emerge as a religious life is in decline.

This chapter is an investigation of some pertinent strains of Jewish and Christian religious life. This material is not an apology for Judaism and Christianity, as if the previous chapters have set up the problem for which this chapter will supply the answer. Judaism and Christianity fail to be the answer not because they are false answers but because there is no one answer. Neither Judaism nor Christianity is the answer because there are innumerable answers to many different questions, some of which have yet to be asked.

With some combination of fate and choice, a person takes up a life as Jew, Christian, Moslem or Hindu. Living within one of the world's faiths can be a blinding experience which narrows vision and produces intolerance. However, living in the midst of a religion and presuming one is beyond it because one has consciously forgot it also has its illusory side. Putting aside Christian dogma and announcing the end of the Christian era may not be a sufficient way to get out from under the repressive aspects of the Christian past. A person brought up in a milieu inundated with one religious tradition cannot easily throw off that religion and take on another. American Protestants do not suddenly become Zen Buddhists no matter how disillusioned they may be with Protestantism and how attractive Zen Buddhism may appear. Religiously as well as culturally a person has to grow into new forms of life according to an organic pattern of development. The process can be telescoped to some extent and a "conversion" may appear with dramatic suddenness. Nevertheless, one cannot adopt a religion as if one were buying a suit of clothes or working out a mathematical puzzle.

The realization that individuals cannot easily be converted from one religion to another has emerged among Christian missionaries in recent decades. Of course, it was always recognized that converting the pagan to Christianity is a difficult job, but something more than that is meant here. Many missionaries came to see that the attempt to convert individual non-Christians is itself undesirable. The supposed successes were very often people who, having been cut off from their own historical roots, acquired the facade but not the substance of a new religion. The result very often was an unhealthy syncretism which did not seem to improve either the religious or non-religious aspects of a community's life.

The missionary experience had a dramatic effect on the theology of the Christian church. If it did not provide a new theology it did much to stop the old one. Particularly in Roman Catholicism the missionary experience had a major part in turning the tide of Vatican II. The missionaries had experience on their side which was not as impressive-looking as doctrinal elaborations but in the long run counted more heavily. Seminary professors could continue teaching that the "ordinary way of salvation is the church" but such words did not even hold up as a debatable proposition in the situation of radical pluralism.

The triumph of the missionaries, however, undercut the role of the missionary. Missionaries who had gone out into the fields to "win souls for Christ" had no alternate rationale for being missionaries when the old theology collapsed. Many theologians contend that the missionary, as potential leader in the international struggle against oppression, has a better reason for existence than ever before. Such a total shift of viewpoint, however, would require a long period of assimilation and implementation. What seems to have happened to many Christian missionaries is that they have been caught in a personal and ecclesiastical time lag. One cannot live for long with a viewpoint that is seriously at odds with the institution one is in. I shall return to the question of church structure at the end of this chapter.

For the present I wish to draw from the above discussion these two conclusions:

232

1) The concept of the one true church has not been disproved in theory and is still given lip service in practice. Nonetheless, where this belief is tested in experience, even by the most dedicated members of the church, it evaporates. If the church were to be consistent in its supposed belief that Christ-church-sacraments are desirable or even necessary, then it would have to increase its pressure in proportion to the opening of the world since the middle ages. Any movement in that direction, however, would be repugnant to most Christians, including the most dedicated Christians.

2) It is not easy to change one's religious affiliation. From the standpoint of Christianity this fact works both ways. If individuals joining the church does not make much sense, neither does individuals leaving it. An individual by reason of an extraordinary set of circumstances might be better for leaving but this is not generally the way that the religious life of mankind is changing. A person can change his residence or employment with relative ease; he can also change his political party. But changing one's religion is another kind of challenge.

In religious change a person has to begin from wherever he is, something that itself takes a long time to discover. From there he has to grow slowly toward a new alternative. Becoming an atheist, for example, is a long road of displacement and disestablishment. In the other direction, having a religion which transcends all sectarian squabbling is also not immediately available. It is conceivable that there could be a worldwide religion which would be better than any existing religion. But the differences between Christianity and Hinduism will not be overcome by abstracting the things they agree upon and leaving behind the things on which they are in disagreement. As people interact, living with each other, loving each other, talking to each other, they may discover more religious agreement than they had suspected. Conversely, some differences may come to be understood as more intractable.

233

The consideration of Judaism and Christianity in these pages is something more than picking an example of religion. However, the supposition is not made that Judaism-Christianity is the true, the best, or the most comprehensive religious tradition. The only presuppositions at work here are: (1) that Judaism-Christianity is where most people are in the West even if they do not like that fact and even if many are trying to grow away from that heritage; (2) that Judaism or Christianity can be appreciated as the best religion a Jew or a Christian has without implying any negative judgment on other religious faiths.[3]

Some of my above references might be taken to imply that Judaism and Christianity are a single religion. There would obviously be an unrealism to such language since Jew and Christian have more often than not been at odds with one another. The very bitterness of the opposition, however, is symptomatic of the fact that there is a close relationship, perhaps closer than either likes to admit. No more bitter fights take place than those between members of a family. The differences between Jew and Christian may have some connection to the theme of estranged brothers which runs throughout the Jewish scriptures.[4]

There are limits to the capacity of language to bind together what is bifurcated in reality, but it is possible for language to aid in overcoming a split. For centuries Roman Catholics and Protestants battled each other, at first with arms and later with words. It was not very realistic to speak about a "Christian church." Until 1960 the Roman Catholic church would not officially use the word "church" to refer to Protestant groups. Even now it is common for Roman Catholics to use the word church as coextensive with Roman Catholicism. It cannot be denied

3. See: John Walgrave, *Person and Society* (Pittsburgh, 1965), p. 167: "In order that one may be tolerant in the full sense of the word, he must realize on the basis of his own experience what it means to have a conviction and cherish it."

4. See: Joseph Ratzinger, *The Open Circle* (New York, 1966), pp. 28–35.

234

that an enormous gulf remains and that there is not a church but a variety of churches. Catholicism is rapidly diversifying but there is still a discernible difference between Catholic and Protestant institutions. Still, one can refer today to a Christian church tradition while admitting all the differences.

The split between Christian and Jew is more serious: it is of longer standing, has involved more acrimony, and touches deeper personal issues.[5] On the same account, the healing of this split might be of greater importance. For my purpose the understanding of this split is of crucial significance. The understanding of an historical division does not cause the division to be overcome but it does help people to live with the division while they examine how much unity or division they desire. I state the case in this very restricted way because it may not be desirable to put unity even as a theoretic ideal. Or, the kind of unity that is ultimately desirable may be discoverable only as people move together in some common search.

The attempt of Christians to embrace Jews has not been received with unbounded enthusiasm by all Jews. The reason is not hard to find. Black men in America discovered that integration into the white man's society on the white man's terms is a form of destruction. This fact remains even when the white man sincerely intends otherwise. A suppressed minority cannot carry the burden of sudden and complete integration. Individually the suppressed people may be as intelligent and capable as their oppressors but they cannot immediately overcome the structure left over from the past. A human integration requires groups who do the integrating and who bring to the process comparable powers for action. An oppressed minority by definition lacks these powers. A process of integration must therefore proceed through three or four steps in which repression is gradu-

5. For Jewish-Christian relations in the early Church, see: Walter Burghardt, "Jewish-Christian Dialogue: Early Church versus Contemporary Christianity," in *The Dynamic in Christian Thought,* ed., Joseph Papin (Villanova, 1970), pp. 186–207.

235

ally eliminated, new self-identities develop and mutual activities are allowed to grow.

Christians who sincerely repent of past Christian attitudes toward Jews are fumbling today for a way of speaking. Some of the ways which may seem to give recognition to Jews may turn out to be embarrassingly inadequate. High flown language which seems to exalt can be a surreptitious way of controlling the other and not allowing him to speak for himself. Just as many who wish to keep women in their place speak glowingly of the "mystery of woman" so also can Christians easily refer to the "mystery of Israel" and presume that this is a compliment. As W. C. Davies has pointed out: "No one wants to be a mystery in someone else's religion."[6] A schism theory regarding the Jews may be an improvement over past theories but schism supposes that one party is in schism. Few Christians, one would imagine, are ready to consider the possibility that Christianity is the one in schism.

During recent decades the term "Judeo-Christian" has come into prominence. The term is perhaps a legitimate and helpful one for describing a line of cultural development. It is very questionable, however, to use this phrase as a description of religion. Christianity did come to dominate the cultural development of the West but that does not mean that the Christian religion either displaced or succeeded the Jewish religion. The term Judeo-Christian originated in the nineteenth-century higher criticism. "The Jewish was latinized and abbreviated into 'Judeo' to indicate a dimension, albeit a pivotal dimension, of the explicit Christian experience. It was rather more a coming to terms on the part of Christian scholarship with the Jewish factor in Christian civilization. It was no less, for all its efforts to be scholarly, an exhibition of what Solomon Schechter called 'Higher Anti-Semitism,' for the Jewish in the Jewish experience was all but

6. W. C. Davies, "The Jews in an Ecumenical Context: A Critique," in *Journal of Ecumenical Studies*, V (Summer, 1968), p. 488–506.

obliterated, being retained, rather like a prehensile tail, in the larger, more sophisticated, economy of Christian truth."[7]

The peculiar difficulty which Christians have always had is that the Jews should have stopped existing. According to the plan, the "Old Testament" was completed and fulfilled in the "New Testament." Accidental as those terms old and new testaments may seem to be, they candidly express the difficulty inherent in a Christian religion. The "Old Testament" Jews pose no difficulty for the Christian church; in fact, the Israelites of old are praised no end in Christianity. It is contemporary Jews who are the stumbling stone. It is not just the historical burden of anti-Semitism that makes it difficult for Christians to come to grips with Judaism. The existence of the Jews is a threat to the foundation of the church. In many ways it is easier for Christianity to admit a legitimacy to Buddhism or Shinto than to Judaism. Any rightful place to Judaism threatens the legitimacy of Christianity. "The roots of Christian anti-Semitism need be traced no further than Christianity itself; Christians have been anti-Semitic because they have been Christians. They thought of themselves as the people of God, the true Israel, who had been faithful to the inheritance of ancient Israel. Judaism, in the Christian view, had no reason to exist once Christianity came upon the scene. We must learn, I think, to live with the unpleasant fact that anti-Semitism is part of what it has meant historically to be a Christian, and is still part of what it means to be Christian."[8]

The Second Vatican Council admitted the special relationship of the church to the Jews but only because at the same time they kept the pressure against the Jews. For many Jewish leaders the debate surrounding the Declaration on the Jews was insulting.

7. Arthur Cohen, *The Myth of the Judeo-Christian Tradition* (New York, 1971), p. XVIII.
8. Robert Wilken, *The Myth of Christian Beginnings* (Garden City, 1971), p. 197; see: Charles Glock and Rodney Stark, *Christian Beliefs and Anti-Semitism* (New York, 1966), pp. 60–80.

They found the pattern of discussion to be bizarre. The church gave evidence of wishing to move away from its formerly belligerent stance but church leaders could not face the painful and frightening reality of the situation. They could not do what was called for, namely, to express the church's repentance of anti-Semitism and to track down the theological cause at its root. Instead, they debated whether the Jews should be forgiven and whether contemporary Jews could be exempted from the crime of deicide. The fact that the final judgment was pro-Jewish did not remove the embarrassment of the fact that Christian leaders thought that they had a debatable issue.

The reactionary forces in the Roman Catholic church, who were not overly jubilant at the exoneration of the Jews, were at least being consistent with their theology. Of course, they would not vote in favor of anti-Semitism but they did try to and did succeed in keeping the burden of proof on the Jews. So long as the Jew is forced into defending his right to exist, the Christian position remains secure. But the Jew will never be neutral in a Christian scheme of things; once the Jew is admitted into full citizenship the whole Christian scheme begins to crumble. From the start and to this day there is a struggle for life and death between these two close relatives. Joseph Klausner wrote: "Judaism brought forth Christianity in its first form (the teaching of Jesus), but it thrust aside its daughter when it saw that she would slay the mother with a deadly kiss."[9]

The theological reason why Jews and Christians have not only failed to cooperate but have been deadly enemies is closely related to the main topic of this book. For coping with the problem, the concept of revelation in Judaism is not wholly adequate and in Christianity is patently inadequate. The Christian attitude toward the contemporary Jewish community is the key test for the adequacy of Christian understanding of revelation. The Jewish issue has often seemed peripheral to Christian theology but

9. Joseph Klausner, *Jesus of Nazareth* (New York, 1925), p. 376.

it is the stubborn fact which resists explanation and throws in doubt all other explanations.

If God was revealed in the lives of Old Testament people and if the promises of God are not withdrawn, then what of the contemporary Jewish people? What is one to make of a Church that bases its claim on a revelation that supposedly brought to a close the "Old Testament?" The church and synagogue do not fit smoothly together. Christian attempts to find a place for Judaism almost inevitably make Judaism the question and negative counterpart to the positive Christian answer. I am claiming throughout this book that there is no way out of the problem from within Christian theology. Christian anti-Semitism will disappear only as "Christian revelation" disappears.

The above description of Jewish-Christian relations may sound unduly pessimistic but it is meant only to be unsparingly realistic. There has been great progress in recent years, much greater than in the course of previous centuries. Given the size of the problem, the progress may be as rapid as could possibly be expected. The 1967 war was both a temporary setback to friendly relations and a reminder that Christians and Jews are still far apart. The state of Israel is for many Christians an incomprehensible problem while for many Jews it is the heart of the problem. Nevertheless, one can still be hopeful that Jew and Christian will continue to grow in understanding and friendship.[10]

The theological advance requires the development of a category of revelation that would subsume both Judaism and Christianity. A Jewish revelation and a Christian revelation will always be at odds with each other. But a universal revelation that both Judaism and Christianity point toward would bring the two peoples together. A revelation embodied and expressed in Christian and Jewish peoples would still involve some conflicts

10. See: Krister Stendahl, "Judaism and Christianity: A Plea for a New Relationship," in *Cross Currents* XVII (1967), pp. 445–458.

but not wars or persecutions. The dialogue would not be between old and new testaments but between contemporary Christians and contemporary Jews. Both groups should be turned outward toward other men and toward the realization of what God calls them to be. "All men are dependent upon the revelation yet to come. Christians as well as Jews depend on the future coming and manifestation of him who is God's Messiah and their common hope. Rather than being divided like possessors and paupers or like soft-hearted and hard-hearted people, Christians and Jews are united as fellows-in-waiting."[11]

We are far from a mutual acceptance of formulas like the above statement. Perhaps it is necessary to step back further from words which carry strong overtones in one tradition or the other. The Christian change in its concept of revelation would be the more drastic one. The change, I am suggesting, must be worked out through the re-establishing of its relation to Judaism. It would be salutory for Christians to begin their religious education by reading some writing of contemporary Jews. The procedure would almost certainly give them a better picture of Christianity.

My concern here is not so much with the "Old Testament" as with the Jewish community that arose in ancient times and is still very much alive today. References in Christian writing to "Late Judaism" are inaccurate and insulting because they assume that Judaism was a moribund and insincere religion at the time of the apostolic church.[12] The Jewish religion was not on the way out of existence at the time of Jesus. It survived the destruction of the Temple, it overcame the persecution of the middle ages and it has withstood the savagery of the twentieth century. The recognition of this fact makes it less easy to speak of the

11. Markus Barth, *Israel and the Church* (Richmond, 1969), p. 22.
12. For a good corrective on this point, see: Frederick Grant, *Ancient Judaism and the New Testament* (New York, 1959); see also: A. Roy Eckardt, *Elder and Younger Brothers* (New York, 1967), p. 87.

phenomenon of Israel as if that were a collection of documents about a people who disappeared long ago. Judaism is in fact an extraordinarily complex phenomenon about which any generalizations are hazardous.

Modern Judaism is the product of a long and rich development of biblical thought. It possesses a normative tradition embodied in the Mishnah and the Talmud, as well as the *Responsa* and the codes of the post-talmudic period. By the side of this dominant strand are the aberrant tendencies, sectarian and heretical, that were never without influence and cannot be ignored.... In the modern era, as every informed observer knows, the various schools conventionally subsumed under the headings of Orthodoxy, Conservatism, and Reform, do not begin to exhaust the variety of religious experience and approach which are competing for attention in the market place of ideas in the Jewish community.[13]

For my limited purpose it is not necessary to unravel all of these distinctions nor to get consensus at all points. I am trying to provide some reflection on the category of revelation from the perspective of Judaism. Whether all Jews would agree on these points is less important than the fact that these points do originate from within Judaism. To this day at least part of Judaism is a continuing witness to these aspects of revelation.

First and most strikingly, Judaism testifies to the fact that there is a religious life: God is God, man is man, and man is God's creature. The extraordinariness of the Jewish religion is its combined affirmation of God's otherness together with the belief that God is intimately involved in human life. Israel appears on the stage of world history as a religious people whose origin, sustenance and destiny are tied into the religious life of her people. There failed to develop in Judaism the split between a religious elite and the mere layman which has characterized most religions.

To the present day Judaism has continued to remind the

13. Robert Gordis, *The Root and the Branch* (Chicago, 1962), p. 62.

world of the meaning of the religious. I use the adjective rather than the noun for reasons which have been discussed earlier and are particularly pertinent here. For the Jew it is not the Jewish religion which is the important thing but the religious response to God. Thus, in Judaism the word religious did not develop the negative meaning that it picked up in Christian writing.

Jewish leaders stood aghast during the 1960's while Christian theologians rushed in the direction of "secularity."[14] Not that the Jews were unfamiliar with or unattracted by the secular. Rather, the Jews were all too knowledgeable about the secular developments of modern times. Largely under the pressure of Christian persecution, Jews had formed early alliances with the Enlightenment forces. What was anti-Christian held some chance of being pro-Jewish.

The Jews did not do badly in the process of secularization. It was experienced as liberation not from their religious tradition but from political and social oppression. At the same time Jews were aware that the modern secular world is not the messiah.[15] At best the this-worldly concentration was ambivalent in the progress of human freedom; at worst the enlightened modern age can unleash the most demonic forces. No contemporary Jew needs reminding of this latter fact. "The doctrine of the divine superman died at Auschwitz," wrote Ulrich Simon. Unfortunately, that judgment is not entirely accurate. Perhaps to any clear-minded person that doctrine should have died but there is evidence that the doctrine of superman still survives.

Christian writing in the 1960's which opposed secular and religious could have been avoided had these writers considered the Jews. Here in the living flesh were people who were among

---

14. See: Emil Fackenheim, *Quest for Past and Future* (Boston, 1968), pp. 278–305; Jacob Neusner, *Judaism in the Secular Age* (New York, 1970), pp. 42–81; Frederick Schweitzer, *A History of the Jews Since the First Century A.D.* (New York, 1971), pp. 156ff.

15. Borowitz, *loc. cit.,* p. 88.

the most religious people and at the same time among the most secular of people. There was something very confused about the terms of an argument that pitted religious against secular.[16] Christian theologians tried to win total and easy victory by aligning Christian faith and secular society against repressive religion. The implication here was that Christianity could be reformed if it could only divest itself of its Jewish roots.

At the most extreme, Christian writers concluded that God had to be done away with.[17] The God who had emerged from the Jewish scriptures was judged to be a transcendent ruler who represses man. Jewish commentators were understandably outraged at this implication that their religious life was at the root of the troubles:

Who is this hostile God, foe of human freedom and source of every repression? He is not and never has been the authentic God of Israel: not in the Hebrew Bible, not in the rabbinic writings, not in the history of Jewish religious thought until this day. He is not the God of the psalmist when he delights in the divine commandments (Ps 119:47); not in the God of the rabbinic sage who declares that 'when the Torah came into the world freedom came into the world'; not the God of the ordinary Jewish worshiper who daily proclaims that it is in his love that God gave commandments to Israel. The enemy-God is a caricature. The authentic God of Israel is he who in his transcendent otherness does not need man and yet chooses to need him; who in his love makes man free and responsible, and thus in commanding demands a free response. He is, in short, a God of grace. But must a Jew tell a Christian about grace?[18]

The Jewish religious life was to free men from internal and external bonds by relating mankind to the just and loving creator of the world. Innumerable explanations can be offered as to

16. See: Peter Berger, "A Sociological View of the Secularization of Theology," in *Journal for the Scientific Study of Religion*, VI (Spring, 1967), pp. 3–16.
17. See: Fackenheim, *op. cit.*, p. 299.
18. *Ibid.*

why such an exalted notion of God came from this people. The fact remains, in any case, that the Jewish experience has transformed the notions of divinity and revelation for all time. In Jewish faith God is clearly in charge. The worst illusion of men is to think that they can escape from this God, manipulate his favors or understand him through their constructed images. For the Jew "faith begins in embarrassment, in being overwhelmed, in being silenced. ... He who seeks a God to suit his astuteness, to appease his vanity, to satisfy his curiosity, will find at the end a figment of his imagination."[19]

In Judaism God is wrapped in awe and mystery, fraught with background and surcharged with foreground.[20] The progressive revelation that the Jew sees in history does not lead to all things becoming clear and unmysterious. On the contrary, it leads to greater awareness of the mysterious, inexhaustible character of the divine and the ambivalent, complex nature of the human. Such a religious life does not end in the antimonies of law or freedom, fear or love, structure or spontaneity. Christians have repeatedly misconstrued the Jewish position because of the presumption that law restricts freedom and fear excludes love. "Nothing so divides Jews and Christians as does the Law/Gospel dichotomy. That is not because Jews are compulsively bound to a meticulous set of legalistic trivia, but because Jews cannot conceive of a religious community or life without some degree of structure and discipline."[21]

A loving and fearful God demands from his creatures both fear and love. His people live by his gracious attitude but he is inexorable in his demands. Neither as under threatening law nor as secure in the guarantee of the covenant did Israel understand itself. Nowhere throughout Jewish tradition is there that pro-

19. Heschel, *Insecurity of Freedom,* p. 67.
20. See: Hart, *op. cit.,* p. 284.
21. Richard Rubenstein, "Cox's Vision of the Secular City," in *The Secular City Debate,* ed., Daniel Callahan (New York, 1966), p. 137.

fusion of talk about love that inevitably tends toward mawkish sentimentality. Instead, there is almost everywhere a sternness of realism touched with the gentleness of irony.[22]

In Israel's view there cannot be a separation between the Father of Mercies and the King of Judgment. This awareness of God as judge is tied to a conception of human life in which each human being is responsible in an ultimate manner. The God of Israel is preeminently a God of justice but the word justice here has a more exalted meaning than it is usually given today. We have tended to oppose justice to love and to think of the former as merely a preparatory virtue. Furthermore, our view of justice is based on the image of a cumbersome legal process that often degrades people caught in it. But the God of justice was the one who judged justly, that is, the one who saw things as they are, set things in order and dealt compassionately with all life.

A God who is unimaginably exalted is one capable of meeting a person in the smallest details of his life. In Jewish tradition the concrete, individual experience, in all the depths of its particularity, lights up the breadth and greatness of the universal condition of mankind. Rather than opposition between the particular and the universal there is correlation. This is a truth more evident to artistic or religious people than to scientific or philosophical peoples. The Jews understood their self-hood and people-hood as an embodying of humanity. Such a conviction does not come from deduction but from a transformation of experience. "As Jew he is a human being, as human being a Jew. One is a *jüdisch Kind* with every breath. It is something that courses through the arteries of our life, strongly or weakly, but at any rate to our very finger tips. It may course very weakly indeed.

22. Martin Buber, *Two Types of Faith* (New York, 1961), p. 137: "God demands from Israel that it should fear him and love him—fear belongs to love as the door belongs to the house—like fear that does not flow into love, so love that does not comprehend fear is only one of the ways of serving God as an idol."

245

But one feels that the Jew in oneself is not a circumscribed ter-
ritory, but a greater or lesser force flooding one's whole being."[23]

If we are to speak not of an abstract humanity but of human
persons who live in the flesh and in the moments of space and
time, then a divine revelation must find expression there. As we
have seen in the revelational act between two humans, progress
manifests itself in the direction of concreteness and particularity.
The human being who searches for love and meaning in his life
cannot find these qualities in a general truth. Attempts to sever
the person from national, racial, ethnic and cultural roots only
succeed in doing violence to the individual human being.

Judaism's grasp upon this fact is embodied in her belief that
she is a chosen people, elected by God to serve as an object les-
son to the nations. The concept of a "chosen people" has always
been a questionable one, seeming to imply an arrogant self-
righteousness. The situation is clouded by explanations which
fail to grasp the meaning of the word revelation. Thus, Leo
Baeck writes: "Until the detractors of Israel can show a Bible,
a line of prophets, or a religious history comparable or equal to
Israel's, its claim to a unique religious significance—the possession of Revelation—cannot be denied."[24] This statement of
claims is defensible until the author comes to the summary
phrase, "the possession of Revelation." This phrase does not express the claim of Israel; *possession* is not a word to go with
revelation in Jewish tradition. It was precisely this error which
the prophets constantly opposed: the equating of "chosen people" and "possessors of revelation."

Some misunderstanding of the word chosen is probably unavoidable but a clarification of the term can be made. Like several words investigated in chapter two (e.g., power), the word
chosen has two meanings which go in opposite directions. The
confusion cannot be cleared up by a simple definition nor by the

23. Rosenzweig, *op. cit.*, pp. 56–57.
24. Leo Baeck, *The Essence of Judaism* (New York, 1961), p. 21.

introduction of another word. The word chosen is the proper word here. It signifies that mysterious paradox of human life that the all must be chosen in the particular. The ambiguity of life can be escaped from only by flattening out the human. The denial of chosen moments, chosen places and chosen people may appear to be in the direction of liberal, democratic principles. Instead, the denial would eliminate the variety, diversity and rhythm which are essential to human life. Furthermore, it leads to the denial of individuality and the reality of time. If all of human life is equally available at any one time then we are dealing not with living persons but with abstract humanity.

Israel's claim was that she is a chosen people despite the fact that many people, both inside and outside of Israel, would misconstrue the claim. The false claim would be to maintain that a group has been chosen because they are better than everybody else. In this view those people are chosen who merit it. To be chosen then makes one secure that he is in possession of truth and salvation. One is thus chosen to the exclusion of all the others. "Radhakrishnan has remarked: 'The Jews first invented the myth that only one religion can be true.' One sees what he means; but the analysis is not, I think exact. What the Jews asserted is that only one God is real, which one may regard as just as reprehensible, but is not quite the same idea."[25] W. C. Smith is carefully noting here what may seem like a fine distinction but it is the difference between understanding the Jewish claim to be chosen and completely missing the point.

The reason for the concept of the chosen is indicated by Smith's pointing out that the claim was not one true religion but one true God. The Jews wished to speak of what confronted them in their experience and lifted them out of their selfishness. Their experience was of having been chosen not because they were probably the best but because they were possibly the least. Anyone can love the most lovable things, but only a supreme

25. Smith, *Meaning and End of Religion*, p. 32.

lover can love what is slight and unattractive. Thus, the quality of the divine is manifested by the choice.

If Israel had been a philosophical people it would be easy to suppose that religion simply adds a few nuances to the best idea of God men work out in their minds. But a people not given to abstract theory, who bring forth the most astounding religious conceptions, challenge our entire scale of values.[26] Perhaps the ultimate truth of life is not found by an educated elite surveying the skies. Perhaps ordinary people in their ordinary lives are capable of participating in the ultimate truth of life.

The choice of Israel, therefore, is not an exclusive but an inclusive one. She is chosen because all are being chosen. So that the chosenness of all may become evident, the least must be the most dramatically chosen of all. In the choice which excludes, the chosen one is given something to possess as his own because he has merited it. In the choice which includes, the chosen is moved to receive and thereby to share what is the birthright of all. The failure to clarify the word revelation has consistently blocked understanding of this distinction. Revelation is not something one is given; revelation is a relation in which one participates. The Jews do not claim to have revelation but they do claim to dramatize with their lives the relationship to the one God to whom all are called.

This attempt to try to point to the highest while claiming no credit for oneself is a difficult one. It might even be called an impossible task saved from complete failure only by continuous reformations. In ancient Israel a succession of prophets reminded the people of what it meant to be the chosen of God. Since biblical times new prophets have continually been needed to remind the people of their calling. They do not announce security to the chosen ones but instead remind the chosen people that

26. For a piece of fiction which brilliantly dramatizes this point, see Flannery O'Connor's short story entitled "Revelation" in *The Complete Stories* (New York, 1971), pp. 488–509.

they should be the ones most aware that no security belongs to them.[27]

Prophet is simply the notion of chosen people carried to conclusion. On the surface it may seem that the prophet claims to have a truth that no one else has. In appearance the prophet seems to be a loner, separated from any community. On deeper examination it becomes evident that the prophet is not at all an isolated, self-righteous loner. "The prophet does not leave the community, though he may be thrown out of it; but he turns one element of the tradition against a distorted tradition in which this element has been forgotten. The prophet does not intend to create a new community, and just for that reason he often does it against his will. The prophet needs solitude, not the loneliness of separation, but the solitude of him who takes the group spiritually with him into his solitude in order to return to it bodily."[28]

The prophets in Israel who look toward the one God and the one human race can be extremely harsh in their judgments on the Israelite community. The prophets threaten, or more exactly they bear the threat, of the destruction of Israel. Those who have the greatest mission stand under the greatest threat of judgment.[29]

The prophet demonstrates with his life, his bodily gestures, his explosive words and his passionate feelings. He tries to convey more than language can contain. He tries to stun people into awareness of their bond to all men and their responsibility before God. "The prophet is a man who feels fiercely. God has

27. For a criticism of Heidegger's misunderstanding of the prophetic movement on this point, see: Buber, *Eclipse of God,* p. 73.

28. Paul Tillich, *Biblical Religion and the Search for Ultimate Reality* (Chicago, 1964), p. 48.

29. Paul Tillich, *Theology of Culture* (New York, 1964), p. 36: "The threat which we hear first in the words of Amos is the turning point in the history of religion. It is unheard of in all other religions that the God of a nation is able to destroy this nation without being destroyed himself. In all other religions the god dies with the people who adore him."

thrust a burden upon his soul, and he is bowed and stunned at man's fierce greed. Frightful is the agony of man; no human voice can convey its full terror. Prophecy is the voice that God has lent to the silent agony, a voice to the plundered poor, to the profaned riches of the world. It is a form of living, a crossing point of God and man. God is raging in the prophet's words."[30] The prophet is in sympathy with the divine pathos refusing to give up on man but also refusing to compromise the demands of justice. The words of the prophet, threatening and liberating, sorrowful and joyful, fierce and compassionate, are startling and mysterious eruptions from a divine-human communion.

The key word that has been used to identify the special place of Israel in revelation is the word history.[31] I have indicated in the first chapter that the term "historical revelation" is misleading when it leads to a distinction between historical and non-historical revelations. Nonetheless, the word history is quite crucial to the discussion. The Jews did not discover one kind of revelation called historical but they understand revelation as historical. They did not discover a tract of history called sacred; instead they helped to discover history.

If history is going to serve as the comprehensive category in this area, its meaning has to be stretched beyond the meaning of its ordinary usage. The word history is commonly used to refer to records of past events, or, more restrictively, to a scientific sifting through the documents of the past. However, some wider meaning for the word is allowed into ordinary discourse. History refers to the entire stretch of the past in which men have experi-

30. Abraham Heschel, *The Prophets* (New York, 1969), p. 5.
31. See: Alan Richardson, *History Sacred and Profane* (Philadelphia, 1964); Van A. Harvey, *The Historian and the Believer* (New York, 1966); Friedrich Gogarten, "Theology and History," in *History and Hermeneutic* (New York, 1967), pp. 35–81; James Robinson, "Revelation as Word and History," in *Theology as History,* eds., James Robinson and John Cobb (New York, 1967), pp. 1–100.

enced the world. There is implicit in this broader meaning a realization that human life is materially, spatially and temporally limited but that there is process, continuity and (possibly) progress in the human arena. This belief in the character of human life may have been embodied in other peoples but it finds a very clear expression in Jewish religion. The discovery that revelation is historical was concomitant with the discovery that human life is historical.

There might have been other routes to the discovery that to be human is to be historical but for the Jews it was a religious path. The affirmation of the historical character of the human was not easy to attain. It meant the acceptance of human limitations. What is real is not eternal archetypes nor ideas in the heavens but the frail, little piece of bodily life that is the human being. The experience of flux and the awareness that one is limited to a bit of disintegrating flesh have been unbearable for most of the race. Religions have often given solace to frightened people by telling them that there is a better world outside the flow of time and the contamination of matter. Religious rites have often been designed to provide escape from human limitation and to put man in touch with the realm of the sacred and immortal. In this view, everything significant has already happened before the "fall" into time. The best that could be done now was to return, if not in fact at least in ritual, to the beginning. Final salvation could be achieved only by escaping from the change and suffering of this world.[32]

Against this strong tendency, Israel countered her own experience. She traced her origins to a meeting with God in the spatio-temporal, everyday world. Israel did not leave time to find a God who transcends time. Israel believed that God found her and communed with her. This belief implies much about the kind of God Israel met and also much about the nature of space, time, matter and fragile human life. Over the course of cen-

32. See: Mircea Eliade, *Cosmos and History,* pp. 141–142.

turies much would be demanded of Israel but at the beginning the initiative was not hers. The notion of God was fairly clear from the beginning and has not varied much since then: "He is the One who is infinite, yet relates himself to finite man; who in his power does not need man, yet in his love chooses to need him; who in his self-sufficiency does not require the world yet wishes to require it—and bids man do his will in it."[33]

The transcendence of God refers not to his encasement in a realm separate from time but to his power to transcend all attempts to manipulate him. The common conception of revelation outside Israel was the extra-temporal bestowal of divine instructions. Such a conception of a divine revelation was unthinkable for the Jews. What was always at stake was a relationship of the divine and human, possible only with the involvement of God in human limitations and the expression of revelation in space-time categories. Israel is "the proof that God is not ashamed, either of having created matter and time or of using history and miracles, and that, man need not be ashamed of these things either. Thus Israel gives reason for joy in men and things as they are and reason to be cautious about all idealistic plans, schemes and systems."[34]

The sense of God is tied to an increasing awareness of the greatness of man, not because man is great alone but because he is befriended by one so great. The small things of the human situation are taken with utter seriousness by God. If God has such an interest in human life, should not man also? Where the human seems to fail it is not to be condemned or put aside. God did not disdain to deal with faltering, sinful men. The scriptures and the Talmud sensed that good impulses and bad impulses are intertwined.[35] Evil or sin was not a failing which was unforeseen in the original plan. Man has always been failing as far

33. Fackenheim, *op. cit.*, p. 275.
34. Barth, *Israel and the Church*, pp. 116–117.
35. See: Gordis, *op. cit.*, pp. 143–144.

back as one can go but God is greater still. Thus, in a very real sense sin is part of the revelational process. If revelation includes all that is human then it cannot exclude sin.

The starting point is a chosen place, a chosen moment and a chosen people in the situation of mankind. This starting point has to be worked out in a process of interaction in which the divine-human communion is expressed, deepened and pointed to. The reason for the long, drawn-out process lies more on the side of man than of God. It is not God who needs fulfillment but man. The message of the Jewish scriptures is to love the fellow man who is created in the image of God and proceeding toward God in a common journey.[36]

A religion of fulfillment implies a process of growth in time. Israel could not acquiesce in an image of time which saw it either as a meaningless circle or as a line running downhill. But that does not imply that they understood time as a line running uphill. Human life is not well represented by any linear images, be they straight lines, circles or spirals. The Jews projected out a future and a past from the present in which they trusted in God. Their experience was not so much of words of promise about things of the future but of human life as promise because it is grounded in God.

The historical situations of Israel were understood to be revelatory of God but that in itself does not necessarily imply a different conception of God and man. An historical event might be the occasion for a divine oracle; an isolated event might convey a truth about God. But what distinguished Israel was the awareness that the process of human life, the total pattern of history, is revelational of God. A God who revealed himself from time to time and then retired to the heavens above would be a God not really involved with history. Such "revelations" would be unhistorical, that is, they would be things deposited

36. See: Morris Margolies, "God and Man in the Tradition of Judaism," in *Jewish-Christian Relations* (St. Marys, Kan., 1966), pp. 46–56.

into history but not of history. Israel came to see that although some moments may be strikingly revelational it should not be concluded that other moments are not revelational at all. The dramatic moments which are most revelatory are reminders that all moments are revelatory for those who can see. Thus, there is a pattern of promise and realization in which small things realized are part of the promise for greater things to come. The pattern is unimaginably complex and no man can put together all the pieces. The Jews did not have a knowledge of the whole pattern but they glimpsed that there is a pattern, a single history of one God and one human kind.[37]

Central to this pattern is the intimacy and reciprocity of the interaction. God does not project a reward for obedient man but is involved with the life of man. God commits himself to man in a way that allows man to bargain, to complain and to remind God of what he is committed to. This kind of intimacy is brilliantly captured in the stories of Abraham, Moses, David, Job and Jonas. Reciprocity is not the same as equality, however. Never do any of the great Jewish leaders forget that God is God and man is man. God may be persuaded but he will not be manipulated. Commenting on the absence of magic in Israel, G. Van der Leeuw writes: "In Israel everything was demanded from God, and by God everything from man. 'In the presence of such a monstrous and frightful God, who united all the might of God and demons, magic completely disappeared: before such a God, who was not only a demon but also God, no charm could avail.' Thus Israel *lives* with its God, in strife and discord, in anger and contrition, in repentance and self-will, in love and faith."[38]

The Jews came to see that there were not revelational events

37. See: J. Coert Rylaarsdam, "The Old Testament and the New: Theocentricity, Continuity, Finality," in *The Future as the Presence of Shared Hope*, ed., Maryellen Muckenhirn (New York, 1968), p. 80.

38. Van der Leeuw, *op. cit.*, p. 638; see also: Walter Zimmerli, *The Law and the Prophets* (New York, 1965), p. 66.

as opposed to non-revelational events. Revelation pertains to the total life of the community. God was to be found in the fleshly, temporal existence of the people. The conclusion to which this belief tends, particularly in light of the meaning of chosen, is that the total life of all humanity is the revelation of God. Going backward and forward, inward and outward, there are no lines which separate revelation and non-revelation. When the Jewish world met the Greek it was open to incorporating Greek philosophy within the one "wisdom" of God.[39]

In looking forward, Judaism could see that God would speak in many tongues. Since the movement was not in the direction of things becoming clearer and less mysterious, there was no reason to expect that at some point God would strip away the veils and exhaust the divine truth. The process was moving in the direction of a deeper, more incomprehensible love worked out within the tension of divine-human relationship. There would always be need of prophetic voices to remind men of their calling to bind and to heal, to love and to serve. "The word of God never comes to an end. No word is God's last word."[40]

Concomitant with Israel's awareness that the divine-human revelation is to continue into the future is a projection of it backwards. The Hebrew scriptures often speak as if revelation began with Abraham. With some reflection, however, it becomes obvious that the community of God and man did not begin then. Abraham, father of the nation, is the prophet raised up to bring men to awareness of what God has always been doing in human life. "The apocryphal *Book of Jubilees,* written before the beginning of the Christian era, could not conceive of untold generations of men before Moses living without a divine revelation. It therefore attributes to Noah, who was not a Hebrew, a code of conduct binding upon all men."[41]

39 See: Samuel Sandmel, *We Jews and Jesus* (New York, 1965), p. 39.
40. Heschel, *Insecurity of Freedom,* p. 182.
41. Gordis, *op. cit.,* p. 46.

255

This reading backwards into history cannot stop with Noah. The conclusion to this way of thinking is the one reached in Genesis, namely, that every man, animal, vegetable and mineral is expressive of the revelation. The creation story was inevitable even though it took a long time to emerge. From the beginning of time there is one world dependent upon the one God. The creator God of Judaism does not retire in fatigue leaving the world in the hands of a demiurge or vegetative divinity. There is a single creative process which includes man, beast and cosmos.[42] There is no discontinuity between man and the universe or within man himself. The single pattern is centered not on salvation from sin but on the creation of new life. The entire scope of history is good but is exposed to failure and in need of criticism.

Judaism's sense of revelation led to a notion of revelation as commandment or rule of life. Christians have seldom been able to grasp this, preferring to disregard Judaism or to ridicule it as legalistic. It was the rootedness in the concrete actions of life that enabled Judaism to escape the common understanding of revelation in Christianity: truths revealed by God to be believed by men. There have been numerous Christian attempts to overcome this narrow conception of revelation as doctrine but there has been little appreciation of the Jewish way which insists upon a rule of life as the alternative. The Christian use of the word "commandment" has led to an almost complete discrediting of the word. Conservatives have tried to enforce "the ten commandments" while liberals have whittled them away. Neither side could feel the Jewish sense of life as command and response.

In Judaism there is only one command but it must find detailed expression in the life of a community.[43] It is with one's

42. See: Mircea Eliade, *Sacred and Profane,* pp. 122–127; Van der Leeuw, *op. cit.,* p. 165.

43. See: Matthew O'Connell, "The Concept of Commandment in the Old Testament," in *Theological Studies, XXI* (Sept., 1960), pp. 352–403; see also: Dietrich Bonhoeffer, *Ethics* (New York, 1965), p. 283: "The

whole life that one answers to God's command. The important thing is to be aimed in the right direction and on the way. A command is something which one person addresses to another and which demands a response. An ethic of commandment is far removed from an impersonal, legalistic system. It can produce a slavish and fear-ridden religion but it can also produce freedom and joy if entered into with the right spirit. The Torah (inadequately translated by the English word *law*) is the total pattern of activity which is to the pious Jew his joy and crown. "The Torah is not an *objectivum* independent of the actual relationship of man to God, which could bestow of itself life upon the one who receives it: it does that only to one who receives it for its sake in its living actuality, that is, in its association with its Giver, and for his sake. To the man who engages in it for some other reason the Torah 'breaks his neck'."[44]

Jewish tradition has consistently asked the question: What should a man do? rather than: What should a man believe? When creedal statements have been drawn up they were usually done by individuals rather than by councils of authorized officials. For example, the medieval philosopher Moses Maimonides composed a creed which consists of thirteen articles of belief.[45] Whereas the Jews borrowed and adapted the word *philosophia* (a life of wisdom) they have been uneasy with the word theology because this study seems to imply precise doctrines about God.

Jewish life is therefore surrounded by a "fence" of custom not lightly to be changed. Attempts to bring Jewish prayer life "up

---

commandment of God permits man to be man before God. It allows the flood of life to flow freely. It lets man eat, drink, sleep, work, rest and play. It does not interrupt him. It does not continually ask him whether he ought to be sleeping, eating, working or playing, or whether he has some more urgent duties."

44. Buber, *Two Types of Faith*, p. 93; see also: Heschel, *Man's Quest for God* (New York, 1954), pp. 100–110.

45. See: Solomon Schechter, *Studies in Judaism* (Cleveland, 1958), p. 87.

to date" can have debilitating effects upon the stability and continuity of the tradition. There is really no way to restore a tradition once it has been seriously disrupted. Many simple, prayerful gestures which have endured thousands of years must somehow be preserved for the sake of a common humanity. The Jews have preserved detailed rites and customs not because these are revelation but because they provide a space in which people can live in relation to God. The idea is best exemplified in the Sabbath, a moment of harmony which anticipates the messianic time. The attempt to preserve the Sabbath by fencing it in with restrictions has the intention of celebrating the peace which is to reign between man and man, man and nature, man, nature and God.

Judaism, as a religion of activity and time, is also a religion of the community. The individual is not neglected, but at the center of Jewish concern is the family, the nation and the human race. The survival of Judaism in the face of overwhelming power has depended on the tightly knit communal structure. Great attention has recently been paid to the distinctive power of groups and group process. The bands of Jewish nomads who took on the mega-machine of ancient Egypt were already a dramatization of community power.[46]

The Jewish faith has survived because people practiced it and because they were initiated into the details of the community's life. A disciple of a Hassidic master when asked whether he visited the master to hear his words of wisdom answered: "No, I want to see how he ties his shoelaces." Such communication does not require elaborate educational institutions. It does require stable family situations and a cohesive community. The cataclysmic changes of the contemporary world pose a peculiarly dangerous threat to the survival of Judaism. It has survived the

46. See: Lewis Mumford, *The Myth of the Machine:* vol. 1: *Technics and Human Development* (New York, 1967), pp. 231–233; Herbert Richardson, *Toward an American Theology* (New York, 1967), p. 132.

brunt of armies and the butchery of persecutions but it may face a greater enemy in the disintegration of family ties and social tradition.

Enough has been said of Judaism here to assert that the initial description of revelation given earlier in this book is not incompatible with Judaism. By saying "not incompatible" I am beginning with the minimum. To some extent the earlier ideas on revelation are derived from Judaism. In the main, however, those ideas have been presented to stand on their own and in a way which leaves them open to clarification, correction and elaboration by Judaism. Thus, the process goes both ways. If Jews would recognize as their own some of the ideas presented earlier there could be eliminated some ways of speaking which distort their position. Without diluting their claim to be a holy people, chosen by God, they could affirm the revelation of God among all peoples.

In the other direction, Judaism offers an invaluable contribution and corrective to any general category of revelation. Deriving revelation from general experience brings inclusion of a sense of the "other" confronting the human. The Jewish religion is a protest against the tendency to reduce that "other" to an impersonal or sub-personal force. In Judaism the "other" comes to meet man and there is never any doubt as to who is in charge. At the least, this "other" has all the capabilities that distinguish man as personal. There is no way to prove that there is a personal God who created the world, speaks to man, and draws all things to himself; nevertheless, the existence of the Jews, who have stubbornly refused to become extinct, is powerful evidence that this alternative cannot easily be dismissed.

Judaism stands as an extraordinary embodiment of the religious meaning of revelation. Nonetheless, it is a limited expression which for its own health needs to be considered in relation to other religions. Some of the formulas used within Judaism need challenging from other sources. Since Judaism has heavily

259

relied on its ethical life, liturgical practice and sense of tradition, it may be in an advantageous position to think radically about the philosophic-religious question of revelation. It has fewer rigid doctrinal formulations than Christianity to overcome.

While Jews can learn something from receptive contacts with Christianity, it is more crucial for Christians to understand Judaism and to understand Christianity from within Judaism. If Judaism taken alone is an incomplete religion, the same can be said with more certainty of Christianity. From the beginning of its existence Christianity had to recognize itself as an offshoot of the Jewish religion but it has always experienced difficulty in living with this fact. In turning now to Christianity I am not entirely leaving Judaism. I am picking up one strand of development that stems from Judaism.

2. A Personal Strand

The obvious connecting link between Judaism and Christianity is the figure of Jesus but the link both unites and separates. It is almost impossible for Jews and Christians to make an accurate evaluation of Jesus. Each faith distorts the picture. Christians are, prevented from seeing by centuries of dogmatic elaborations which in popular piety simply made Jesus into God. Jewish judgment is obscured by centuries of persecution in which Christ was the slogan of attack on all things Jewish.

Better historical scholarship can ameliorate some of the problems but it will never resolve the difficulties. What is urgently needed is encounter between contemporary Jewish and Christian religions. Such a meeting would probably strengthen and purify the faiths of both Christian and Jew. Although there probably is no final reconciliation of the two, the real differences might be sharpened and the false differences might fall away. Entrance into dialogue implies that a person admits that his own position might need radical overhaul, that is, new perspectives, different concepts and changed vocabulary.

The Christian positions on Jesus go rapidly in one of two directions, either to a "high Christology" with a string of titles that make further discussion difficult, or else toward a reductionism which is not so much an affirmation of a position as a whittling down of an opposite position. What follows in this section will probably get categorized as "low Christology" but it is not intended to be "Christology" at all. When "Christology" becomes a field of study, an exhaustive kind of infighting is almost inevitable. Whoever wins the battle of high versus low Christologies, the results are not promising for anyone. This struggle does not help either the Christian trying to get in contact with his own religious roots or the Jew who wishes to reclaim the Jewishness of Jesus. In his book *We Jews and Jesus,* Samuel Sandmel notes sadly: "It is my opinion that Jews and Christians are farther apart today on the question of Jesus than they have been in the past hundred years, this despite other ways in which Judaism and Christianity have drawn closer to each other than ever before."[47]

Although there are few attacks launched today against the person of Jesus, he remains the great obstacle to Christian-Jewish unity. Sometimes admiring comments are made about Jesus while harsh comment is reserved for Paul. But these two cannot be completely separated. In the Christian understanding of Jesus, as interpreted through Paul, the Jewish covenant comes to conclusion with and in Jesus. He is the end of the "Old Testament" and the beginning of the "New Testament." In recent Christian writing Jesus is not portrayed as the enemy of the Jews and the destroyer of their tradition. But that claim might be easier to deal with than a corrosive influence which does not negate Judaism but which preempts its past meaning and undercuts its future significance.

Given the narrow framework in which discussion normally occurs, the Jew has little room in which to discuss Jesus. "All the Christian objections to Judaism and the corresponding Jew-

47. Sandmel, *op. cit.,* p. 104.

ish replies pale into insignificance before the point of dispute . . .
which was decisive in the life of Saul of Tarsus: Whether the
Law has not found its fulfillment and been abolished through
belief in the Lord and Savior, Jesus of Nazareth."[48] This statement may in the end be the true statement of differences but we
must ask whether the words *fulfill, abolish, Lord* and *Savior* are
unambiguously clear in the statement. We should not make a
definitive conclusion on what the differences are until a sufficient
exploration of the similarities has been made. It seems safe to
say that the exploration from both sides is far from exhausted.

From the Christian side, many writers are anxious to set the
contrast between Christianity and Judaism: the sharper the conflict, the clearer the choice. Even those who show great interest
in Judaism often do so for the contrast it gives to Christianity.
For example, Jacob Jocz in *Christians and Jews* writes: "In the
encounter with the Synagogue the Lordship of Jesus becomes
alive again. Everything else about the Gospel becomes a side
issue in comparison with this major question. . . . It is only in
confrontation with Judaism that the scandal of the profession
that Jesus is Lord becomes evident and acquires New Testament
proportions."[49] Despite the author's claim that he is not writing
a polemical or denigrating book about the Jews the contents of
the book show otherwise. There has not been much progress so
long as Judaism is used as an easy foil for establishing the greatness of Christianity.

As a start, several points can be advanced from within the
most narrow and orthodox Christian position. The most obvious
point but one still needing repetition: Jesus was a Jew, born of
a Jewish mother and reared in the Jewish tradition. It is linguis-
tically and otherwise difficult to say that Jesus was a Christian
but it is beyond debate that he was Jewish. From a Christian
point of view Israel should be judged a success because she

48. Hans Schoeps, *The Jewish-Christian Argument* (New York, 1963),
p. 40.
49. Jakob Jocz, *Christians and Jews* (London, 1966), p. 4.

brought forth the messiah. Nurtured in the traditions of his people he grew to manhood and carried out his mission from within the Jewish community. Since Christians believe that Jesus is the messiah for all mankind they should also believe that the Jews who long for the messiah are united in faith with Christians, that is, that the Jews implicitly believe in Jesus. Such a formulation is not acceptable and may be insulting to Jews; nonetheless a narrow Christianity even on its own terms ought to lead to closer identification with the Jews.

Even Paul, whom many Jews see as the main culprit, affirmed that God had chosen Israel and that his promises are not revoked. As represented in Romans and Ephesians, Paul sees Christians being grafted into the main stock of God's choice. Paul does place Jesus as the first born of all humanity, the supreme realization of the gift for all mankind. This belief of itself says nothing against Israel. Paul's well-known contrasts between old and new laws may be more understandable when placed in context. For the survival of their own faith today Christians have to search for a way to affirm what is Christian without denying what is Jewish.

The denigration of the "Old Testament" not only means that a part of Christian heritage is lost. It also means that the part which is salvaged is badly distorted. Rudolf Bultmann's attitude to the "Old Testament" simply carries to the extreme what is usually implicit in Christian writing: "To the Christian faith the Old Testament is not in the true sense God's Word. So far as the Church proclaims the Old Testament as God's Word, it just finds in it again what is already known from the revelation in Jesus Christ."[50] Several questions are raised by such a statement, only one of which is his attitude to the "Old Testament." In what sense is the New Testament God's word in the true

50. Rudolf Bultmann, "The Significance of the Old Testament for the Christian Faith," in *The Old Testament and Christian Faith*, ed., B. W. Anderson (New York, 1963), p. 32.

sense? What is the revelation in Jesus Christ? Can any historical figure be understood without his dialogical relation to the tradition and culture that bring him forth?

There is a strange, self-destroying process that happens to the person of Jesus as his Jewishness is eliminated. While words like Christ, Son of God and Lord are used with unrelenting frequency the one to whom these words supposedly apply seems to disappear. It became common in recent theology to refer to the "Christ event" with the presumed intention of stressing the dynamic and historical character of Christianity. The apparent gain is at the expense of eliminating the founder of the Christian movement. Whatever else Jesus of Nazareth was, he was someone and not an event.

The tendency to talk about "Christ event" springs from the premise that revelation is after all a certain set of things God told us. The Old Testament and the life of Jesus were significant in their time and may still serve as teaching aids today. However, it is not necessary to bother with all that because the revelation is clearly available to us in the texts of the New Testament. A typical statement of this position is the following: "For purposes of this discussion let us consider the 'revelation of God in Christ' as being one event. This will spare us a lengthy discussion as to which of the elements in the life, death, and resurrection of Our Lord is the most significant. The important factor at this point is that we have a certain understanding of God in terms of the totality of his revelation through his Son."[51]

The above quotation is from a book called *Scripture and Social Action*. It is a kind of book which is common today, that is, one which tries to relate the revelation of God as contained in the New Testament to the contemporary scene. Following Karl Barth's advice to carry the bible in one hand and the newspaper in the other, this kind of writing claims to be up to date.

51. Bruce Rahtjen, *Scripture and Social Action* (New York, 1966), p. 45.

Unfortunately, this species of literature is inevitably destined to appear as pretentious and arrogant. Who are these Christians who suppose they can deal with the complex issues of the day by using 2000-year-old texts which God bequeathed to them? So long as revelation is an event, or more precisely a truth that comes through an event, Christianity will be an intolerant religion. Christians will continue to claim that they have revealed truths which no one else has. If, in contrast, revelation were understood as personal and social communion, then adherence to the truth one knows implies no intolerance. Even the exaltation of one man to the heights of the divine implies no denigration of any other person or group. In fact, every brilliant man, virtuous man or heroic man lifts the whole race of men higher.

At various times in the history of Christianity there are movements to put Christ at the center of the Christian faith. Each of these movements must be looked at very carefully because very often what is happening is the reverse of what is said to be happening. Christocentric reforms often go in two different directions: a "life of Jesus" piety which invites men backward to walk in the footsteps of the Savior or a theology which makes faith today depend upon a Christ doctrine. The opposition is long standing between the christological theologians and the Jesus pietists. But both of these forms of Christ centeredness abstract themselves from the historical and social matrix of mankind. Both of them speak of Christian relevance to social issues but both have an individualistic concept of revelation which is extrinsically related to social situations. Both of them are antihistorical although they talk at length about history. The Jesusologist tries to recover every historical detail of the master's life; the Christologist constantly relates his doctrine to historical development. But the concept of revelation in both instances is not sympathetic to history. The suppositions that a man who lived 2000 years ago supplies answers to the historical problems of today or that any doctrine is a norm by which to judge history

265

are unintelligible to the man who is sensitive to history as the life of all people.

Reform movements in Christianity have usually sensed that at the center of the Christian faith ought to be Jesus the Christ. It has also usually been assumed that being "at the center" was unequivocal in meaning, but it was not. In trying to determine what the centrality of Jesus Christ means we must consider what the alternatives are. The alternatives are *not* God centered or Christ centered. The centrality of Christ is the way of being directed toward God. Christ and God are not in competition for the center, although they are not to be identified either. Discussion of theological method which pitted theocentric against christocentric missed the point.[52]

The real alternative to Christ centered is some other *thing*, e.g., church organization or written texts. The christocentric project is not an easy one to accomplish. Because Jesus of Nazareth lived 2000 years ago, theology has access to this person mainly through texts. Most struggles in Christian theology are not between Jesus and texts but between texts and texts. This struggle has usually taken the form of scriptural texts versus later doctrinal development. When this occurs the centrality of Jesus Christ may be more on the side of the scripture advocates but not necessarily so. To the extent it is a textual argument the Christ centeredness is likely to be on both sides; but for the same reason, a Christ-centered faith is not found in either set of texts. The New Testament may be the most immediate textual source for historical information on Jesus but it is still *only* a text. No humanly articulated words guarantee the conveyance of truth and no oral or written text contains a person.[53] A theology that is thoroughly New Testament in concept and language may still not defend Jesus Christ against detractors.

52. For a summary of the discussion of theocentric and christocentric theology in recent times, see: Gabriel Moran *Catechesis of Revelation* (New York, 1966), pp. 20–40.
53. See: Piet Schoonenberg, *The Christ* (New York, 1971), p. 93.

I would suggest that the paradox of a religion centered on Jesus Christ is that it might not speak much about Jesus Christ. Great teachers, leaders and prophets do not say: "Go out and quote me and speak endlessly of my accomplishments." They have instead been interested in other people thinking for themselves and acting in cooperation with their neighbor. Religious leaders have tried to show that the man truly in touch with himself and his neighbors will recognize the divine at work in the universe. The great prophet inspires people to believe against sizeable evidence that they can do greater things than he has. He can even inspire them to believe that everything is possible for those who open themselves to the creative vent of being.

If a teacher says: "Do not quote me; this is the way I think out of my own convictions and if I think for myself so should you," who is the true follower: the man who quotes this statement or the man who does not quote it? Perhaps both of them are followers, perhaps neither; it is their attitude to truth and readiness for action that will eventually show who is on the same path as the prophet.

If Christians believe that Jesus of Nazareth surpasses all the prophets, saints and heroes, one should expect them to carry through this process to its conclusion. Certainly, one would not expect a reversal of the prophetic process. The reason for the centrality of Jesus Christ, therefore, is not that he is a substitute for human struggle but that he is a constant reminder that there are no substitutes. No thing could serve that purpose; a thing becomes the exclusive possession of some group. No ordinary person is capable of turning back power and life to all those who are afraid to assume it. It requires a most extraordinary human being to lead men by refusing to accept what leadership seems to mean, to teach men by saying that his message is not his own but belongs to all who can hear, and who is willing though not anxious to lay down his life in the cause of trying to get all people to recognize their sister/brotherhood.

The life of Jesus of Nazareth is intelligible only within the set of themes discussed previously in reference to Judaism. He emerges as the chosen one who affirms the historical character of revelation. The Jewish people understood themselves to be chosen by God to dramatize in their flesh the relation of God to all mankind. Within that people of Israel, Jesus carried this logic to conclusion. It was not possible to be more chosen than he.[54] The divine pole of revelation emerged in the concreteness and ambiguity of a single life. God was not ashamed to affirm a small people or even a single person. The passage of time in all of its impenetrability and suffering becomes bearable in the light of this chosen one pushing to extremity the paradox of the divine-human. The human mind separated from life does not think it should be that way at all. "It seems indecent that an Almighty God would tie himself so firmly into the flux of things, focusing his definitive visitation of man at one simple brief period, the lifetime of Jesus Christ."[55] Many men and many religious traditions prefer to find God by escaping out of time and looking for the infinite that is uncontaminated by structures. The life and death of Jesus fell right into line with the Jewish tradition which turned away from the swift, false transfer into eternity and chose the slow, true confinement in time.[56]

All time and all flesh mediate the divine-human interaction. Jesus represents no intrusion into this process but the one who exemplifies this logic in his person. In this sense, and only in this sense, is he a "mediator."[57] He is not a middle man, a go-between, or a bargaining agent as the term mediator might suggest. He is in fact the denial that a middle man is needed because he epitomizes in himself the immediate contact of the divine and human. Since human life is shown to be open to the

54. See: Pannenberg, *Jesus-God and Man,* p. 197.
55. Ong, *op. cit.,* p. 122, commenting on G. M. Hopkins's *Wreck of the Deutschland.*
56. See: Hans Urs von Balthasar, *A Theology of History* (New York, 1963), p. 30 and also his *Martin Buber and Christianity* (New York, 1962), p. 26.
57. See: Edward Schillebeeckx, *The Church and Mankind* (Glen Rock, 1965), p. 98.

divine, then every life is part of the process of revelation that is always present, personal and social.

As the life of Jesus is an embodiment of the peculiar logic of Israel's history, so his teaching derives almost completely from that world. Each of his ethical teachings has its parallel in the "Old Testament" or the Talmud. Nonetheless, his teachings have an urgency and vividness which give them a character that is refreshingly new.[58] His attitude of faith in God, obedience to the law and reliance upon the promises marked his teaching as authentically Jewish. More than was the case in earlier Judaism he addressed the individual. But such development presumes no disparagement of the prophets who had preceded him. "The sayings of Jesus about love for the enemy derives its light from the world of Judaism in which he stands and which he seems to contest; and he outshines it. . . . But one should not fail to appreciate the bearers of the plain light below from amongst whom he arose: those who enjoined much that was possible so as not to cause men to despair of being able to serve God in their poor everyday affairs."[59]

In this context for the life of Jesus much of the Christian terminology which quickly developed was, to say the least, misleading. For example, saying that he was the one mediator between God and man was not a helpful formulation. He was the man who brought mediation to a personal peak. Henceforth, there was to be no need of things interposed between the divine and human. What Christians meant by saying he was the one mediator was that old forms of mediation were seen to be unnecessary. He demonstrated with his life that the divine is mediated in personal communion everywhere.

Christians also chose to use the word "incarnation" to describe Jesus Christ. If they had wished to restrict the word to that one person then the word should have been put in continuity with other words. Perhaps better, incarnation could have

58. See: Klausner, *op. cit.*, 414.
59. Buber, *Two Types of Faith*, p. 75.

269

been used to describe everyone's life. To say that God became incarnate in Jesus Christ and nowhere else implies that a process with a logic all its own takes over here. It would be better to to use incarnation and revelation as applicable to the same process.[60]

Christian faith would then maintain that just as revelation began with the divine-human interaction of creation and continues to the end of time, so also incarnation is the process which reaches a climactic stage with the appearance of Jesus but continues today. "The first step in any pragmatic reconstruction of this symbol is to reject viewing it as an event which happened in the past and as localized exclusively in Jesus of Nazareth. Instead of speaking of God as having *become* incarnate, it is more appropriate to speak of God *becoming* incarnate."[61] If Christians had kept more in contact with Jewish tradition they would have spoken of incarnation as part of the intention of creation and not as a rescue operation after the introduction of sin.

In the original documents of Christianity there is a variety of languages and images. At times the New Testament speaks of God sending down his son from heaven. This divine being saves mankind from sin through his suffering. The punishment of this one person seemed to substitute for other men being punished. What the New Testament did not say was that this person is God. He was God's anointed, God's son or God's word; these and other phrases could have been compatible with the Jewish tradition of which he was a part.[62]

60. See: Juan Alfaro, "Encarnación y Revelación," in *Gregorianum XLIX* (1968), p. 459.
61. Fontinell, *op. cit.*, p. 250; see also Teilhard de Chardin, *Christianity and Evolution* p. 53: "The incarnation of the word (which is in the process of continual and universal consummation) is simply the final term of a creation which is still continuing everywhere."
62. See: Raymond Brown, "Does the New Testament Call Jesus God?" in *Theological Studies* XXVI (Dec., 1965), pp. 545–573; see also: Rylaarsdam, *loc. cit.*, p. 75: "If Jesus Christ were simply a new epitome

A process began almost immediately that would blur the distinction between Jesus as the messiah of God and Jesus as God. This tendency is often attributed to the Hellenistic philosophy of the time and undoubtedly a case can be made for that influence. However, the desire to have a divine being who would eliminate the problems of understanding the divine is more widespread than Hellenism. There is probably a universal desire to get rid of guilt and suffering by a god taking them away. The development of Christological doctrine would allow Christians to boast that everyone else has only human means and human outlook. Only by being a Christian could one also view reality as God does.[63]

One of the strongest connecting links between Jewish and Greek traditions was the concept of the Logos of God. Apart from Jesus the development of the logos doctrine was occurring among the Jews of the Diaspora. The wisdom which the Jews had proclaimed was also being sought for by the Greeks. Both traditions, despite their strong differences, believed in some intelligible divine logic in which the world was structured. This context was waiting for use by the Christians who wished to announce to all the nations that the desired one had arrived. The messiah of God was said to be the manifestation of the logos. The church fathers believed that the logos is actively present in everything but it is in the life of Jesus Christ that the logos finds full expression.[64]

The subtlety of theological distinctions did not well survive the process of "Christian education." In popular Christianity,

---

of the Word of God, exemplifying new insights into its authority and finality, in relation to the human facts of sin and death, for example, the chasm between our two Bibles and two faiths would not be so great. What makes it great is the Christian identification of a particular event in the order of time, space, and matter as the very Word of God."

63. See: Niles, *op. cit.*, p. 25.

64. On the doctrine of the logos in the church fathers, see: Justin Martyr, *Apologia*, I, 46; Clement of Alexandria, *Stromata*, V, 5, 29; Augustine, *De Magistro*, 11, 38.

271

Jesus became equivalent to God and all distinctions became inoperative. The attempt to preserve the human nature of Jesus was in practice overwhelmed by the assertion that he was God. The Christian conception of revelation was incapable of coping with the intricacies of what councils and liturgy were struggling to express. In turn, as the divine character of Jesus Christ became the one dominant note, the category of revelation became further evacuated. Jesus Christ might still be called the "revelation of God" but this simply meant that God delivered the revelation in the person of Christ, instead of the phrase meaning that in Jesus the receptivity of the human for the divine reached a high point.

Christians believe that Jesus is the revelation of God. This position need not imply any arrogance or intolerance. The claim that Jesus is the greatest single expression of revelation would be difficult to prove. However, even that claim is not an intolerant one. The word which does cause a problem is the one which came to dominate discussion about Christ, viz., uniqueness. The question "Is Christ unique?" is probably the best touchstone of orthodoxy in the modern Christian world. Before one can judge the claim to uniqueness to be true or false, one must investigate the meaning of the word unique.[65]

Unique is a peculiar word in the language. It seems to say that something is completely different from everything else. On second thought, however, it is obvious that this cannot be so. A comparison implies that in some way there are similarities. One thing can be different from another thing only under certain aspects. At the least they are the same in being *things*. Uniqueness would then have to be considered a limit point never reached in which a thing would exclude all shared properties. Although a thing could be unique (or alone) in a class of things, it is literally senseless to say that a thing is a unique thing.

65. See: C. F. D. Moule, "Is Christ Unique?" in *Faith, Fact and Fantasy* (Philadelphia, 1966), pp. 101–125.

The word unique, however, can function in a different direction. One can say that each thing, insofar as it is one thing, is not another. Every individual thing is uniquely itself; in this usage the word is equivalent to individuality. Grammarians protest that the adjective unique does not have degree but popular usage correctly senses a comparative meaning. As one goes up the scale of beings the unity which distinguishes things increases, in this sense the animal might be called "more unique" than the vegetable. This concept of uniqueness makes full sense only when we speak of persons. Each human being is not one of a class but an unrepeatable original. One might debate whether each molecule in a piece of wood is a unique being but there is no doubt about a person's uniqueness.[66]

The claim that Jesus was unique would not be difficult to sustain on the basis of this second meaning. Every human being is unique and to the extent that his human integrity is developed, the more apparent is the uniqueness. The claim that Jesus is the (most) unique revelation of God would mean that his receptivity for divine communion was the greatest known to men. This would still be a big claim, of course, but it is one that might be defensible logically and phenomenologically. It is a claim which does not exclude revelation elsewhere. In fact, it implies that the receptivity which was most pronounced in the life of Jesus is to varying degrees present in every human life.

The common claim to a unique revelation has not been what I have just described. A unique revelation has not meant a unique Jesus but a unique Christianity. Since the "revelation of God in Christ" was understood as that thing which God has delivered to mankind, the claim to uniqueness has meant the possession of a unique thing, i.e., a "Christian revelation." The

66. John Macmurray, *The Structure of Religious Experience* (New York, 1971), p. 12 bases the comparative character of uniqueness on value: "For the more generally useful a thing is, the less individuality it possesses. The more unique anything is—the more it possesses an intrinsic value of its own —the less generally useful it is apt to be for practical purposes."

273

concept of a "Christian revelation" implies the first meaning of uniqueness cited above, i.e., a thing possessing some aspects which are not found in other things of the same class.

A "Christian revelation" will almost certainly be called unique. The only question is how the claim will be pushed; two ways lie open. In the first, it will be claimed that "Christian revelation" alone can legitimately be called revelation. All the other so-called revelations are human inventions which do not reveal God. In the second way, there are many revelations but the "Christian revelation" has some truths which no other revelation has. Christian theology has been edging its way into this second claim because the first is so blatantly intolerant and self-righteous. But the second way is illogical and contrived and does not even achieve the purpose of opening the door to other faiths. A reduction in the quantity of religious truths claimed as exclusively one's own does not represent coming to grips with the problem. As soon as one introduces the concept of a "Christian revelation" one will be faced with a choice between intolerance and indifference. The way out of intolerance is not through being indifferent but by denying that the phrase "Christian revelation" is valid.

In summary, a *thing's* claim to uniqueness rests upon the claim to exclusivity whereas the specifically *personal* claim to uniqueness derives from its inclusivity. Thing-like uniqueness demands unrelatedness; a thing is unique if it possesses some characteristic which is not possessed by any other thing in its class. A person can also work for that kind of uniqueness but it is self-defeating. The more different and unrelated a person is, the less the person has of identity which grows out of relationship. If, in contrast, the person is receptive to other beings he or she will become more and more a unique self. Complete uniqueness for a person would imply a similarity to every being in the universe. A unique revelation would be a divine-human relation capable of being filled out by all that is human and divine. The significance of the figure of Jesus is that he should be the continual reminder that all claims to an exclusively unique revelation are false in principle because they reduce revelation to a thing. In reference to revelation, Jesus' person excludes only the claim to exclusion; it affirms that all reality is revelational.

The preceding discussion of the word unique may seem belabored and artificial. It is. I went into it not because I think that the word unique is particularly helpful here but because the word is so central to Christian formulations of belief. I hope at least to have shown that the question of a unique revelation in Christ and a unique "Christian revelation" are radically different issues. The reason why it is wrong to speak of a "unique Christian revelation" is because there is no "Christian revelation." On the other hand, the use of the word unique with reference to Jesus was not entirely misguided. It sprang from a genuine instinct to exalt both God and man. Given the difficulties of the word, however, I would not recommend its use. If exclusivity is not intended, why is it necessary to introduce the claim to uniqueness? The Christian can claim that he gets decisive help to make sense out of his life in the figure of Jesus. He can even claim that some definitive breakthrough in human history occurs with this person. The word uniqueness adds nothing but a claim vis-à-vis other religions and the claim is almost certainly premature. A great deal more dialogue between religions is needed before any one can make the claim which uniqueness implies.[67]

In any dialogue with other religions Christianity stands in a

67. For example, O'Collins, *op. cit.*, p. 44: "Outside Christ there is no revelation. Outside official Christianity there can be revelation, but it is always a divine disclosure which comes from and leads to Christ.... Whether explicitly recognized or not, Christ constitutes the only true light which enlightens every man." The first and last sentence are misleading, to say the least. Christian belief that revelation is supremely embodied in Christ does not imply that "outside Christ there is no revelation." Statements like this one are patently insulting to people who are not Christians, a fact which should make Christians examine whether they are saying what they mean to say.

275

very good position with reference to its founder. Instead of jumping to all kinds of conclusions that indicate an insecurity, Christians could concentrate on communicating an inspiring portrait of the human situation in Jesus. Where this communication might lead cannot be predicted. The Christian ought not to be worrying about that but how to make available to those who are not Christians some appreciation of the Christ figure. Instead of having to fight off competitors to Jesus, the Christians would probably find a great receptivity to the person of Jesus. If the main part of Christian tradition does not do this, then the Jesus figure is likely to re-emerge in many weird forms. For all their talk the Christian churches do not seem to grasp the strength of this central element. Great religious leaders of our own time do not think of themselves in competition with Jesus. Mahatma Gandhi wrote: "I refuse to believe that there now exists or has ever existed a person that has not made use of his [Jesus'] example to lessen his sins, even though he may have done so without realizing it. The lives of all have, in some greater or lesser degree, been changed by his presence, his actions, and the words spoken by his divine voice.... And because the life of Jesus has the significance and the transcendency to which I have alluded, I believe that he belongs not solely to Christianity, but to the entire world."[68]

The claim by Christians that Jesus is the "fulfillment" is as problematical as the claim to uniqueness. In the early church fulfillment was first used in reference to the Jewish scriptures. That claim was quickly broadened to include a fulfillment of Greek philosophy. Gregory of Nyssa wrote: "The Jewish dogma is destroyed by the acceptance of the Logos and by the belief in the Spirit; while the polytheistic error of the Greek school is made to vanish by the unity of the Nature abrogating this imagination of plurality. While yet again, of the Jewish con-

68. Quoted in James Douglass, *The Non Violent Cross* (New York 1968), p. 56.

276

ception, let the unity of the Nature stand; and of the Hellenistic, only the distinction as to persons."[69]

In Christian writing today the claim to fulfillment is made in reference to all other religions. Whereas the church fathers could base their claim on dubious exegesis, it is difficult to see what the basis of the claim is today. But the underlying question here is the nature and meaning of "fulfillment." As I indicated earlier, if fulfillment of the Jewish scriptures were to mean that the promises were withdrawn or are no longer valid, then it should not be said that Jesus or Christianity fulfills Jewish history. There is a real sense, however, in which every great person fulfills the past of his people, not in the sense of abrogating but of expressing the hopes and promises of the tradition. Each prophet is a fulfillment though he is also a promise to some greater fulfillment. Fulfilling old promises means living them to the height of perfection, thereby making them new again.

There is little doubt that Jesus as a most faithful Jew was a fulfiller of Jewish hopes. The problem for the Jews was the Christian claim that with Jesus the messianic age had arrived. To the Jews who were suffering persecution the claim seemed patently false. The Jews and Christians were perhaps saying different things: The Christians that the messiah had come, the Jews that the messianic age had not come. Discussion could not get beyond this point. Jews cannot say that Jesus is the messiah but the term messianic era might have some flexibility.

Christians believe that in Jesus of Nazareth a decisive historical breakthrough occurred. Nonetheless, the messianic traits of one person do not make a messianic era or a messianic society. If there is to be a messianic age it is still in the process of coming to be. Even though Christians refer to Jesus as the Christ they have also spoken of the Christ to come. Norbert Lohfink

69. Quoted in Jaroslav Pelikan, "De-Judaization and Hellenization: The Ambiguities of Christian Identity" in Papin, *op. cit.,* p. 124.

can write: "The statement: 'In Christ God acted finally in history' and 'in Christ God will act finally in history' must both be combined to form the Christian understanding of history."[70] The only place where this Christ of past and Christ of future can be joined is in the religious experience of the present. Jews and Christians remain divided not only on whether Jesus is *the* Christ but whether there is *a* Christ. But Jews should be able to understand that belief in a Christ at the end of history quite logically includes a belief that the Christ has found embodiment in the flow of history.[71]

It should be evident that even if one claims that Jesus is the most perfect fulfillment of human hopes, it does not follow that Christianity is the fulfillment of other religions. It is doubtful that it makes any sense at all to say that one religion is the fulfillment of all the others. In any case, the Christian religion is only a limited expression of the "kingdom of God" which Jesus asserted was close at hand. Christians and non-Christians both look forward to the realization of such a world. Christians cannot claim to follow perfectly the Christ that is past and they certainly cannot claim to possess the Christ that is to come. Neither can Christians claim to have the key to understand all other religions as mere forerunners or distortions of the one true faith. If there is a one true faith it has yet to be realized.[72]

It will be helpful here to comment further on the life of Jesus as an exemplification of faith and a realization of love.

70. Norbert Lohfink, *The Christian Meaning of the Old Testament* (Milwaukee, 1968), p. 136.

71. See: Teilhard de Chardin, *Christianity and Evolution*, p. 181: "The more, indeed, we think about the profound laws of evolution, the more convinced we must be that the universal Christ would not appear at the end of time at the peak of the world, if he had not previously entered it during its development, *through the medium of birth* in the form of an *element*. If it is indeed true that it is through Christ-Omega that the universe in movement holds together, then, correspondingly, it is from his concrete germ, the Man of Nazareth that Christ-Omega (both theoretically and historically) derives his whole consistence."

72. See: Allen, *op. cit.,* p. 155.

He emerges within a long list of prophets who feel called to speak some hard truths for which they are likely to suffer.[73] The religious prophet is obsessed with awareness of God but not in a narcissistic way. His whole self is turned outward toward the universal community where the truth has to be realized. Speaking of the true religious man, Erik Erikson writes: "What is true now will, if not attended to, never be true again; and what is untrue now will never, by any trick, become true later. Therefore I would interpret, and interpret with humility, the truth-force of the religious actualist thus: to be ready to die for what is true now means to grasp the only chance to have lived fully."[74]

Jesus lived at one of the great turning points in human history, the so-called axial period. It was an era marked by the rise of new groups of people ready to turn away from the possession of material goods toward some higher ideal of the human. As the Buddha several centuries before him had set in motion the religious quest, so Jesus inspired a following. The life of Jesus created a new way of life among those who found his teaching and example to resonate in their lives. Even among the enemies of Christianity the ideal of the Christ figure has not found adequate substitute.

In the terms of modern historical scholarship we have a very limited knowledge of the life of Jesus. Attempts at writing a biography have all but been abandoned. The limited knowledge seems to shake up scholars more than it does the ordinary folk. The latter seem to find the gospel story adequate. A. N. Whitehead wrote:

The essence of Christianity is the appeal to the life of Christ as a revelation of the nature of God and of his agency in the world. The record is fragmentary, inconsistent and uncertain.... But there can be no doubt as to what elements in the record have evoked a

73. See: Urs von Balthasar, *Martin Buber and Christianity,* p. 104.
74. Erik Erikson, *Gandhi's Truth* (New York, 1969), p. 399.

response from all that is best in human nature. The Mother, the Child, and the bare manger; the lowly man, homeless and self-forgetful, with his message of peace, love and sympathy; the suffering, the agony, the tender words as life ebbed, the final despair; and the whole with the authority of supreme victory.[75]

There is one particular point about the ethical attitude of Jesus which needs comment. Many Jewish writers are severely critical of what they call an ethic of self-abnegation. To an ethic of self-abnegation they oppose an ethic of self-fulfillment as the only workable social ideal.[76] This objection carries strong weight against some Christian rhetoric which condemns "self-assertion" and glorifies "self-abandonment." It is fairly evident that there are overtones of meaning with each of these words which may vary from one person to the next. Self-fulfillment may not be incompatible with self-abandonment depending upon the meaning of these two phrases.

Even though differences will remain between Christians and Jews, it should be possible to clear away some of the ambiguity here. Christian theology has not been able to sustain a social concept of revelation and is thus prevented from having a social ethic. Christian teaching has been caught on the horns of the dilemma: self-assertion to deal with the terrible evils of the world or self-abnegation to provide a Christ-like witness to God. The alternatives are almost never placed in such bold contrast but such a dilemma does flow from the notion of faith and revelation in much of Christianity.[77]

The way out of this difficulty lies in the direction of developing an adequate anthropology with a social meaning of revelation. From the description in chapter two of this book an ideal

75. Alfred North Whitehead, *Adventure of Ideas* (New York, 1967), p. 167.
76. For example, Klausner, *op. cit.,* p. 391; Gordis, *op. cit.,* p. 155.
77. An individualistic notion of revelation tends to produce an overgrown institution of Church to house it; see: Walter Rauschenbusch, *Christianity and the Social Crisis,* ed., Robert Cross (New York, 1964), p. 185.

emerges of what a mature, healthy, adult, virtuous, responsible and morally good person is. "For almost all, the model of human excellence—sometimes assumed, sometimes clinically proved—is that of a self-determination from within, motivated and shaped by love for those around us."[78] I am not presuming that this ideal is a scientific one to which a Jewish, Christian or Hindu ethic must conform to be valid. It could be maintained in fact that this modern ideal draws heavily upon religious traditions, especially the Christian gospel. This is not to claim that a religious document can establish a scientific ideal.

The nature of interaction between religion and science on this issue will always remain debatable. The most that I wish to establish here are the following three points: (1) There are some lines of convergence about what constitutes a human and ethical ideal. (2) This ideal is not a rationalistic catalogue of powers to be developed but involves abandonment, receptivity and the risk of losing one's life if necessary. (3) The Christian following of Jesus may push to the limit the paradox of willingness to give up one's life to save it, but this ethic is not entirely different from nor completely opposed to ethical ideals found elsewhere than in Christianity.

It would help if Christians would stop speaking in falsely posed antimonies, delighting in the alternatives which make human choice prematurely clear. No one should be told that the choices are: to give oneself to faith or to follow one's reasoning, to surrender to God or to assert oneself, to follow the world or to follow Christ. In these and a dozen other formulations, phrases from the New Testament are wielded to set up contrasts. The process is one more manifestation of that biblicism which presumes that the "Christian revelation" is the catalogue of truths Christ left to Christians. The startling phrases of the New Testament abstracted from the flow of Jewish and world

78. Langdon Gilkey, *Naming the Whirlwind* (New York, 1969), p. 380.

history can be weapons in the hands of unhealthy people who, as Max Scheler said, because they love no one think they must love God.

At times even Christians realize that the process has gone awry when texts are used in racist or reactionary ways. But the aberrations are intrinsic to the process. The fact that Christianity has thought of *preaching* as one of its central activities is indicative of its unworkable and distorted ethic. Preachers cannot grasp that telling people what to do may be part of the problem instead of the answer. The preacher delivers a text to people and the medium would be inadequate no matter what the message. Unfortunately, the message often makes the preaching worse. It tells people to imitate Jesus (who in the next breath is presented as a superhuman being who could not possibly be imitated) and to live by New Testament texts.

If anyone were actually to do what the preacher demands it would mean giving up the attempt to figure out what to do with his life. Beyond that it is not clear at all what the preacher is advising by words like conversion, faith, self-abnegation, etc. In the middle ages "renouncing the world" may have meant that an individual gave himself over to a tightly knit group such as a monastic community. For some people it was undoubtedly an unhealthy, masochistic life; for others it was probably a blossoming of their persons despite the particular restraints. In any case, the choice was never what the exaggerated rhetoric seemed to make it: God or the world, pleasure or asceticism, self-love or God's will, etc. Life has always been more complicated than that and it continues to become more complicated still. But one thing has become clearer: a religion of documents and preaching which opposes self and other, self and God is invalid.

I am trying to suggest that a rapprochement is possible between a Jewish and modern ideal of self-fulfillment and a Christian ideal of individual responsibility. Jesus of Nazareth was one of the supreme individuals who tried to show with his life that the affirmation of the individual is not in negation of the community but is carried out in, with and for a community. He was willing if it came to it to lay down his life even though his sense of what he had to do conflicted with a repugnance for suffering and death.

When he was forced to the limit he did lay down his life for his brothers; he did it because he wished to and willed to do it.[79] Set within the flow of world history his life could have been a powerful impulse toward the era of universal peace and justice. In some ways it has had that effect but in many other respects the Christian church has failed miserably. Because the church "possessed Christ" it jumped over all the intermediary steps and came up with final answers before the questions had been asked.

Jesus could have been the focus of the comprehensive affirmation of God and world, individual and community, personal and impersonal nature, but Christianity often turned him into the opposite. It might almost be said that he came too early. People were not ready to understand the reality of individuality without doing injustice to one's neighbor, to nature and to ethnic and national traditions. The sense of individual was a kind of potion on which men could become drunk. On the other hand, perhaps it was necessary for the human race to experience a rampant individualism before it could fully grasp the relation between person and community. It is useless to speculate on what might have been if history had been different. But it is very pertinent

79. See: Lynch, *Images of Hope,* pp. 125–126: "I do not say that it is clearly said in any particular proposition of religious thought, but it seems half accepted—without propositions—by the religious mind that wishing is not quite the best thing in the world and that having one's own wishes might possibly be the worst thing in the world. There is, for example, a fondness for the isolating of that one prayer of Christ in his agony: *Not my will but thine be done.* Seldom cited are such phrases as one that explains why he was put to death. *Quia voluit,* the Vulgate reads: because he wished it."

to criticize the Christian church, which to the extent that it conceives of itself as "the one true church established by Christ to save mankind," perpetuates much of this inadequate ethical and human ideal.

It is appropriate at this point to introduce a topic which is fundamental to Christian faith, that is, what Christian tradition called the resurrection of Jesus. The word resurrection is a very problematical one which I shall discuss. But the New Testament was written and Christianity came into existence on the presupposition of what was called the resurrection. The documents of the New Testament are written in the light of that belief by people who believed that Jesus had "risen."

It might be more logical to place this discussion before the preceding comments on Jesus but that procedure can be a block to considering the life of Jesus. Since the whole New Testament is influenced by this belief it cannot be entirely put aside in any discussion. However, an explicit and detailed treatment of the matter needs preparation. What was at issue in the history of Judaism and in other religions forms the background for consideration of Jesus. Any neglect of this background will almost inevitably lead into the resurrection of Jesus becoming an unintelligible, brute fact, the most extraordinary incursion of God into the world. Then the whole of Christianity is precariously hung from this datum, with the reason for accepting the doctrine being that the bible says it's so. Any questioning or doubting of this demand is taken as a manifestation of lack of faith.

The world is not without many people who are looking for strange beliefs like a man coming back from the dead. All the problems of life become manageable or minor if everything can be solved by one herculean effort at faith. Of course, there remains a constant problem of believing in this one strange bit of information but the problem is a single, consolidated one. With enough fear, anxiety, guilt and good intention, it is possible for a human being to believe anything. The doctrine of the resurrection of Jesus can function this way, that is, as a trump card which enables one to escape from living. Although the belief is not evident or even intelligible to most people, it is made patently true within the believer's own system. Thus, the resurrection was made into an obvious fact which anyone with an open mind could see. The fact that the Jews did not see it was taken as proof that they are close-minded. The Jews' failure to accept the resurrection proved that they were wrong and the Christians were right.

Many Christian writers recognize that this simplistic opposition is not tenable. They have difficulty with miracles of any sort and the resurrection strikes them as the most incredible of the lot. However, they do not have much room to move. Discussion of the resurrection quickly becomes a battle of exegetes agonizing over every detail of the fragmentary and confusing texts of the New Testament. The possible results are severely limited by the restricted starting point. Conservative exegetes are likely to conclude that although the evidence is sketchy there is no reason why people should not continue to believe what they have always believed. Liberal exegetes are likely to come up with some vague formulas which do not exactly deny the old but certainly do not affirm it. The belief that "Jesus arose in the faith of the Church" is not something Christians would ever have opposed but it is also not what they have believed. If the resurrection simply means that the apostles were inspired to preach about Jesus, there are more direct and clearer ways to say just that. It would seem that one should candidly admit that Christianity was founded on an egregious error. That is a possible conclusion for a scholar to come to but if he does then it is puzzling why he does not say that. It is even more puzzling why he keeps speaking as if the New Testament were the source of religious truth for the world.

The whittling down of a belief until it can be turned into

285

something else is not well named "liberal." The process does not break Christians out of their narrow confines to make contact with others who are searching for meaning and love. On the contrary, Christian reinterpretations of the resurrection have turned Christianity in on itself to where it possesses the kerygma. Herbert McCabe pinpoints the issue: "There are Christians who hold that the resurrection of Christ means that, although he died, he still lives on in the faith of his followers—a faith expressed by word and sacrament in the church. The basic catholic objection to this is that it makes of the resurrection a religious event, one that makes a difference primarily to what happens in the church; whereas for the catholic tradition the resurrection is a cosmic event, it means that Christ is present to the whole world whether believer or not. The resurrection meant not just that a church was founded, it meant that the world was different."[80]

The claim which is expressed here is an enormous one but at least it is fairly clear what is claimed and why it is important. My presumption is that this belief must be intelligibly connected with the tendencies in Jewish tradition, the searchings in other religions and the best drives which can be located in contemporary experience. Biblical exegetes may object to this procedure since they prefer to approach the texts of the New Testament with a clean slate. That procedure, however, makes presumptions about the nature of the New Testament which are highly questionable. It also makes dubious presumptions about the relation of knowledge and experience. In positing a wider experience as the measure of this Christian belief I am trying first to determine not whether the belief is true but what the belief means. I am not interested here in whether "modern man" can believe in the resurrection of Jesus after the invention of the electric light. I do not think "he" should be asked to until it is decided what is meant by resurrection.

80. Herbert McCabe, *What Is Ethics All About?* (Washington, 1969), p. 142.

The best of our experience points to the affirmation of the individual and the community as both having a permanent value. The individual emerged out of the collectivity of the whole as the flux of time came to be accepted as real. Truth, meaning, life and love are not to be found except in a history which embraces all who have lived and will live, a history that is truly of the world. The drive of this world is toward a unity but a unity which constantly reveals greater diversity than we had imagined. There is an "instinct" here which stands on the side of life against death and being against non-being. This bias toward living is one which has existed and still exists today without visible support from religious belief. But religions at their best, including Jewish and Christian forms, have supported this instinct. Despite the powerful evidence of seeing each individual die, religions have stubbornly refused to admit that the evidence is conclusive. There is a different kind of evidence which supports the human desire to live.

Jewish history was and is a way of looking at the whole universe. From personal experience the people of Israel came to trust in the process of history. The Jews believed that there is a point of unity toward which history moves. Magic, as a way of manipulating divine favor or of skipping over the finite structures of the universe, was thereby excluded. The choice was to accept man, the world and God in the movement of life or else to look for an escape hatch.

Jesus of Nazareth stood squarely in this tradition of affirming life in the face of death. He arrived at a culminating moment in the history of Judaism and the world scene. It was now clear that not only a people struggles to overcome death but that each person is confronted with the problem of his own death. A God who abandons each person to the grave would not be worthy of trust by each person. If the universe is worthwhile, then the most significant differentiation within it cannot be plowed back into the whole. The Christian faith grasped this fact. Focused in Jesus of Nazareth the Christians saw something

287

new about the divine in relation to the human. "Easter is not an episode; it is both a culmination and a new beginning. Resurrection is an assertion about God before it is a puzzling reported fact about Jesus. And the persistent heart of the puzzle is due to the fact that the first shines through the second, and has never been understood in the historical mind of the church in any other way."[81]

There is a problem, as I have indicated, with the word resurrection. The people who were living at the time of Jesus tried to express something about God and the world; they used a word which was available at that time. The word is burdened with certain associations and connotations which have become more troubling over the centuries. Looking back from today, one could speculate about resurrection being an unfortunate choice of term. But it will not work to put aside the word today as if it had not been a key word on which the whole tradition was built. However, if the word cannot be disregarded, neither should it be shouted at people as if there were no problem with it. When the question is asked: Was the resurrection an historical event? the temptation is to give an immediate answer of yes or no. But in addition to "historical event" not being a self-evident phrase, the word resurrection probably makes the question unanswerable.

The matter at issue, however, is not so unclear as much of the historical and exegetical argument would suggest. Men at the time of Jesus, as well as men before and since then, have wished for the triumph of life over death. They have wished to believe that death was not the end of everything. There have been several ways to express this hope but each way that speaks directly of it has severe limitations. Two words that were commonly used dealt with the question in very different ways. Those words were immortality and resurrection. These two words got run together in the history of Christian thought but they were originally derived from two contrasting anthropologies.

81. Joseph Sittler, *The Ecology of Faith* (Philadelphia, 1961), p. 40.

The word immortality denies the reality of death. It is almost impossible to say that "men are immortal" because very obviously men die. However, it is possible to say that the soul or the spirit is immortal. This belief almost always implies that a man is composed of two parts: a soul and a body. The body part ultimately is not significant and is hardly real at all. A logical conclusion to this belief is that a human being is hardly real if it is the soul or spirit which survives. The immortal, unchanging soul is bothered with its material connection only for a time. A doctrine of immortality thus denies the personal, social and historical character of reality. The doctrine fails to affirm the dignity and value of the human person.

The Jews at the time of Jesus and the Christians of that period had no intention of denying the personal, social and historical character of the universe. Pharisaic Judaism and early Christianity made use of another word to express their hope: resurrection. The origin of the word is impossible to trace here but it has both Greek and Hebrew connections. The word varied in meaning from one group to another. Among some gnostic groups it meant that the soul had arisen when it received the gnosis that separated it from ordinary life.[82] In any case, the word bears within itself the image of rising or standing up, with the added touch that one is rising *again*. Most literally it seems to suppose that a person stands up in the tomb and comes back to life, that is, reverts to his previous state. This image hardly does justice to what early Christians were trying to affirm. Nor would a man coming back from the dead seem to be of any special help to anyone.

The larger context of the question must be kept in mind. Christians were trying to say something about God and a personal universe. They pressed into service the word resurrection though they must have realized themselves that the word was in many ways misleading. St. John tells the story of Lazarus as a

82. See: Willi Marxsen, *The Resurrection of Jesus* (Philadelphia, 1970), p. 132.

sign of what was to come in Jesus' life but with no thought of making the return of Lazarus an instance in the same class as Jesus' resurrection. The Christian intention was not to say that Jesus had returned but that Jesus' life and teaching had been authenticated by God. They believed that Jesus did not come back to life on earth but that he passed to some new life with the God who did not discredit him by abandoning him.[83]

The resurrection texts of the New Testament are products of the interpretation of the experience of the community. This statement is not a denial of the truth, realism or validity of the texts. The whole New Testament is an interpretation of the experience of the authors. The resurrection texts may have more imaginative detail written into them than most of the remainder of the New Testament. But what is affirmed by these texts and indeed witnessed to by the *existence* of the New Testament is not obscure. Jesus of Nazareth did not cease with death. He continues in some way that is beyond our imaginations (though not beyond our desires). To say that the early church believed that "Jesus arose into the kerygma" is little short of equivocation. If someone wishes to maintain that that is all that happened he can do so without great difficulty. He should also admit that the apostles were wrong in their belief. The inadequacy of the word resurrection cannot obscure the fact that the authors of the New Testament believed that Jesus of Nazareth still is. It was not first a question of "preachers of his word" but the person whom death did not stop.

If the question is clear in regard to Christian belief, the next obvious question is why anyone should believe such a story. To which question I would respond that one should not believe stories but that one should believe in people and the universe. Strange stories can become acceptable if they make some sense

83. See: Ulrich Wilckens, "The Tradition—History of the Resurrection of Jesus" in *The Significance of the Message of the Resurrection for Faith in Jesus Christ,* ed., C. F. D. Moule (Naperville, 1968), p. 70.

out of the marvelous, surprising and incomprehensible world. If a story is a response to an almost universal quest, one should be wary of ever pronouncing the story false. If experience becomes richer and wider on this basis and if experience is bearable at all for some people only on this premise, then one can never dismiss this way of looking at the universe.

The resurrection of Jesus, therefore, is not one of a long list of miracles (virgin birth, bread and fishes, Lazarus in the tomb) to be dissected on the same principles. Resurrection was the light in which the New Testament came to be. Just as "creation" is a culmination of Jewish belief in God and his relation to the world, so resurrection was a new creation story to express something further on the divine-human relation. Creation/Resurrection was not an account of what God once did but is a description (in inadequate words) of the present relation of God and the universe. Christians believed that resurrection was a modifying or perfecting of the creation belief. In Jesus of Nazareth a breaththrough was made in affirming decisively that not only the universe and the group are God's but the individual person as well.

The resurrection of Jesus did not enter into the historical stream as a brute fact to be taken on faith against all reason. It was rather a focusing and dramatic embodiment of what is everywhere present. Religions have constantly expressed the sentiment that man must endure. In early Jewish religion and in early stages of other religions it was not clear that "man" meant the individual man and woman. But once the individual person has surfaced it is impossible to go back. If there is not "personal" survival then the universe for the person is absurd. It does little good to tell a person to trust in God and the future if the person's ultimate future is simply to go down to the dust again.

In the latter part of the Hebrew scriptures (2nd Isaiah, Daniel, Baruch, Ezra) the doctrine of creation was being modi-

291

fied to include resurrection.[84] The Jesus story continued in that direction. In the eyes of the Jews the Christian belief foreshortened and thereby distorted the hope for a messianic age. But the hope of Jew and Christians, as well as many other religious traditions, is not radically different here. It is the hope that being ultimately is "gracious," that in the end man is not simply done in and that annihilation is not final victor. Religions did not first come up with the doctrines of soul, spirit, immortality, resurrection, etc., and then overextended into the literal what should have been figurative. Men have desperately wanted life, have sensed that there is a way out, and then have expressed this hope in a variety of imagery. None of the images is adequate but each of them is a protest against the finality of death.[85]

The hope of resurrection is an affirmation of life in spite of death. It does not deny that death is real, horrible and disintegrating but it maintains that life is stronger than death. The deeper the experience of life, the greater is the demand that life triumph. "There is no meaningful hope for the body we *have* but only for the body we *are*. In love we break through the deadly category of having and arrive at the category of affirmed being. Herein alone lies resurrection hope in accord with the Christian faith."[86]

The experience of love for a human being is the way in which a person grasps that unity and differentiation are not opposites. The final choice is between an undifferentiated impersonal unity and an organic unity which does not obliterate the

84. See: Moltmann, *Theology of Hope,* pp. 208–211.
85. See: Van der Leeuw, *op. cit.,* pp. 311–312; Teilhard de Chardin, *Christianity and Evolution,* p. 206: "The more life is individualized, the more it finds an absolute irreversible need in itself. Expressed in positive terms, this means simply that the only form of universe compatible with the presence and persistence on earth of a thought, is a system psychically convergent on some cosmic focus of conservation and ultra-personalization."
86. Jürgen Moltmann, *Religion, Revolution and the Future* (New York, 1969), p. 58.

centers of personal consciousness which helped create the universe. Love is the irrefutable testimony that the second alternative is both possible and necesary. Love destroys the security of plans for the future because it reveals that men are mortal and that they die one by one.[87] The one who loves intensely in this life finds it extremely difficult to believe that anything survives death. The lover simply finds it harder still to accept that death is the end of all.

The effect of the hope which is concomitant with love is a deeper immersion into life combined with a readiness to die if necessary. One man may express this attitude by the words: "I live life as if I were never to die" while another person may express this attitude by the words: "I live life as if I were to die at any moment." In both cases the person is dominated by life without pretending that death is not real. This realistic attitude of believing in life in the face of death was beautifully expressed by Dietrich Bonhoeffer:

Wherever it is recognized that the power of death has been broken, wherever the world of death is illumined by the miracle of resurrection and of the new life, there no eternities are demanded of life, but one takes of life what it offers, not all or nothing but good and evil, the important and the unimportant, joy and sorrow; one neither clings convulsively to life nor casts it frivolously away. One is content with the allotted span and one does not invest earthly things with the title of eternity; one allows to death the limited rights which it still possesses.[88]

The Christian expression of hope has much in its favor but its whole pattern needs affirmation in the context of all human experience. In my *Theology of Revelation* I developed as a central theme that the divine-human revelation is summed up in the "consciousness of the risen Christ." I think that within the confines of a Christian theology this thesis is still vaild. Christian

87. See: May, *op. cit.*, p. 101
88. Bonhoeffer, *Ethics*, p. 79.

theology seems to be to be unintelligible when it lacks this focus in the present. Of course, "consciousness of the risen Christ" needs connecting links to everyday experience. Not only this phrase but all the statements of Christian theology are liable to sound like magical formulas or pious clichés unless Christian theology is worked out within a broad, ecumenical context.

The demand here is not for a superficial "relevancy" which limits one's world view on the basis of what modern man can supposedly believe. The gradual elimination of the resurrection hope by rationalizing it away does not make Christianity palatable to modern man. Wild, surprising, illogical life and meaning may be what the closed-in world could best use. Perhaps Christians should concentrate on trying to articulate the deepest desire for human victory. The rationalists have had their day and been found wanting. "The good shepherds meantime have all faded into the darkness of history. One of them, however, left a cryptic message: 'My doctrine is not mine but his that sent me.' Even in the time of unbelieving this carries a warning. For he that sent may still be crouched in the body of man awaiting the end of the story."[89]

3. A CONTEMPORARY RELIGIOUS COMMUNITY

In this last section it remains only to say a few things about the form of a Christian and/or religious community in light of everything that has preceded. When the topic of revelation is discussed in the Christian church, the discussion usually centers around scripture, doctrine and dogma. It should be obvious by this point that the revelation question has little connection with Christians passing down revealed truths. It cannot be denied and should not be forgotten that questions of tradition are important. Continuity with the past, authority in an institution and a common language for a community are life-and-death issues for a

89. Eiseley, *Invisible Pyramid*, p. 149.

religious group. But before any approach is made to these issues it should be made clear how the word revelation is related to each of those words.

Christian theologians and church officials have not dropped the claim that somewhere there is a something called "Christian revelation." The identification of revelation with any *thing* is a cul-de-sac. It implies notions of truth and authority which cannot be sustained. The Catholic church's claim that revealed truth is "infallible" was a logical conclusion from this premise. Of course, infallibility has little chance of surviving as a meaningful doctrine but the premise of the doctrine goes unchallenged. Is "papal infallibility" invalidated because there is a "paper infallibility" or the infallibility of some "word of God" somewhere?[90]

If the common Christian premise is granted, the best that can be done is to blur some distinctions and temper the claims. Specific church doctrines or individual scriptural statements are not often called revealed truths. Nonetheless, it is constantly assumed that the gospel of Christ is the revelation while leaving rather vague what gospel means in this context. The question of doctrines and messages is never going to be handled adequately until doctrine is put subsidiary to wider concerns. Revelation concerns the way people live much more than the way Christians talk. The main thing to be considered, therefore, is the structuring of human, religious and Christian communities so that the divine-human relation can emerge and be better expressed.

The question of structure is a painful one for the churches to face but the subject is unavoidable. As soon as the religious element in life is expressed in any organized fashion, problems of social structure and institutional organization have to be dealt

90. Hans Küng, *Infallible? An Inquiry* (Garden City, 1971) directly challenged the concept of infallibility in Roman Catholicism. A problem of method remains in the way Küng approached his subject. He measures infallibility against a "Christian revelation" given in scripture.

with. We have seen previously that although the "religious dimension" is considered in a positive light today there is at the same time a widespread attack upon and a rejection of traditional religious organizations. Erich Fromm was not voicing an uncommon sentiment when he wrote: "The question must be asked, not from an antireligious point of view but out of concern for man's soul: Can we trust religion to be the representative of religious needs or must we not separate these needs from organized, traditional religion in order to prevent the collapse of our moral structure?"[91]

Organization of any kind is a problem for religion because organization seems to intrude on an area of life that is peculiarly personal and in need of spontaneity, freedom and flexibility. Because of its claim to truth and finality, the organization of Christianity has additional problems. The Christian church made immediate claims of a supra-national mission to bring all men to the one fount of truth. By elevating itself above the tribal, racial and national loyalties of humanity it could avoid much of the troublesome conflict that divides people. But the union might also be premature and the unity might be one of mind and talk rather than one of flesh and people. A cerebral union requires strong, external supports; people are held together by a rigid, closed institution. This objection has always been the central reproach of Judaism to the Christian church: "You talk about the leaven, about a spiritual people, and you ramble on about freedom, but you, with your church, have nothing to offer the nations and peoples of the world—nothing but your missions and the directives of your pastoral letters—while your freedom is only obedience to the clergy."[92]

Some people believe that the Christian structure is irreformable and that it is arrogant simply because it is being consistent

91. Erich Fromm, *Psychoanalysis and Religion*, p. 33.
92. Martin Buber as quoted in Urs von Balthasar, *Martin Buber and Christianity*, p. 85; see also: Kenneth Cragg, *Christianity in World Perspective* (New York, 1968), p. 113.

to its fundamental beliefs. Insofar as the church thinks of itself as the possessor of the final truth of history it does have an insoluble problem on its hands and it is a dangerous problem for people outside the church. However, I have tried to show that there are other strands within Christianity itself and it is possible that they might finally become the dominant strain. In particular, the belief that Jesus constitutes the complete revelation did not imply that the Christian church is possessor or depository of a complete revelation. Christians believed that the church was "necessary for salvation" but they also believed that their God was the God of all mankind and not only the God of Christians.

In recent years there has been a slow but steady movement of the Christian church toward a dialogical position with non-Christians.[93] Implicit in a genuine dialogical attitude is the recognition that one does not have the complete and final truth, even though this fact may not be immediately admitted. At first, dialogue may simply indicate that one wishes points of contact so that one can more effectively convey the truth. If the conversation is not to become a charade, however, the dialogue will become a true exchange in which the truth is born in the process of interchange.

At first Christians began admitting that they did not possess every detail of "divine truth." Gradually they reduced the number of revealed truths which they alone possess. Despite the unreality of the language in light of numbers, it was long maintained that the church is the "ordinary way of salvation." The fact was accepted that God could provide other "extraordinary ways" beside the church. But what happens to a rule when eighty per cent of cases become exceptions to it?

In recent Catholic theology a way out of the artificial language was sought with the term "anonymous Christian."[94] Al-

93. See: Baum, *Man Becoming,* pp. 83–84.

94. See: Karl Rahner, "Christianity and Non-Christian Religions," in *The Church* (New York, 1963), pp. 112–135; Klaus Riesenhuber, "Rahner's Anonymous Christian," in *Theology Digest XIII* (Autumn,

though well intentioned, the phrase compounded the difficulty. Christians may think it is a compliment to a Jew or Hindu to be called an anonymous Christian but to most people the phrase is neither clear nor complimentary. Christian theologians were trying to assert that some of their old claims were true while at the same time admit that the truth was found among all men. The choice of terms was not very felicitous. The word Christian to most people does not first denote a follower of Christ but a member of a church. Thus, anonymous Christian seemed to make people members of a church which they do not wish to belong to. If non-Christians had been called "anonymous followers after the messianic era initiated in Christ" it would still be a questionable claim to make but the claim would be less misleading and less likely to insult. There would seem far more logic in calling Christians "anonymous Jews" rather than the reverse.

Although the choice of terms was unfortunate, Karl Rahner must be given due credit for courageously pushing the rethinking through the term anonymous Christian. Some people who readily criticized Rahner's term could not understand that he was trying to deal with the central issue of the traditional Christian claim. Some of those who dismissed his phrase continued along their own path of arrogantly assuming that Christians have the message which non-Christians need. Rahner was admitting by his terminology that revelation is everywhere and that if the church has any role it must be drastically rethought in light of this fact. At the time of Vatican II, Rahner pointed out that a new meaning for revelation was implied in what was being said about non-Christians. He noted: "It is still impossible to foresee all the theological consequences of these simple statements of the Council, which were scarcely debated, and not noticed at all by press and public opinion. But they are there,

---

1965), pp 163–171; Anita Roper, *The Anonymous Christian* (New York, 1966).

they will produce their effect and promote the growth of quite new attitudes in Christians."[95]

Rahner was correct in this prophecy but the unforeseeable consequences are still very slowly emerging. At some point the word revelation will have to undergo a complete transformation. Just prior to the statement quoted above, Rahner wrote: "It will have to be shown that the other "revelation" may not be discussed or denied in favour of this historical, explicit, verbally formulated revelation and that revelation cannot simply be identified with the latter."[96] That statement puts it mildly to be sure. If any use of the word revelation requires quotation marks it is that verbalization which Christians have wrongly equated with revelation. It is not really that the word revelation must somehow be extended from the past into the present nor that the word revelation must somehow be extended outside the Christian sphere. Rather, the primary meaning of revelation must henceforth be the present, social and practical reality whose definition is not the prerogative of Christians. When it comes to the crucial question of revelation, ecclesiology has yet to have its "copernican revolution."[97]

If Christians are interested in preserving, expressing and deepening revelation then their primary concern ought to be with establishing religious communities that experience revelation. In recent years with the growing interest in the question of community the churches have been quick to assert that they are communities. Undoubtedly the word community can be extended to include human groups of all kinds. For the most part, however, the churches appear to be huge, bureaucratic institutions mainly intent upon their self-survival. At the beginning of mod-

95. Karl Rahner, *The Christian of the Future* (New York, 1967), pp. 96–97; see also his *The Church After the Council* (New York, 1966), pp. 61–64.

96. Rahner, *Christian of the Future,* pp. 96–97.

97. The image is developed in Richard McBrien, *Do We Need the Church?* (New York, 1969).

ern times the church was faced with the choice of being inside or outside the new mainline of institutional form. The church chose to conform by adopting the bureaucratic pattern.[98] This tactic enabled the church to survive but it has also made desperately necessary a new form of community structure for today. It has become increasingly clear that man cannot live on bureaucracy alone. Whether bureaucracy will survive as the dominant form of economic life cannot be explored here. But the religious life of mankind definitely requires some alternative to the bureaucratic model.

At the base of bureaucracy lies the isolated individual split into parts and functions for the sake of efficiency. At the base of religious organization there ought to be groups of persons who are always growing toward greater wholeness. In order for a human group to function as a personalizing unit, size is a crucial factor. The basic communal unit of church would ideally be larger than two but probably not larger than twelve or fifteen. These small groups, of course, are not an answer to the enormous social problems which face the world but they might be the *sine qua non* to an answer. Without such cellular units any organization formed to grapple with big problems is liable to add to the problem. Within the small group the individual can receive affection, support and solace. This experience of community is critically important for people who think they have a "mission" to others. People dedicated to helping others are often blinded by their own unconscious needs. There is no substitute for being loved if one intends to go out and convert the world to God.[99]

In a small group there can be direct participation by every member in the life of the group. Reaching a consensus within a group is never easy for human beings but if the size of the

98. See: Berger, *The Sacred Canopy*, pp. 138–153.
99. See: Gabriel Moran, *The New Community* (New York. 1970), pp. 54–74.

group and its environment are favorable, decisions can be and should be made by the group. Communication occurs when we are mutually deciding what mutually involves us in risk. The era of unilateral decision by the surrogate parent must come to an end in religion. It will come to an end not by the leader listening and then deciding but by the growth of the small groups who change the dynamics of communication. Leadership in a small group emerges according to "charismatic" principles rather than by appointment. Obviously, priest or minister would cease to be a profession and full-time job. There is no reason why every man or woman in the religious community should not play that role for a time.

The need is not only for small groups but a connection between small groups.[100] The best image today is probably that of a "network." The small groups have a unity among themselves when they vest some decision-making power in a central (not higher) body. Such central power ought to be directly and simply accountable to the small groups. John Gardner has remarked that in our day complexity has replaced secrecy as a way of preventing people from getting control over their lives.[101] Some systems are not closed but they are not open either; they are simply too complicated for anyone to change. A Christian church needs to develop the means by which people can effectively participate in the decisions which direct their church. It is not so much by intention that church leaders have made a farce out of words like collegiality, subsidiarity and shared responsibility. Their positions isolate them from feeling what the new demands mean.

The failures of the Christian church, however, cannot be easily unloaded on a few church leaders. Those who have never

100. On the need for a *federation* of small cells or communes as the basic social structure, see: Martin Buber, *Paths to Utopia* (Boston, 1958), pp. 129–138.
101. Gardner, *op. cit.*, p. 40.

faced the problems of administrative and organizational jobs often have a naive understanding of what can and should be done with the church organization. If there is going to be a church in the twentieth century it cannot avoid these tasks. People enamored of small groups are often so anti-institutional that they oppose all larger organization. The worst part of the anti-organizational spirit is that it produces such terrible organization. If no one plans and corrects organizations they simply grow up in confused and chaotic fashion. People will say "let's have a loose association with a minimum of structure." Because the concern is for having the least structure instead of having clean, efficient, workable structure, the organization is doomed from the start. People are always amazed that in a very short time they have more organization than ever. The destructive cycle begins again or else people leave in search of a world of persons unencumbered by bureaucracy. There is no way to avoid bureaucracy today except by planning and executing an organization that goes beyond bureaucracy. It is possible to avoid at least the worst features of bureaucracy but that is not an easy accomplishment. The key to developing post-bureaucratic organization is the use of communication media among cells, groups and teams of people.

In the past the Christian church simply expanded, becoming more powerful as it acquired people and wealth. The growth did not proceed by the grafting in of cells but by the incorporation of vast numbers of individuals. Success had its price. Without the means to prevent the dichotomy, the church quickly became a two-caste society. The idea of an elite who were in charge of handing down revelation logically accompanies the notion of revelation as *something* given to the church by God. Which of these two notions came first is hard to say but once the direction was set one reinforced the other. If it is believed that God's revelation was written down in the first century then this belief has the advantage of stimulating people to learn to read.[102] It also has the disadvantage of excluding illiterate people from direct contact with revelation. The educated, clerical class became the authority on revelation and the remainder of Christians became the "church taught." The tendency which was inherent from the beginning became solidified in the middle ages. The perfection of this system is the pyramid in which the higher the authority the less the human contact. Each cleric was to be in touch only with the higher superior from which God's revelation proceeded in an unobstructed channel. Thus, the notion of revelation was not just non-communal; it was anti-communal. The human experience which is today called community has always been a threat to a "Christian revelation."

The Protestant Reformation was a passionate protest against the corrupt power system that had been centuries in the making. Despite the good intentions and some sound instincts on the part of the reformers, the protest was of limited success. It was faced with the option of church or scripture, and the latter seemed by far the better. The reformers did not want to have a religion in which each man would sit at home reading his bible. They wanted the word preached and lived in the assembly of believers. In practice, unfortunately, there was not much difference between the two procedures. In a world fascinated by print, God's word became the book, i.e., the Christian bible.

A "return to scripture" as a way of criticizing the church could be part of a great reform movement. Considered in isolation, however, the return to scripture represents a regressive tendency. Christianity's temptation from the start has been to identify revelation with the written and spoken words which it possessed. Words which come up from life and illuminate personal action can be the highest human reality. But words that are passed down by "authorities" to regulate life can be the most exploitive and obstructive of human realities.

102. See: Jean Leclercq, *The Love of Learning and the Desire for God* (New York, 1961).

In the early ages of Christianity and throughout the medieval period, the flowering of the liturgy served as some protection against the cerebralization of revelation. Despite the superstition and despite the clericalization of the liturgy, enough of it remained with the general population to prevent the complete identification of revelation and written truths. Christianity survived in art, music, architecture and drama as much as in theological and catechetical books.

The Protestant reformers, while cutting through much of the superstition, tended to reduce religious practices to rational activity. For the elite class of reading Christians the loss may have seemed negligible but the religious life of a people does not live on words alone. The growth of a clerical class who possessed the word was inhibitive of the development of a religious community. Protestantism, far from doing away with the class, solidified it. The isolation of the Catholic priest was the strength of a system which made a man become a non-human agent of grace and truth. The fact that the role was not human at least gave hope of eventual self-destruction of the system. The marrying of the clergyman has the effect of obscuring the fact that the profession should not exist in the first place. It is ironic that conservative Roman authorities have resisted "optional celibacy" since it would almost certainly solidify the status quo.

Most Catholic and Protestant churches have been deficient in any experiential sense of community. Some of the smaller Protestant sects have done better than the other churches on this score.[103] Most of these smaller groups, however, have a rigid approach to the Christian scriptures which is not consonant with a fully experiential approach. The bigger churches have been better organized and more rational; an experience of community was excluded by design. The churches became images of the other structures in society which they supposedly challenge. At the base there has been the private individual or the nuclear family and at the top the corporation with its power brokers

103. See: Reuther, *The Radical Kingdom.*

and portfolio. The church retained its medieval attachment to the land as if religious community were exclusively a geographical issue. The primary meaning of the word church became the enormous buildings which often have neither beauty nor functionality.

It is not my purpose here to address the whole matter of church structure. I am simply trying to indicate that a particular kind of church structure and a particular notion of revelation are reciprocally related. The institution which has existed for centuries has not been inappropriate for the meaning of revelation which has accompanied it. Significantly changing the institution changes the meaning of revelation, just as significantly changing the meaning of revelation requires a change of the institution. One of the sure signs that the meaning of revelation has not changed much in Christian theology is the fact that the actual communal structure of Christianity has changed so little.

Catholicism has been under intense pressure in recent years to initiate structural change. Small changes have been made within sub-systems of that church but there seems to be little tendency to do away with the outdated concepts of "clergy, religious, lay." The pope writes letters instructing the world on the way a democratic society should be structured but little has happened within the Catholic church to move in that direction. Very little challenge is offered to pope, bishops and clergy concerning the functioning ideal of authority, an ideal which is incompatible with an adult, communal and democratic institution.

Every human organization or institution requires an exercise of authority. No group can maintain itself unless there is a basis upon which power is exchanged and directed. Authority pertains in the first place not to the giving of orders but to the legitimation of power.[104] A person is not the authority but persons are

104. See: Robert Dahl, *After the Revolution: Authority in a Good Society* (New Haven, 1971), pp. 3–58; Robert Johann, "Authority and Responsibility," in *Freedom and Man,* ed., John C. Murray (New York, 1965), pp. 141–151.

necessary to exercise authority. The office or role of authority goes beyond the particular person who holds office. Everyone who exercises authority has the right not of himself but from some other source.

In most of the history of the West a chain of authority has been imagined that would allow the present ruler to trace his exercise of authority to the founding fathers of the group.[105] The Christian church adopted this notion of authority and in the Catholic church it is still the dominant idea. If authority concerns the dispensing and protection of a revelation from the founding fathers, then this notion of authority is obviously the ideal. If revelation is not the truth handed down by the founding fathers then the church becomes freer to imagine other ways of exercising authority.

A continuity with the past is not lightly to be dismissed. Religious bodies today should be more attentive than ever to their past traditions. The question of authority, however, is not exactly the same issue. In establishing credible authority today it is more important to be accountable to the human community being served in the present than to make claims of continuity with a divine establishment in the past.

Because revelation was conceived of as a number of truths given to the church, the commands of legitimate authority came to be equated with divine commands.[106] Gradually, the entire structure became divinized so that any criticism of church was regarded as disloyal and irreligious. Particularly in post-Tridentine Catholicism, the one supreme virtue was obedience and obedience was interpreted to mean submission to the "princes" of the church who were God's "vicars" on earth. When the princes surrounded themselves with symbols of divinity, this was con-

105. Hannah Arendt, *The Human Condition* (Chicago, 1958), pp. 188–236.
106. See: John Cameron, *Images of Authority* (New Haven, 1966), pp. 2ff.

sidered a virtue of the office because it reminded the faithful of their duty to obey.

All of the men who are in these church positions today do not seek out pomp and splendor for themselves. However, this is not an adequate defense. To the extent that they accept the trappings of office and refuse to break through the stereotypes, they perpetuate the divinized authority image which alienates men today The issue is not mainly one of continuity with the past tradition. Or, if one wishes to talk about the past, one has to choose which past traditions are worthy of continuity and imitation.[107] If one is interested in a direct line of continuity to Jesus, does the line run through Francis with his brothers and sisters of the earth or through a renaissance pope with his cathedral, villa and servants?

A religious community today must be made up of people who are both priestly and prophetic. In the past, the prophet and the priest were often opposed to each other: the prophet standing for change and future, the priest representing stability and status quo. The two roles remain to this day and they also remain in tension. The reason why priests and prophets should not be fighting today is because both are roles and not people. The same person can at one time be priestly and at another time be prophetic. Priesthood is not a profession for a man to acquire as his own; it is a role which each man and each woman can play some of the time. Likewise, prophecy is not something for a small number of deviants to undertake as their private thing. The prophet is indeed called by a special personal revelation, as Max Weber said, but in the framework I have presented everyone is called by a special personal revelation.[108]

The functions of prayer leader and challenging spokesman

107. See: Yves Congar, *Power and Poverty in the Church* (Baltimore, 1964), p. 139.
108. See: Max Weber, *On Charisma and Institutional Building*, ed., S. Eisenstadt (Chicago, 1968), p. 254.

of a group are in principle open to every individual in a group. Perhaps some people who demonstrate a striking capacity for one role or the other might become executors of the role on a permanent basis. Such a development must avoid confusing the person with the role and must not lead to the exclusion of the community locus of priesthood and prophecy.[109]

The Catholic phrase "priesthood of the laity" was well intentioned but it was practically a contradiction in terms. Laity existed because there was a priesthood, that is, the operative meaning of laity in Catholicism is the class of non-priests. If the church were serious about re-establishing the biblical meaning of laity as the priestly people, the first step would be to do away with priesthood as a class of people. Hardly anyone seriously advocates this in Catholicism, perhaps in part because Catholics feel that it has been tried and found wanting in Protestantism. It is true that Protestantism, despite eliminating the word priest, did not fully succeed in eliminating the dichotomy. The era of the Reformation was perhaps not ready for the kind of communal change demanded in the twentieth century.

The question can certainly be raised as to whether any religious group can survive if it does away with the classes of priest and prophet. The question is equivalent to the one which runs throughout this book: Is it possible to have a post-critical religion? No one doubts that it is possible to have vague religious feelings or general religious attitudes in the twentieth century. The question is whether there can be a specific and effective religious institution which frees people. The final evidence is not yet in to give an answer to this question, but one of the things which needs testing is the assumption of the priestly and prophetic roles by each religious person.

The leaders of the Christian church have seldom been able to grasp the objections leveled at their structure. Many people today are looking for a religious community where they could

109. See: Slater, *op. cit.,* p. 28.

pray and play together and raise a challenge to inhuman structures of contemporary society. Such religious people are often turned away from any Christian church because it seems to be characterized by the same authority split which these people are trying to oppose elsewhere. The churches have generally moved from authoritarian dictatorships to paternalistic bureaucracies but this move has not really improved things. The Christian leaders feel that they have just about gone as far as they can in democratizing church structure. In this regard they are acting in consistency with their beliefs. What they cannot imagine is the elimination of the class of people who are divinely ordained to pass down divinely revealed truths. However, if there is no "Christian revelation" then there is no need for a group whose special preserve is the protection of "Christian revelation."

Both Catholics and Protestants tend to identify revelation with the New Testament writings. It is common to see the word revelation used interchangeably with gospel and scripture. Often, the scripture is even referred to as the "revealed word" of God. Catholics and Protestants traditionally divided over whether scripture contained the whole revelation or whether there had to be additions made to this scripture from a parallel oral tradition. The long controversy came to a culmination during the 1950's and early 1960's.[110] The controversy was resolved as much as it could be by both sides rethinking their own formulations. Roman Catholics came to give greater prominence to the bible, even to the point of adopting the Protestant principle of *sola scriptura*. From the Protestant side there has grown up a greater appreciation of the place of tradition in the composition and interpretation of scripture.

The effect of all this writing was to bring Catholics and Protestants a little closer together. But the whole scripture-tradition controversy turned out to be an intramural squabble. There is

110. See: Gabriel Moran, *Scripture and Tradition* (New York, 1963); Josef Geiselmann, *The Meaning of Tradition* (New York, 1966).

little evidence that the controversy forced a rethinking of the *Christian* assumption about revelation. The presumption that revelation is a Christian thing goes practically unchallenged. The big problem remains where to locate *it*. The Catholic move to locate it all in scripture had the advantage of paring away some of the excrescences too far from the center. It could be argued, however, that the de-emphasis of later developments and the insistence upon the adequacy of scripture solved the difficulty too easily.

The job of determining the genuine meaning of revelation was given over to biblical exegetes. At least in principle the issue now seemed clear: whatever agrees with scripture is revelation. The "revealed truths" were made fewer but the essential problem of any document being a revelation from God was worsened. The rich, variegated life of Catholicism was now brought under the judgment of one criterion. The supposedly liberal movement in Catholicism was in fact a restriction of the meaning of revelation. It is not so surprising as it might seem that some of the early leaders in this movement (e.g., Jean Daniélou, Louis Bouyer) have been vigorous opponents of more recent church developments.[111] It is not so much that they have turned reactionary as the fact that the placing of revelation *sola scriptura* was not unambiguously liberal in the first place.

Having made the above point, I must emphasize that scriptural study was one of the important breakthroughs in Roman Catholicism. Over the centuries scripture had taken second place to tradition as a source of revelation. In practice this often meant that the church officials became the third and most important source. As George Tavard described it, "Scripture serves to illustrate the doctrines which the hierarchy has decided to define, while theology is used to support decisions that need not contain

111. For example, see: Louis Bouyer, *The Decomposition of Catholicism* (Chicago, 1969); Jean Daniélou, *The Faith Eternal and the Man of Today* (Chicago, 1970).

their own justification."[112] What biblical exegetes could do was to show that this whole procedure was invalid on the basis of historical scholarship. The bible simply could not back up what was being propounded as the revealed truth of God. What biblical exegetes could not do was to devise a viable alternative to the discredited procedure of post-Tridentine Catholicism.

The way out cannot be defined by the bible because the situating of that book is a major part of the problem. Revelation is a word that must first be defined from the present, social, practical experience of mankind.[113] As I have indicated, Christian tradition makes a sizable contribution in filling out the meaning of the word but only if Christianity can accept its position of being a contributor toward interpreting a reality which goes beyond it. Revelation (and Inspiration) is what transpires in every present community. The Christian scriptures are one verbal expression of that reality. In being written documents they are limited in what they can express and convey. What they do provide is a guide for further developments within Christian theology.

The New Testament makes no pretense itself of being a collection of revealed truths from God. There grew up in the early church a collection of oral and literary pieces which expressed

112. George Tavard, "Scripture and Tradition," in *Journal of Ecumenical Studies V* (Spring, 1968), p. 323.
113. The alternative to this radical revision of revelation is to do away with the concept altogether. John Charlot, *New Testament Disunity* (New York, 1971), p. 198, agrees with these alternatives: "The old theory of unity posited a revelation of truths, of a body of doctrine, a deposit of faith, at the beginning of Christianity. The fact is that such a deposit or body of doctrines cannot be found in the New Testament; rather, only a great variety of contradictory theologies. The doctrines of revelation and inspiration must either be radically revised or simply rejected as no longer useful or intelligible. Inspiration and revelation would seem to be simply theoretical constructs of the old theory." My only objection to statements like this is that Christian writers then go back to business as usual as if the elimination of revelation and inspiration was one of many problems within Christian theology. If revelation is eliminated, then books on the New Testament cannot establish the basis of Christian belief.

311

the faith of the community. This writing drew heavily from the Jewish scriptures while in turn this writing added to that "Old Testament." "Like every previous addition, this one again changed the pattern of meaning in the Old Testament as a whole. Thus, to use paradoxical language, one could say that in the sense of the dogmatic doctrine of inspiration the New Testament was one of the 'sacred writers' of the Old Testament."[114] These new writings together with the old came to be regarded as the Christian bible, "a structure so unsystematic and various and a style so figurative and indirect that no one would presume at first sight to say what is in it and what is not."[115]

It makes no sense to draw a line at the point where revelation ended and the development of doctrine began. Despite its misleading dictum that "revelation closed with the death of the last apostle," Catholicism was closer to the truth than Protestantism was on this point. Catholic theology saw a single process of development which goes back before the writing of the New Testament. At some point the early church drew a line and established a canon of books as authentic expressions of the church's faith. But this line does not mean that the canonical books have revelation in them and the non-canonical books do not. Any book can be a verbal expression of the revelation which is everywhere present. The books which found their way into the New Testament were those that had some guarantee of apostolic authorship.[116] They have held a special place henceforth in the life of the church even though there is great diversity in the quality of the documents. It is amazing, Nietzsche once said, that when God wished to write a book that he learned Greek and more amazing still that he did not learn it better.

I have said that Catholicism was closer to the truth in seeing a single process that moved from biblical to non-biblical works. In

114. Lohfink, *op. cit.,* p. 38.
115. John Henry Newman, *An Essay on the Development of Christian Doctrine* (New York, 1960), pp. 90–91.
116. Karl Rahner, *Inspiration in the Bible* (New York, 1961)

this perspective, doctrinal elaboration could have the positive value of giving further insight and adding true judgments to Christianity. In practice, the effect has often been a negative one. Conciliar decrees, theological treatises and episcopal pronouncements may only obscure the stark, simple message of Christianity's founder. To their credit, councils and popes often recognized their limitations and worked mainly to preserve the original gospel from destruction. Ecclesiastical councils often met in the midst of opposite errors and simply pronounced both of them wrong.

One can understand why the Protestant Reformation and lesser renewals in Christianity have tried to go back to the simple images of the gospel. But centuries of thinking cannot simply be stripped away. The rereading of the New Testament can be a help to pushing forward but the bible must not be approached with a nostalgia for doing away with life's complexities. The doctrinal problems which the Christian church has struggled with are unavoidable. Every religion that moves beyond a couple of people has to face the difficulty of finding a common speech and developing a doctrine. The process must be carried on despite the risk of obscuring the truth that one is fighting to express.[117]

There is a role of setting up safeguards to protect the truth from violation. If bishops and councils over the centuries have succeeded at this task, their work can be called a success. Of course, there is a positive function of thought and speech but that is not a job for a few leaders. One must feel some ambivalence toward Vatican II's attempt to be positive. Since it was not a council truly representative of the church, its attempt to present a whole platform of contemporary Christian belief must be judged presumptuous. Perhaps it should have stayed with

117. See: Edward Schillebeeckx, "Faith Functioning in Self-Understanding," in *The WORD in History*, ed., Patrick Burke (New York, 1966), pp. 56–57.

what most councils before it tried to do, namely, condemn the errors of the day which are clearly at variance with the Christian gospel (e.g., racism and war). Or, if the council wished to be positive it could have changed the structure by which bishops and councils come to be so that Vatican III would have a real chance of being an ecumenical council of men and women.

In a well-structured religious community each member would participate in his own way in "doctrinal development." People who have more intelligence and better education might make more of a contribution, but the contribution of some should not be to the exclusion of anyone else. In earlier centuries the poet and the painter did as much as the theologian to develop Christian doctrine. Theologians and councils have seldom recognized this fact. Otherwise, they would be more attentive today to the beauty, mystery and appropriateness of their work and not just concerned with the truth value of statements.[118]

A community uses a common language for its existence. The relationship is bilateral. A group of people that is a community will show it by activity and speech that manifest commonality of experience and purpose. Conversely, a unity of language is indicative that a group of people represents a real community. The way for an individual to become a part of the community 's to be immersed in its language.

The word unity here should not be interpreted monolithically. A human unity has a great deal of diversity built within it. A human language should flower in imagery, paradox, tension and spontaneity. When unity of language is taken to mean that everyone makes the same sounds and repeats the same formulas, there will be unity but not human unity (i.e., community). The unity will be of an impersonal institution in which officials decide what is speakable. "In the nineteenth century, when his-

118. See: Karl Rahner, "What Is a Dogmatic Statement?" in *Theological Investigations*, vol. V (Baltimore, 1966), pp. 42–66; see also: William Lynch, *Christ and Apollo* (New York, 1960), pp. 139–140.

torical consciousness broke through in the secular disciplines, expressing the radical historicity of thought, the Church made itself the defender of some of the most cherished theses of eighteenth-century rationalism. Theologians took the view that the truths of revelation, at least, were indubitable, universal, and immutable. They claimed unrestricted currency for their select body of axioms which, in the nineteenth century, came to be called 'dogmas.' "[119]

Throughout this book I have been trying to strike a death blow at this conception of revelation as indubitable, universal and immutable truths. The purpose of doing this is not to destroy the Christian religion but to recover whatever of it is salvageable from its modern rationalistic form. Those who defend dead systems of belief will protest that they are the last defenders on the outposts of faith in a godless world. The threat to the old system is great indeed but faith, revelation and God are not the main contenders; one must be a little suspicious of defenders of God against a godless world. "The effort to maintain orthodox belief," writes Robert Bellah, "has been primarily an effort to maintain authority rather than faith. It was part of a whole hierarchical way of thinking about social control, deeply embedded in traditional thinking."[120]

The words orthodox and heretical have a doubtful future but these words express what should be of concern to a religious body.[121] If a group has anything to offer, it ought to be able to draw some distinctions about its way of living and thinking. It ought to be able to say who is part of the group and who is not. The boundaries will be blurred in many places and the limits should be subject to continual change, but limits do exist for any functioning group. It is to be suspected that those who say

119. Avery Dulles, *Survival of Dogma* (Garden City, 1971), p. 117.
120. Bellah, *op. cit.,* p. 221.
121. See: Karl Rahner, *On Heresy* (New York, 1964); John Macquarrie, "Some Thoughts on Heresy," in *Christianity and Crisis,* Dec. 26, 1966, pp. 291–294.

that there should be no boundaries are insufficiently conscious of their own ideologies and not respectful enough of other peoples' wish to be different.

In modern times it has become more obvious that the person who assents to a formula is not necessarily part of the group. Conversely, the person who challenges or rejects certain sanctified formulas may be not only a loyal member of a group but one of its most creative and helpful members. Thus, there is no computer programed basis on which to test an individual's adherence to the group. The Christian church, like every other community, has to live with the ambiguity of not always knowing who belongs and who does not, who is a true prophet and who is only a destroyer.

The effort must be made to determine who is in and who is out. However, heresy is not cured by administrative procedures or loyalty oaths.[122] Not only does that kind of action force out the wrong people, it also helps to breed a latent heresy within. Dressed in the formulas of orthodoxy, Christian groups can spout forth racism, warmongering and hatred for other groups. A religion that has turned revelation into a collection of dogmatic truths is helpless before these corrosive attitudes which are always careful to keep themselves within standard orthodox formulas.

The need for leadership remains but it is a different kind of leadership than the Christian church is accustomed to. Someone has to organize things, get people together and encourage them to carry on their work. There have to be free spaces for thought and discussion, zones of freedom where people can imagine new things, experiment with different approaches and occasionally make mistakes. The role of the leader here may look simple but it is not. He is to be a non-interferer who sees that creative individuals can get together and that less imaginative people do not move in on them prematurely. These "immunities" have been

122. Karl Rahner, *Nature and Grace* (New York, 1964), p. 130.

JEWISH AND CHRISTIAN EXPERIENCE

built into parts of modern society but the Christian church is generally deficient on this count. A bill of rights for the religious community cannot be presented here but the preface to addressing the issue would be a de-divinization of current structure. What has been humanly created can be and should be humanly changed.

A main job of a community leader is precisely not to define and not to bring to conclusion the religious issues. There is need to stimulate further dialogue which will pick up more of the past. The history of development is one of narrowing as well as expanding; it is a history of forgetting as well as remembering.[123] Dialogue cannot be carried on between the past and the present; dialogue is what living men in the present do. But if there is any depth and sensitivity to their interaction, if there is search and discipline in their discussion, then the past will function in the present.[124]

The past cannot be lived but neither should it be cast aside as irrelevant. What Catholic tradition at its best struggled to do was to face the whole past tradition. When it tried to draw definitive conclusions from this wildly variegated past, the statements often seemed artificial, contrived, and downright dishonest. I am suggesting that the intention is still valid and that the project is more important than ever, namely, to be concerned with accepting our whole past. In distinguishing all doctrine (including the New Testament) from revelation, a different kind of unity can be sought and a different kind of continuity with our past can be maintained.

Revealed truths or a "Christian revelation" would have to

123. See: Piet Schoonenberg, "God's Presence in Jesus: An Exchange of Viewpoints," in *Theology Digest* XIX (Spring, 1971), pp. 29–38; Karl Rahner, "The Development of Dogma," in *Theological Investigations,* vol. 1 (Baltimore, 1961), pp. 39–78.
124. See: Karl Rahner, *Grace in Freedom* (New York, 1969), pp. 173–174; Edward Schillebeeckx, *God the Future of Man* (New York, 1968), pp. 1–58.

317

take the form of a logical unity in which each truth is logically compatible with all the others.[125] In contrast, the unity which is demanded by a present, social and practical revelation is a human one which is subject to discontinuities, riddled with misapprehensions and afflicted with dead ends. But through it all the human community survives, remembering in one century what it had forgotten in another. There is never the necessity of denying doctrines even though every doctrine is not of equal value. The definitive value of any doctrine from the past would only be determinable from the end of history.[126] A religious community has as a primary mission today to prevent the closure of judgment on the past and the collapse of imagination in considering the future. As for the present, perhaps all that human beings can do is to try to care for each other and refuse to resign to meaningless and death.

125. See: Wilken, *op. cit.*, p. 100: "The Eusebian construction of the past made it difficult for men to see either the diversity of the Christian past or the changes that had taken place over the centuries. By extending tne authority of the apostles to later Christian generations, the unity that men had projected onto the first Christian generation, namely that of the apostles, was made to embrace the whole of the Christian past. The irony of the Eusebian view is that in stressing the unity of the tradition—one unchanging faith—it led to a hardening of division and disunity. For if diversity could not be tolerated, the only way of explaining differences was to say that divergent views contradicted or opposed the true faith."
126. See: Scheler, *On the Eternal in Man*, p. 40.